GOD AFTER GOD

GOD AFTER GOD

The God of the Past and the God of the Future
As Seen in the Work of Karl Barth

ROBERT W. JENSON

Fortress Press
Minneapolis

GOD AFTER GOD
The God of the Past and the God of the Future: As Seen in the Work of Karl Barth

Fortress Press ex libris publication 2010

Copyright © 1969 Robert Jenson. All rights reserved. Except for brief quotations in critical articles or reviews, no part of this book may be reproduced in any manner without prior written permission from the publisher. Visit http://www.augsburgfortress.org/copyrights/contact.asp or write to Permissions, Augsburg Fortress, Box 1209, Minneapolis, MN 55440.

The Library of Congress has catalogued the original publication as follows:
Jenson, Robert W.
God after God; the God of the past and the God of the future, seen in the work of Karl Barth / Robert Jenson.
p. cm.
Includes bibliographical references
ISBN 978-0-8006-9788-4
Barth, Karl, 1886-1968. Römerbrief.
God (Christianity)—History of doctrines—20th century.
BT102 .J47

The paper used in this publication meets the minimum requirements of American National Standard for Information Sciences—Permanence of Paper for Printed Library Materials, ANSIZ329.48-1984.

Manufactured in the U.S.A.

For Kari

Contents

Foreword ix

Preface to the 2010 Publication xi

Acknowledgments xiii

Part One — The Death of the God of Past History

    CHAPTER ONE — The Dialectic of the *Commentary on Romans*   3

    CHAPTER TWO — The Self-Cancellation of Historical Religion   24

    CHAPTER THREE — The Word-Event in the *Commentary on Romans*   39

Part Two — God of and Against Religion

    CHAPTER FOUR — Epochal Possibilities   51

    CHAPTER FIVE — The Christological Reversal   67

    CHAPTER SIX — Against Religious Theology   79

Part Three — God Who Happens

    CHAPTER SEVEN — The Doctrine of the Trinity   95

    CHAPTER EIGHT — God's Being in Time   123

Part Four — The God of Future History

    CHAPTER NINE — Ambiguities   139

    CHAPTER TEN — The Futurity of God   157

    CHAPTER ELEVEN — God as Word   180

Notes   195

Index   213

Foreword

This book may be read in several ways. It may be read as a dogmatic proposal, and any who read it so will be closest to the personal concern which led me to write. The subject of the book is: what does "God" mean in the Christian faith? A dogmatic *proposal,* as distinguished from a treatise on received teachings, is necessarily also a diagnosis of the state of theology. This book may therefore be read for its information about and analysis of theological situation, and I hope that those who find my suggestions for the future repellent or even unintelligible will at this level nevertheless not have wasted their effort. Finally, the story of our theological situation is still very largely the story of Karl Barth and his reception, despite rumors of his antiquation recurring annually since 1923. The root and problem of our task remains the "dialectical theology," of which Barth's *Commentary on Romans* is the compendious document. And the theologian who sets out to solve or cut the knot tied in 1922 and looks about for helpers and competitors in the task, will find few of the format of Barth himself and none at all who are independent of him.

Thanks are due and gladly given to: my wife, who has read and criticized every word; Lawrence Grow, a former editor of Bobbs-Merrill, who initiated the project; and Robert Amussen, the editor-in-chief of Bobbs-Merrill, and his entire staff.

Preface to the 2010 Publication

When a small seminar of graduate theological students recently proposed to read *God after God* with me, I warned them that it was the weirdest of my books. Revisiting it to prepare for the session, I found that judgment confirmed. But I also found that I agreed materially with most of what I had then written.

Readers should consider the date of publication. It was written during the famous "sixties" and displays the rhetorical and conceptual hijinks of the period. Some readers may enjoy this, others deplore it. I have since become—I think—rather more sober, though there are those who suspect that this is only a disguise.

It was the time of "radical" theologians—proclaimers of the death of God and such. My intent was to beat them at their own game and just so come full circle to a theology more faithful to the gospel than had recently been possible. And I thought I had been prepared for the venture. My dissertation on Karl Barth had been accepted in 1959 and part of it published as *Alpha and Omega* in 1963. But I had learned and thought much while reading Barth that did not appear in the dissertation and had criticisms that would have been out of place there. Barth, I thought, was ambivalently perched between the "religious" version of Christianity that he set out to overthrow and the insights that made his thinking constructive. He was at once the perfecter of religious Christianity and its nemesis. Or so I then thought and some days still do.

Those "radical theologians" are interlocutors in *God after God*. Most are now forgotten; readers need not worry if they have never heard of them. Some deserve their fate and some do not; I will not here sort out the names. One major figure is now neglected and should not be: Thomas Altizer. To find out why I think that, I direct readers to the book here before them.

If *God after God* is so thoroughly rooted in its period, why should anyone now read it? If indeed one should, it is because we ourselves are so thoroughly rooted in that very period. Those shaped by its discontents and assumptions now run government, the information and entertainment services, and even big business. As for the church, the nihilistic nostalgia hidden in current "progressive" theology and church practice found its American form in the pathologies of the sixties. Clinging to the past under cover of rhetoric about new insights is the very brew Barth despised, and it again dominates the life of our churches. In *God after God* I tried to expose this heart of our late-modern problem with Christianity. If my book is now granted a second chance, perhaps some good may come of that.

I was surprised and much pleased when Fortress Press proposed reprinting another of my older books, *Visible Words*. But I was absolutely astonished when they proposed reprinting this one. I am grateful for both proposals and particularly to the editor in charge of the project, Josh Messner.

Acknowledgments

Permission to quote copyrighted material has been graciously granted by:

Christian Century Foundation, Chicago	for "Theology Is Not 'American'" by Nels Ferre, *The Christian Century*, Dec. 26, 1962
Christian Kaiser Verlag, Munich	for *Widerstand und Ergebung*, by Dietrich Bonhoeffer and *Theologie der Hoffnung*, by Jürgen Moltmann
EVZ—Verlag, Zurich	for *Der Römerbrief und Kirchliche Dogmatik* by Karl Barth
Fortress Press, Philadelphia	for *Christ the Representative*, by Dorothee Sölle
Gütersloher Verlaghaus Gerd Mohn, Gütersloh	for *Grundzüge der Chistologie*, by Wolfhart Pannenberg
Harper and Row, New York	for *The Reality of God*, by Schubert Ogden
Herder and Herder, New York	for *The Future of Belief*, by Leslie Dewart
Macmillan Co. Inc., New York	for *The Invisible Religion* by Thomas Luckman and *The Secular City*, by Harvey Cox
Müllerschön Verlag, Bad Cannstatt	for *Hermeneutik*, by Ernst Fuchs

Neukirchener Verlag, Neukirchen	for *Eschatologie und Geschichte in der Theologie der jungen Karl Barth,* by Tjarko Stadtland
Vandenhöck & Ruprecht, Göttingen	for *Grundfragen systematischen Theologie,* by Wolfhart Pennenberg
Verlag, J.C.B. Mohr, Tübingen	for *Gottes Sein ist im Werden,* by Eberhard Jüngel
Zwingli Verlag, Zurich	for *Zukunft und Verheissung,* by Gerhard Sauter

Part One

*The Death
of the God of
Past History*

Chapter One

The Dialectic
of the
Commentary on Romans

I

"The No which meets us is *God's* No. What we lack is just what helps us. What shuts us in is new country. What cancels all the truth of the world is also its foundation. Exactly because God's No is complete, it is also his Yes."[1] This is the dialectic of Karl Barth's *Commentary on Romans,* a wild, boring and fascinating spin of contradictions which has made believers discover they were unbelievers and atheists unsure of their rejections, a hypnotic dialectic which alternately energizes and immobilizes, and sometimes both at once. Over all who still experience Christianity as a religion, it has lost none of its destructive power. And—since this dialectic works both ways—it will, if given opportunity, find new victims among the searchers for nonreligious faith.

There is no way but to keep quoting. *God* occurs in this rhetoric as the pure "negation of the creature."[2] He "acknowledges us as his in that he takes and keeps his distance from us."[3] He is "known as the unknown, speaking in his silence, merciful in his unapproachable holiness, calling for responsibility by bearing all, demanding obedience by working all, graceful in his condemnation—not man and just *therefore* the first and last truth . . . of man."[4]

Christ is the one "who bridges over the distance between God and man—in that he tears it open."[5] At the goal of his life he is a "purely negative entity . . . who precisely in that he offers . . . all thinkable human possibilities to . . . an invisible other, is the fulfiller of . . . human possibilities."[6] The *revelation* which occurs in him is a "hindrance, disturbance and negation of our life . . . , a curse on our creatureliness, a manifestation of divine wrath, a work of Ungod, the god of this world. . . . But we see . . . in God's wrath his justification . . . , in death life, in No Yes. . . ."[7]

Faith is "respect for the divine incognito, love for God in consciousness of the qualitative difference between God and man . . ." acknowledgement of "the bounding of the world by a contradictory truth. . . ."[8] Such an acknowledgement produces a mode of life which is absolutely dialectical: "Our experience is that which is not our experience: our religion consists in the cancellation of our religion. . . . Nothing human is left which would be more than empty space. . . ."[9] The believer "is what he is not, knows something that he does not know, does what he cannot do. . . ."[10] "To be brought down by God means, since God is God . . . , the possibility of rising again. . . ."[11]

What is evaporated in the emptiness these contradictions open up is everything that Europe and America have known as religion. Almost apart from its particular doctrines, the *Commentary on Romans* was an event. The crisis of "historical religion" achieved language—this time *within* the theology of the church. In the present situation of American theology, it may seem superfluous to speak of the crisis of religion as if it were something remarkable. But, as I will argue later, the merely a-religious piety and theology of our avant-garde was secretly still all too religious, and that is why we have tired of it so quickly. We have not attained, in theology, the fundamental and sophisticated anti-religious polemic of the *Commentary on Romans*. There is a sense in which American theology has not yet had its "Barthian" period; until it does, we will continue merely to attenuate religiosity rather than to overcome it. Whether the deep crisis comes to us under the name of Barth is of course of minor importance. But that, under whatever name, we must become much more radical in faith and doubt is indisputable. If a belated reception of Barth's work as the event it was could help, a book or two could be excused in the process.

II

We are not concerned here with Barth as a person, though he is a fascinating one. Only so much biography is needed as will place the

Commentary on Romans in time.[12] In the great days before the First World War, young Barth, a native of Switzerland, studied with Harnack and Hermann at Berlin and Marburg, served a term as pastor of the German-speaking congregation at Geneva, and in 1911 went to Safenwil, to be pastor of a congregation of farmers and laborers. There the duties of his pastoral office broke down the liberal theology in which he had been trained. Or rather, it broke down his Christian religiousness.

The defining character of liberalism, as Barth came to look back at it, was that it took the Christian *religion* as its starting point. It began with religion, i.e., with man's strange propensity to reach beyond himself and beyond the realities which limit his life to a unity and completion which everything in life drives him to seek but does not provide. Then it tried to grasp the faith as a species of this genus. Christianity, said liberalism, is the highest religion. It is the form of religious existence which most appropriately achieves the goal of all religion, continuity of our lives with that beyond our lives which justifies them.

It was not those elements by which we often identify a theology as "liberal" against which Barth revolted: alliance with historical-critical biblical study, or dislike of metaphysics. What Barth found to be sand under his feet was a foundation which liberalism shared with all branches of post-reformation Christianity, including confessional and speculative theology and the theologies of the awakening. In one way or another all begin with a phenomenology of human existence, by which religion is established as the necessary center of life. Then it is shown that religion always appears as some particular religion. Finally, the special character of the Christian religion is analyzed, and some attempt is made to show why it is the best one, or at least the one which history dictates for us. The pattern of theology and piety which collapsed under Barth began by fixing religion as an essential phenomenon of life, and *then* asked what the coming of Christ had done to and for this. It began by asking after the meaning of life, and *then* asked how Christ might help achieve this. It began with the story of *man-the-seeker,* and then looked for Christ's role in the story.

How this prior insight into the goal and plot of life was obtained varied from school to school. It could be obtained by phenomenological analysis, by speculation, by pondering history, or from the Bible as a source of anthropological and theological information in its own right. But to Barth's revolt, these variations make no difference—and that he perceived this is not the smallest part of his importance.

In trying to preach and teach in the unrarified air of Safenwil, Barth discovered two things, or rather, two sides of one thing. He discovered the complete irrelevance of this religious Christianity for the actual content of most men's lives, the uselessness of talk of "the higher things" or "authentic existence" for the problems of working conditions and elementary justice which plagued his congregation. He sat in his study on Sunday morning, watched the people out walking on their day off, and wondered why they *should* come in to hear him. He discovered, that is, the same thing that religiously enthusiastic young pastors still regularly discover, and turn to clinical work or non-directive counseling or teaching *about* religion or a nervous breakdown: that he had nothing much to say.

Every Sunday, he had to preach—from a text. So he discovered the second thing: that the Bible is not about man and his religion at all, but about something much harder to understand—God and his coming Kingdom.

Therefore, Barth became an active socialist and a theological searcher. He worked for social justice and struggled to understand the Bible, with its talk of a "Kingdom of God" which is "not of this world." It is important to see that his socialism and his theological unease were for him not two events but one, that the disillusionment with liberalism which I have divided under two headings was but one experience. Throughout the whole development which began at Safenwil, Barth's search for the reality of life in this world and his search for understanding of God's transcendent Kingdom have not been two "emphases" which he has tried to "balance," but one search.

If we could really get hold of this, we would be well on our way into Barth's true radicalism and specific theme. We would also have understood that almost nothing of what people have spoken of in America or England as "Barthianism" has much to do with the thought of the man from Basel.[13] From the very beginning Barth's theological search has been for a proclamation of the transcendent God whose transcendence is *not* that of the terminus of our alienation from the things of this world, and of the religious quest in which we enact that alienation, but rather the transcendence which limits us *to* the tasks of time, and just so frees us from and for them. The kind of "otherness" of God which Barth is popularly supposed to have carried to an extreme is exactly what he has made his target. It is what he means by "religion."

The documents of Barth's struggles at Safenwil were two successive editions of a *Commentary on Romans,* written to master his own pastoral task and published almost on second thought. The first is historically interesting, but it was the second, published in 1922, that made the history and became the rallying point for that strange group, united in little but rebellion, who have been tagged the "dialectical" theologians and from whom all contemporary theology springs.

The book is one long attack against the presumption that religion —the sum of the attitudes and ideas and resignations and efforts by which I seek to transcend the antinomies of life—is continuous with faith. It is an attack on the theory and practice of faith as the flowering of religion, on finding the Father of Jesus Christ by pursuing that self-transcendence by which man accomplishes his own meaning, on identifying God as the one who appears at the terminus of man's search for his true self. In the Christian *religion,* God appears as the addressee and answerer of man's question after himself, posited by the necessity of asking the question. He appears as an element in man's explication of his existence, as the secret of what man seeks in seeking the meaning of his being here. He appears as the element of the transcendent in man's understanding that he himself is self-transcendent. The God who thus appears is the God of the *Christian* religion simply because he appears in the course of a religious quest which has been determined by the story about Christ.

It is vital to see that the attack is on the continuity of faith and religion, not of faith and life. It is vital to see that what is meant here by "religion" is exactly our *alienation* from time and our life in it, our quest for another reality which will make up the radical insufficiency of this one. Barth did not even propose that we do without religion. For the self-transcendence which is our humanity cannot occur without our positing a goal to our quest, and the goal which *we* can posit must be just such a sublimated world, just such a religious object. Barth wants only to say that this God is not the Father of Jesus Christ. What Barth attacks is any presumption of continuity between the religion we cannot avoid having and the faith proclaimed by the Christian gospel.

It is also important not to get lost in terminological confusions. If by "religion" one means that fundamental directedness to a purpose beyond our present grasp, which is the essential reality of man, then there is no polemic against religion in Barth. By "religion" he means the phenomena which occur as we enact that directedness, which he claims will inevitably be one or another attempt to evade the realities of time, a quest for an eternity which must be a false eternity just because it is posited as the escape from time.[14] Whether one chooses to call the fundamental structure of transcendence "religion," and regard its manifestations as perversions—and so to refrain from polemic against "religion"—or to restrict "religion" to the quest for escape from time in which this transcendence is in fact always enacted—and so to join Barth in attacking the unity of faith and religion—is in one way a purely terminological decision. Yet the decision one takes will probably reflect one's habit of mind. The "catholic" mind is always concerned to avoid dualisms, and will choose the first course. The "protestant" habit of mind will make the second choice. In candor, let it be said that this book will reflect a protestant mind—and will indeed be a sort of argument for its superiority as a pattern of believing reflection.

If, at least provisionally, we are allowed Barth's sense of "religion" then we can say that what occurs in the *Commentary on Romans* is the self-destruction of the *Christian religion*. Faith and religion, the God of the Gospel and human self-transcendence, turn against each other; and the possibility of carrying out the religious quest *by way of* the events of which the Gospel tells, falls away between them.

III

The contradictions which thus explode the Christian religion are generated from one basic contradiction which Barth carries through all reality, or rather, between all that we take to be reality and God. This is the difference of time and eternity.[15] "If I have a 'system, it consists in what Kierkegaard called the 'infinite qualitative difference' between time and eternity."[16] On the one side is man, on the other God, and the division is death.[17] The meaning of eternity for time is cancellation, *crisis,* "the unrolling of all being by its . . . not-being."[18] Time and eternity touch only in "the critical moment" of Christ's resurrection, or what is the same, of faith.[19] Here time touches eternity "like the tangent of a circle, without touching. . . ."[20] The moment has no before or after, it has "no extension on our level."[21] It has no content;[22] there is no special "God's history as a . . . quantity of history at large."[23] Thus this moment is *cancelled as time*— and just this is its meaning: it is the moment of time's *crisis*. So also the moment cannot be any particular moment among others. It is "the continuous crisis of all history, not a history in or alongside history."[24]

Out of this metaphysic, Barth generates contradictions to attack "religion qualified with the predicate of faith,"[25] as "the betrayal of Christ."[26] As Socrates generated contradictions to drive apart the Athenian citizens and the civic and intellectual ideals which they supposed to be theirs, so Barth pries apart the religion—not the actual life—of Christendom and the God it claims to worship. As Socrates questioned away the assumption of continuity between justice as known in Athens and justice as it is in itself, so Barth will hear of no continuity between the question we are for ourselves and God's question—which is the answer—to us. Time and eternity, each defined as the negation of the other, are assigned as the modes of being of man and God, so that every human possession of God, every continuity of human self-transcendence with its own fulfillment, every theological assertion or religious attitude or practice of piety, is made inwardly impossible.

To begin with, "religion" is understood in the broadest and most favorable possible way, as "the human possibility of receiving and keeping an impression of God's revelation, of . . . following and depicting the . . . movement from the old to the new man, in the visible forms of human consciousness and human creation, of assuming . . . an attitude which corresponds . . . to God's ways and . . . making this visible."[27] Just so, religion is "a before and after the moment, which yet is supposed to be not altogether unlike it. . . ."[28] Thus in religion the reduplication occurs in which "this side of the abyss which separates man from God, revelation changes from eternity into temporality . . . , the beyond becomes a second metaphysical something over against a 'this side'—and just so a mere prolongation of that 'this side.' "[29] Religion, although it is our reception of God's revelation, is nevertheless *our* reception, and therefore a phenomenon of the reality this side of the "line of death, that separates . . . time and eternity."[30] It is "the highest pinnacle and perfection" of the human, "but not its overcoming . . . , not even as authentically Christian religion."[31] "Also those religious experiences that we have . . . of the crucified Jesus belong to the things which Jesus passed by to die."[32]

"In direct confrontation stand: the nearest invisible reality, God's grace, in which God's freedom reaches for man . . . , and the farthest visible reality, . . . religion, apparently the same relation of the same man to the same object . . . , only that . . . it is this side of the abyss."[33] Yet religion cannot be willing to *stay* this side of the line, for it is the attempt "to experience eternity temporally, to think, discuss, depict and represent it. . . ."[34] Also "genuine . . . religion, the religion of Abraham and the prophets, the religion of the *Letter to the Romans* and obviously of books about the *Letter to the Romans*,"[35] is "the relating of ourselves to the one to whom *we* cannot relate ourselves" and so essentially involves "a titanic forgetfulness of the distance."[36] Religion is essentially a mixing of time and eternity.[37] "God's eternity, related to man's temporality, qualifies this as sin; man's temporality, related to God's eternity, becomes sin. . . ."[38] This is true not only of the perversions of religion; the titanism is precisely that of the church's necessary and proper talk of trying "to hear and speak God's word."[39] The tragic paradox is that what we, in the spiritual-historical reality of this man in this world, cannot and must not refrain from because it is "the act of our turning to the foreign land that is nevertheless our home, is *as* an act . . . the betrayal of its own presupposition. . . ."[40]

Thus religion is the attempt to crown our temporal quest with the "pathos of infinity."[41] "Our pride demands, besides all else, the availability of a higher world. It cries for a deeper foundation, for transcendent praise and reward. Our lust of life longs for pious hours, for prolongation into eternity."[42] The result necessarily is "one or another prolongation of nature to supra- or subnature (metaphysics), one or another middle-region of visible invisibilities. . . ." That is, the result is "Not-God, the God of this world (who can be named Life, Reality, Kingdom of God, The Beyond, etc.). . . ."[43]

Religion is, in short, the high point[44] and the visible experience and event of man's fall to the temptation "You shall be as God."[45] "The slaves' uprising of man against God comes to visible expression precisely in religion."[46] Nor is negative religion, like that of the *Commentary on Romans,* excepted. "Whatever directs itself to the world of religious phenomenon is pervaded by the same air . . . : religious affirmation *and* anti-religious negation . . . , Amaziah *and* Amos. . . ."[47]

It may well be inevitable that our fall is thus enacted. But the enactment is not and will not be faith nor the stuff of the Christian Gospel. The believer will have a religion, "but all that cannot . . . be the power of obedience, in which he . . . says yes to God." Christ is our Saviour exactly in that he came "under the Law," i.e. carried the religious possibility to its conclusion as prophet, wise man, teacher, friend of man and Messiah—and dies to all this to live as God's Son. In the "dead Christ" of religion, the "last and highest human possibility, the possibility of being a believer, a pious, enthusiastic and praying man, found its fulfillment through its total elimination. . . ."[48] Grace occurs when "the religious possibility, seriously taken and in full power and development, is sacrificed."[49] The true church would be a church "daring enough . . . to cultivate . . . religion by undismayed relativizing of all religion, the pious man . . . by tirelessly confronting him with the heathen, publicans, Spartacists, imperialists, capitalists and other unsympathetic types—whom God has justified."[50]

IV

Reference to Socrates was not merely illustrative. Since Socrates first persecuted the Athenians, his heirs have never been rid of him. His dialectic has recurred again and again to make inwardly impossible every new abiding city in which western man has tried to come to rest. The dialectic of the *Commentary on Romans* is such a recurrence, this time in the theology of the church. Socrates generated endless contradictions to demolish the claims of Athenian opinion to be knowledge of the point of life. Just so—not similarly, but *just* so—Barth generated contradictions to demolish the claim of Christian religion to be faith in God, to be knowledge of the meaning He promises us. I am not trying to praise Barth as a "second Socrates"—evaluation is not the point at all.

Barth's dialectics are born of a basic contradiction between time and eternity. So also were Socrates': "What is justice?" he asked, and dialectically exploded every given answer by showing its partiality and relativity to historical circumstances, and its consequent inability to make plausible the absolute and timeless claim which justice must have on us. Unless Plato has utterly falsified the death scene, Socrates meant by these conversations to wean himself and his hearers from captivity to time and to prepare for the eternal.

Moreover, Barth's dichotomy of time and eternity came to him at the end of the same tradition in which Socrates stood. Although his use of it in the *Commentary on Romans* was doubtless justified by success in expounding the test, the dichotomy came not from the *Letter to the Romans* but ultimately from quite a different testimony of faith, the revelation which Parmenides of Elea received early in the 5th century B.C. from a certain goddess.

Carried by the chariot of the Daughters of the Sun, Parmenides passed from darkness to light—and saw the goddess. The goddess spoke: "You must learn all: the reliable heart of balanced truth, and the opinions of mortals in which there is no true belief."[51] This is a description of the experience of an initiate into the mysteries; the knowledge the goddess will give is *saving* knowledge.

To be saved, Parmenides must know that there are only two patterns of thought and that only one leads to truth: "the one way, that 'is' can be truly said and never 'is not,' . . . attends on truth; the other, that 'is not' can and must be said, is . . . wholly unthinkable."[52] We need not mind the logical errors involved in this assertion that negations are always meaningless; the existential content is our concern. Parmenides stipulates this: "What can be thought is the same as what is real."[53] Here is double security. On the one hand there can be nothing beyond our grasp, no mystery we cannot transcend by seeing through it. On the other hand, unreality cannot be experienced, and so need not be feared. The enemy is our own unreality, death; salvation is assurance that death is an illusion.

If only "is" is a possible predicate, all "that is real is . . . deathless." And time, which is the mode of coming into being and passing away, is an illusion. Reality is eternity's moment without before or after.

"Neither was being nor will it be; it is all simultaneously now."⁵⁴ Yet we do have the illusion of time.⁵⁵ Salvation, therefore, is the resolute turn from this illusion. It is the choice of eternity. The content of our first great philosophically conscious religiosity was a call to refuse to believe in death.

Overcoming—or evading—death by positing a timeless reality set above our stories in time has remained the structure of what we have in the West called "religion." Parmenides did not explicitly say how, if the difference between time and eternity is as absolute as he makes out, we can stand between the two so as to make such a choice. But there his goddess put us, in the contradiction of time and eternity.

Socrates taught us how to live there between. His religious opinions amounted, apparently, to the conviction that we should have few such opinions. He eschewed any metaphysical system on the lines of Parmenides. But what he *did* in his thinking and questioning was to make the move from time to eternity to which Parmenides was called. His endless questions exposed how we bind the words— as "justice" or "beauty"—by which we grasp the meaning of our life, to partial and passing realities. Just so, each question was a step above such temporal limitations. The dialectic was intended to open our aspirations to the eternal reality which alone can fulfill them.

Thus Plato rightly saw Socrates as the incarnation of the religious possibility.⁵⁶ And he turned his vision into art, in the dialogues, especially in the *Symposium*. The guests at this most famous of drinking parties speak in praise of Eros. Although these speeches are parodies, when they are done, "Eros" has been made the name of man's search for completion in all its well-guided and misguided forms. Eros *is* religion. Then Socrates speaks. He first dialectically attacks the praise of Eros as himself wise and beautiful, i.e., the claim that our search, just as we conduct it, carries its justification in itself. Then, under the guise of what he has "heard" from a prophetess, he tells the myth of man's quest.

Eros, Socrates says, is not a god. Nor is he a mortal. He is something midway between mortality and immortality. Just so he is a "demon," an unstillable spiritual energy—for all value is in immortality, mortality is unfulfillment, and Eros is child of both.⁵⁷ In the grip of Eros, "the philosopher" step by step abandons the temporal objects of his life to seek immortal values, until "suddenly he sees an amazing essential value . . . which always is and neither begins nor is destroyed. . . ."⁵⁸

So far Socrates' speech. Then Plato's miracle of art occurs. For as we read we remember that Socrates came late to the party because he was in a trance, we see Alcibiades enter to tell his tale of deep yet wholly sublimated love with Socrates—and suddenly we see that

Socrates himself is Eros. If we then read Plato's story of Socrates' death, the image is complete. Socrates becomes an icon, of life as the journey from time to eternity, of life propelled on by their contradiction. He becomes the icon of the overcoming of death, which has ever since been on the screen of all western religion.

Aristotle completed the pattern. Often taken as the prototype of the scientist-philosopher, he was equally a religious thinker.[59] He taught that the philosopher, that is himself, was a man who, out of awe and to overcome the threat of the awful, sought to grasp the eternal principles of the world. Suspended between possession and lack, the philosopher rises to fulfillment by the power of "Mind," by participation in divine and therefore changeless truth. So far, Aristotle is purely Socratic. His particular place among the founders of our religion was that he described its appropriate God.

Aristotle's great question was: what is the being of beings? What is true of anything that is, just so that it is? His answer was: that in anything which is *changeless,* that in which so long as it is what it is, it always is just what it was.[60] The hidden unrest in all Greek philosophizing was the question: Can it be that all things pass away? Aristotle answered: No. That in the world which does not cease to be, which does not die, is what grants reality to the world. "Being itself neither comes to be nor passes away."[61] There is reality in things which does not change, of and in which one can be *sure*. In this sureness, we can be secure from death.

Yet none of the objects of our knowledge and activity satisfies this definition of reality. All of them are subject in one respect or another to change and time. And so our search for security from time carries beyond nature to God. God is the absolutely *present* being, who fully satisfies Parmenides' postulate. He is the purely Present to himself and all things, without past or future. He is the exemplary fulfillment of the meaning of all beings: never not to be. In him, the denial of death is triumphant.[62]

V

Barth's *Commentary on Romans* was, therefore, wholly religious, and in the great western tradition. Its theme is the theme of Parmenides, its practice that of Socrates, its understanding that of Plato, its God that of Aristotle.

Eternity is "the meaning of all history,"[63] which "in fact runs through all history . . . and could always have been seen."[64] Just because the moment of apprehension of the eternal is "not a moment in time,"[65] "it is the red line that runs through the world's reality. . . ."[66] From the moment of apprehension of eternity, all times are contemporary, and all, without regard for historical distinctions, have meaning as possible occasions of this knowledge.[67]

Every word of this is pure religious platonism. And when Barth specifies *what* is the relation of time to eternity in the moment of crisis, the platonic element triumphs altogether. "The passible, recognized as such, is the *likeness* of the impassible."[68] This recognition occurs in the dialectic. Even the negative side of this, that the temporal reflects the eternal exactly by way of what it is *not,* that it is when we recognize the temporality, and so nothingness, of temporal realities that they point us to eternity, does not necessarily contradict Plato. And Barth can complete the correspondence by even adding the motive of remembrance: faith is "seeing the profane, relative and finally meaningless pattern of history; but also its meaning as likeness, witness and remembrance of a wholly other world. . . ."[69]

Just as in platonism, no particular historical event can be the union of time and eternity in any exclusive sense, not even the one we call "Jesus." "The meaning of every epoch is directly related to God."[70] "Always and everywhere . . . men have been made sick by God and so become well. . . ."[71] The knowledge of God is thus a possibility running through all history, as its inner meaning.[72] Jesus is merely—though "merely" is the wrong word—that historical point "at which the others are known in their connected meaning as the line . . . of history."[73] Thus "the visible meaning of Christian faith is the knowledge that the line of death which runs through the life of Jesus is the law and necessity of all human life. . . ."[74] The only suggestion of something other than pure platonic religion in all this, is that Jesus lights up the rest of temporal reality in this way only "by virtue of his effacement, departure and disappearance. . . ."[75] But even this *could* be said of Socrates.

Yet all this platonism operates somehow in reverse. That time is the likeness of eternity is surely pure religious platonism. But here the sense is always *"only* a likeness." The mortality which the dialectic uncovers running through all things once drove us to seek eternity; now it blocks all such attempts. And so the dialectic, which once was the reality of our life between time and eternity, here functions as the endlessly ingenious impossibility of living there between. The difference of time and eternity, which once propelled our thoughts on the way from time to eternity, here blocks the pathway between the two—in either direction.

The purpose of the dialectic is here to "expose the true nature . . . of this whole realm between."[76] The realm between is discovered to owe its existence to just what Parmenides was called to, man's refusal to believe in death.[77] But what Parmenides took as heroism acquires quite different qualifications here: in the pious man there lurks the "unabashed and ineradicable bourgeois—who does not want to die."[78]

The dynamic of our lives, which Barth also names "Eros,"[79] derives from the insoluble problem of our finitude[80]—just as Plato said. We are driven onward by "the thought of an infinite divine harmony beyond our world,"[81] by the postulate of the meaningful completeness which time lacks. We cannot avoid this drive, "as surely as man's unavoidable remembrance of his lost direct relation to God must become a psychic and historical occurrence."[82] The "religious *a priori*" is clearly affirmed.

In this journey between time and eternity we are in the realm of the demons, of what is neither God nor man, just again as Plato said. But the value of this description is reversed: according to Barth this is the realm of "mediated, derived, indirect, lordless divinities, powers and principalities, who discolor and dim the light of the true God," of "divinized natural and psychic powers" who "are now become gods, and rule our life's atmosphere as Jupiter and Mars, Isis and Osiris, Cybele and Attis."[83] What arises "in the middle between here and there" is "the religious fog or porridge, where by means of the most various, more or less sexually tinged . . . , mixing processes, sometimes purely human and animal happenings are elevated to be experiences of God, and sometimes God's being and action are 'experienced' as human or animal occurrences."[84]

For we who seek infinity are finite, and "the infinity which we can think out for ourselves is defined against our finitude and therefore itself but infinitude finitude. The harmony which we postulate is relative to our disharmony and is therefore merely the fata morgana of our desert wandering."[85] Eros, in all his manifestations, is Not-God, the god of this world. For he is merely "the highest affirmation of the reality of this world . . . despite the glorious attributes with which our pathos decorates him."[86] Just because Eros is the dynamic of our search for something other than this temporal world, he is merely "one thing in contrast to another, a pole to a counterpole . . . a god who is *not* wholly free, unique . . . and victorious. . . ."[87] The true God "never is nor will be identified with what we name, experience . . . , or worship as God. . . ."[88]

The punishment of this frivolous undertaking is that it succeeds, that Jupiter, Mars, Isis, Osiris, Cybele and Attis do jointly rule our lives.[89] But this Not-God is "made in the image of man" and so subject "to man's critique, and even denial, as soon as an Ivan Karamazov comes along."[90] Therefore this god cannot give our life meaning. In his service, man is alone with his own lack of meaning, to face "the meaningless rule" of the religious powers.[91]

The progress toward eternity which we make in our religiosity is thus illusory—also when the religiosity is genuine. "Everything that must be said of men in general must also be said of men of God. . . . There are no saints. . . ."[92] "In this world, there is no other man than just the old man."[93] This old man, the subject of the religious activity, can be a believer only in negating his religion, only in that "he subjects himself to this No," only in "the will to emptiness, in conscious persistence in being negated."[94]

VI

We may ask: what has made the difference? What has turned the dialectic into this massive critique of its old achievements? What has turned the dialectic, by which we once climbed to heaven, into a snare set anew at every attempted upward step? What is at work in the *Commentary on Romans* that did not come from Socrates?

What has reversed the meaning of the dialectic is that its God is not only the God of Aristotle, but also that of *Romans:* the God who "justifies" the "ungodly."[95] And to be justified as ungodly is an utterly different situation of life than the security of being-what-one-was. It is to be what one is not yet, and so to see the "Being" which is immunity to change as the very prison from which we are set free. It is to hope for a fulfillment of life not determined by what has been and so is, indeed, to find the meaning of life exactly in and as freedom from what has been, freedom in every new future from what already is. The one thing that the eternal Now, the eternal Presence, cannot do is justify the ungodly. If the justifier of the ungodly is God, then this Presence is Satan, from whom God frees us. If the justifier of the ungodly is God, then to be God is to have, not to be free of, the future. To be God is then to be the one who can call to and give permission to live by the unexpected.

Here the distinction between life and its meaning is the distinction between past and future rather than between time and eternity. Here the passion of life is hope rather than Eros. Here language is address rather than dialectics. And here the counterparts of Parmenides are the prophets of the Jewish Exile. What Jahweh said to them was the exact contradiction of the goddess' oracle to the Eleatic: "Remember not the former things, nor consider the things of old. Behold, I am doing a new thing. . . ."[96] Or again, "Behold, the days are coming, says the Lord, when I will make a new covenant with the house of Israel and the house of Judah, not like my covenant which I made with their fathers when I took them by the hand to bring them out of the land of Egypt, my covenant which they broke. . . ."[97]

Israel's life had been built upon trust in what God *had* done. He had brought them "out of the land of Egypt"; of a group of wandering tribes he had made a nation with its homeland. As a result of what *had* happened there was *now* a stable situation within which life had meaning. However great the difference may be between a life thus based on a past event in time, and one based on an event in the once-upon-a-time of eternity, and so between the faith of old Israel and the mythic nature-religion of other ancient peoples, this fundamental pattern was the same for both: the great saving change is past, salvation now lies in the continuance of the order then created.

When that order collapsed in the Exile, some despaired of their God, some turned to desperate restorations, and most no doubt tried to go on as before. But the prophets took the collapse of the past as the act of the very God whose revelation that past had been. In his name they preached that there was no more salvation in the old acts of God, no hope in clinging to what already was. Over against the past, and the present order of meanings it had created, Israel was lost and not saved. The old acts of God were but prophecies of his true reality in the future.

Nor did the prophets proclaim the new and different future acts of the Lord as a mere replacement for what had been lost. They attacked all reliance on the past *in order to* clear the way for *a life lived as response to promises.* The faith of Israel was to become a different thing: no longer trust in what had been, but hope in what would be.[98]

The prophets called for a new pattern of life in time. Jesus of Nazareth finally enacted it, as the crucified and risen one. If the creed is correct in summing up his life in the word "crucified," then its content was the abandonment of his life as what had been and therefore was in his possession. The subsequent proclamation "He is risen" is the word that his enactment of freedom from the past is indeed for him the triumph of his future. For us, it is the proclamation that he, who is always ahead of the claim of what has been, who *loves,* will be also for us the future from which we may live, our victory over the past and over death which makes all things past.

Jesus was a preacher of the Kingdom of Heaven. In the true tradition of the prophets, he proclaimed the future of God, the day of God of which all other days are but anticipations. What he said of this day was not original, but he said it in a new way. He spoke of the coming Kingdom in such a way as to cancel the time between the moment of hearing his call and the coming moment of God: those who heard and understood no longer had time to prepare for the Kingdom, could no longer say that they would indeed have someday to reckon with God. Then and there they either became citizens of the Kingdom or found they had already declined.

That is, the possibility of neutralizing God's future, of incorporating it into the present by *planning* for it, was taken from Jesus' hearers. His proclamation asserted God's future as future, as free, unpredictable, uncontrollable and sovereign.

Yet just so he also healed the isolation of the future from the present, healed the unreality of the future. In his preaching, the future in fact now determined the present, determined the present moment's content of responsibilities proposed by the past, and of vetoes imposed on present possibilities for the future by past occasions of fear and refusal of the future. "Your sins are forgiven," he said—and by his word brought it about that what is to come determined the possibilities his hearers might find in their pasts, rather than the usual other way about. He ate with crooks and whores—he did not merely hold out the future ideal of being other than their past had made them, he enacted that possibility as their present reality. Just as the past presented them, they *were* his future brothers.

For his pains, he was crucified. He was crucified by the refusal of the past to give up its rule and be real only in the future. He was crucified by the horror of freedom present in the religion even of the heirs of the prophets. *Such* a union of past and future in the present as occurred in his words and actions, a victory of the future over the past and for the past, was there defined as suffering and death. It was defined as losing one's life, in order to gain it—with the "in order to" representing not a mere calculation, but the ultimate wager on the future.⁹⁹

So the life called for by the exilic prophets was lived—and it was revealed why it was not lived before. Alienated, past-bound, man can be free for the future only in death—and then it is too late. Only the *success of death,* only resurrection, can be the act of life from the future free from and for the past. If Jesus is risen, this life is enacted.

And if he is risen, then he himself is not only an item of the past. Were he not risen, allegiance to him, the attempt to enact the futurity which he enacted, would be itself an imitating of the past—and so self-defeating. But he is risen, which means that we may not only remember him as a past event, but await him as the future: "He will come again with glory to judge the quick and the dead." The word which came to utterance in him will be spoken as the conclusion of the conversation of our lives; involvement in his history of self-giving to his fellows will be the justifying conclusion also of our lives—a self-giving which will never conclude because it will *be* the conclusion. The proclamation that Jesus is risen is the equivalent of Plato's artistic vision of Socrates as the image of eternity. It is a proclamation and not a vision because it is the future and not the eternal that triumphs in it.

It is in general a correct intuition that has so often paired Socrates with Jesus. As Socrates judged time by eternity, so Jesus judged the present by the future. As Socrates lived between time and eternity, so Jesus lived for the present from the future. As Socrates in his death became Eros, the moving image of the changeless deity, so the crucified Jesus is believed as the Incarnation of the Coming One. The different wordings of the two parts of this sentence are dictated by the difference of the two apprehensions of reality. The timeless God can have images, but cannot be incarnate. The God of the future can be incarnate, but cannot have images. Finally, as Plato was to Socrates, so John and Paul were to Jesus.

We may as well use the word, and say the expected thing. The word of the justification of the ungodly apprehends reality as *history*. If I am justified as ungodly, then my life is a constant departure from what I am toward what I am not yet. It is a choice for the insecurity of the non-given, for transcendence in time. Again, if I am justified as ungodly, then I do not justify myself, then the meaning of my life is essentially enacted as a conversation with one other than myself. Then life is inherently antiphonal. For I cannot live by what I am not yet except as I am addressed by one who is what I am not: the justification of the ungodly is necessarily communication. Self-transcendence in time and communication are exactly the two notes of all typical modern understandings of the historicity of human being. Barth has himself given as good a summary as any other: "The history of a being begins, continues and is completed when something other than itself and transcending its own nature encounters it, approaches it and determines its being in the nature proper to it, so that it is compelled and enabled to transcend itself in response and in relation to this new factor."[100]

VII

It is neither surprising nor reprehensible that as the church incorporated the life of the ancient world within itself, it should have identified these two oppositions, that it should have interpreted the eternity of Plato as the future of the prophets. The fathers have been much blamed for "hellenizing" Christianity. But this is simply to blame them, who would have been hellenists in any case, for being Christian. And they did not so much interpret the faith by hellenistic religion, as interpret hellenistic religion by the faith. By this interpretation the fathers created something new, something which was neither simply Christian faith nor a normal religion: the Christian religion, a *religion about an historical, temporal event.*

The single great founder of our religion was Origen.[101] He lived in the great religious crisis of antiquity, in which men came to feel the clash of time and eternity as too great to contain in their lives. Men no longer felt able to stand where Socrates stood, or reach God by dialectic, for our language has a grammar appropriate to time—but God is eternal. Thus the quest of the age was for a bridge between time and eternity, for an Eros who would be more than the mere inner dynamic of the individual's own life, who would be a tangible separate reality between time and eternity to lead us from the one to the other. The quest was for Socrates as a demi-god, for an Image of eternity which we might behold and lean on, and not only be.

Origen proposed Jesus Christ for the role of subsisting Eros—as others proposed various other persons, mythical figures, or abstract entities. He begins with an Aristotelean notion: "God does not have knowledge of himself through a medium, but by virtue of his self-relatedness, being himself both act of knowing and object known."[102] In this act God therefore posits himself-as-the-content-of-his-knowledge, the *Logos*. And "in the Logos, since he is God and the Image of the unseen God, can be seen the Father who begot him. Thus He who looks into the Image of the unseen God is able to intuit also the Prototype of the Image. . . ."[103] Jesus Christ, says Origen, is this Logos-Image.

So far this could all be pure late platonism. But Origen has proposed an *historical* figure as the Logos, so that it is exactly this person's recorded history which is the image in which we see God: the inner-trinitarian life of the Logos is an image of the Father, and "Jesus' deeds are mirrors"[104] of the life of the Logos. As it is events in time which are the revelation, the "eternal" truths of which they are the image are also the *future goal* of these events, they are "the things to come,"[105] the events of the Last Exodus.[106]

Appropriately, Origen replaces the dialectic, as the way of moving in thought toward the eternal, with allegorical exegesis of Scripture. This is, like the dialectic, a way of so speaking about the things of this world that our language opens itself toward the transcendent meaning of this world. But here transcendence is the *goal* of history, rather than its eternal cancellation. Here the opening to transcendence is done by interpreting biblical *history* as the image of its own goal; allegorical exegesis was a dialectic operating not on common opinion but on a *narrative*. It was a sort of dialectic of history.

In Origen we see emerge the familiar outlines of Christianity as we have known it. The picture was completed with the doctrine of man, worked out by a soberer platonist than Origen, and the father of western Christianity, Augustine. "You have made us for yourself, and our hearts are restless until they rest in you,"[107] can stand as the theme for all western Christianity's understanding of man. Man is intrinsically a being on his way home. He is weary and lost, tempted to settle down in some far country, yet drawn ever on by that one for whose fellowship he is destined. The *Confessions* are the first great document of such a journey.

But, "You have made us for yourself, and our hearts are restless until they rest in you," could very well also have been said by Socrates. And the *Confessions* are set in a thoroughly platonic framework. Reality is a structure of levels, rising from brute matter through the level of life to pure spiritual reality, above which is God himself. On this great ladder of being, man is the movable item: united by his spirit to the spiritual and by his body to the material, man is drawn both up and down. If his direction is from God toward material things, he is in sin; if he turns from material things to God he is being saved; grace is the possibility of this turn. The protagonist of the *Confessions* is exactly the erotic philosopher of the *Symposium*.

Yet the *Confessions* are also a document of the apprehension of reality as history. Augustine's record of the way upward takes the form of the first autobiography. It takes also the form of one side of a long *conversation* with God. Augustine's God is one who has spoken to him, who has taken an initiative with him; only in response to this initial address by God has there occurred that journey through life which the *Confessions* describe. "You will not desert me when I call on you, for before I could call on you, you anticipated me [*praevenisti*] . . . with many voices, so that I should hear from far off and turn and call on you who were calling me. . . ."[108] The whole story is a document of "praevenient grace," the initiative of God which opens history—and the one thing most inappropriate to, and unworthy of, Aristotle's God.

Augustine was well aware of the combination he was making. In a famous passage, he described his reception of the entire religious understanding of late antiquity, as this was concentrated in the conception of the Logos. And he specified exactly what he missed in antique religion: "I read there that God the Logos was not born of the flesh . . . but of God. But that the Logos became flesh and lived with us, I did not read there."[109] What he missed was the event in history; this he found only in the Scriptures.

Whether one should call classical Christianity's union of life for eternity and life for the future, of longing for stasis and life in history, a "synthesis" or an uneasy accommodation will always be disputed. In any case, this remarkable thing, a religion about an historical occurrence, survived for a thousand years as the soul of western civilization. Or perhaps that is the wrong way to put it. For a religion is always the religion of a culture. Only by becoming the religion of the West did Christian faith become the Christian *religion;* the synthesis we have just described was the inner transformation attendant on this event.

What was to come of this synthesis could not have been predicted, nor can the Fathers be faulted for it. But if God is to be at once God of history and changelessly eternal, he must be *the God of past history,* and this is what he became in the history of Christian religion. For of all the modes of time, it is the past which can be changeless, if it is not appropriated into a life lived from a future. The God of a *religion* about *history* is neither the eternity of Plato nor the God who comes from and for the future. He is the God of frozen history, the God of what *has* happened. He is the God who has a "plan" of salvation, i.e., a fixed course set by past decisions and events. He is the God of objective past "mighty deeds." He is the God of pre-Exilic Israel become absolute. Moreover, the God of past history is the *moralistic* God, who holds us to what we *have* done and so *are,* over against whom we are defined by the permanent part of our temporality, the past. His meaning for us is guilt.

We may protest that this is not the God we proclaim or worship. We may protest that no theologian of the church has ever so understood God. And our protests would be, so far as they go, correct. Yet the whole world—including ourselves in all but our most theological or saintly moments—has heard exactly the moralistic God in our talk of God and seen the moralistic God in our behavior. All the world thinks of the Christian God as the guardian of morality, with a special attachment to the status quo and the past. This impression cannot have arisen by accident. Whatever we may have wanted to say *about* God, the very structure of our thought of God, behind and above all our explicit talk of his love and forgiveness and newness, has determined that what has been heard has been the voice of guilt.

It was not, therefore, to be expected that the Christian religion could be stable. For under the God of past history no man can live—and as the inner logic of Christian religion works itself out, and the face of this God shows itself ever more clearly, men will rebel against him to save their souls. The eternity of Socrates and Plato meant escape from history. But by being identified with the ruler of history, eternal being is defined by what happens in history, which has to mean by what *has* happened in *past* history. Then eternity is no longer an escape from history, but the barrier shutting us into history, into past history. Now the meaning of eternity is condemnation to live by what we have been and done. Its meaning is guilt. Conversely, the God of the gospel is the God who *both* accuses and promises, condemns and accepts; he is the justifier of the ungodly, of those he has judged. But by being identified as changeless eternity he is prohibited from promising, from justifying freely in defiance of the condemnation he has just spoken. From both sides, the God of historical religion, the God of past history, is a God who always condemns. We must dethrone him or die.

Historical religion, where "religion" has the specific content it does in the West, had to be self-destructive. We need not—and I could not—unravel the shifting circumstances that determined how long the synthesis in fact endured. But since the fifteenth century, the history of the West has been a struggle on all fronts—philosophical, theological, political and ecclesiastical—to halt the breakup we brought on ourselves by creating Christianity as our religion.

The plot of this history of breakup matches exactly the dialectics of the *Commentary on Romans.* And the result is also the same: the Christian religion becomes unable to function as a religion, the religion of the West; and the Christian gospel loses its old language.

Chapter Two
The Self-Cancellation of Historical Religion

I

The *Commentary on Romans* can serve as a theory of the history of the perfecting of historical religion—which is also its self-cancellation. To see the book from this viewpoint, we must study more closely its dialectic of unity and difference between time and eternity.

"Originally, man lived in Paradise, where there is no Over and Under, no Absolute and Relative, no Beyond or This side. . . ." Man is, and is known by God to be, other than God, "the creature as a second reality alongside the Creator." But this difference, real in God, was not supposed to become a content of *man's* own knowledge and will; we were not to affirm the objective distinction of time from eternity, were not to affirm our separation from God. And so long as man does not make his difference from God a content of his life, he lives directly for and with God, for the eternal. God, in whom alone the difference is then real, transcends all such differences.[1]

"But now observe in Michelangelo's *Creation of Eve* the fatal gesture of worship, with which Eve enters the scene, and the warning hand with which God . . . answers this gesture. Here what should not be prepares itself. Eve (truly to her credit; she is the first religious personality) is the first to step over against God, worshipping him but just so establishing her boundaries against him. . . . The 'famous snake' is immediately on the spot, the first conversation *about* God (prototype of all sermons) is held, God's command becomes an object of human pondering (pastoral counselling) . . . ,"² and the fall has occurred.

In that the creature defines himself over against God, the distinction between time and eternity now operates for him, with the fatal meaning the distinction must have for the one who is not God. The creature *in himself* is other than God, and so worthless and negated. The creature is, of course, *not to be* in himself, but is rather to see his life for and from God. But now his independence of God, given for *God* in the very fact of his creaturely existence, is seized as his possibility, and the difference between God and man, time and eternity, is established as the death that it is not for God, but is for the temporal creature.

This fall is the same as the birth of religion. For *that* distinction between time and eternity which we make a content of our temporal lives cannot be a distinction between time and God's eternity, but only a relative distinction within time. This eternity is the projected eternity which is but a negative image of time—and so is born Eros, time's striving to become eternity.

Precisely this striving is thus the struggle *against* the true difference of time and eternity, the struggle against God's being other than we. And so the event we are describing is the fall of and into sin. In that I now, having defined myself over against God, seek a direct relation to him, I do this as a rebellion against the boundary between him and me, and just so disrupt the relation.³ "For if man 'is as God' and knows good and evil," i.e., knows the difference between eternity and time, "this is the destruction of his true direct relation to God, since thereby this direct relation becomes one content of his life among others."⁴

This doctrine, in its knotted convolution of true and false unities and differences between time and eternity, in which every position of unity or duality can be transcended by a different position, is a hard one to hold on to. It results from Barth's holding together a purely religious vision of perfection and an apprehension of actual existence as the justification of the ungodly. It results, that is, from the Christian synthesis. Just so it perfectly corresponds to the beginning point of western history, describing a fundamental and irresolvable ambiguity as the origin of its strange restlessness.

Our history has been a dizzying tail-chase, a restless succession of settlements of the relation between life and its goal, each of which has cancelled its predecessor by showing it undermined by a transcending dichotomy, only to suffer the same fate itself. The development of the Christian religion in the *Commentary on Romans,* and the position in which that development finally puts the Christian, provide a theory also of this history; and we turn back to it.

The religious attempt to overcome the difference between time and eternity is itself possible only as the "impression left behind in . . . history" of God's *genuine* overcoming of the division, i.e., of "revelation." It is "the burned-out crater of God's address,"[5] the unavoidable "historical canalization of God's act on man, an act which itself never becomes history."[6] But why should God thus make possible the rebellion against him? Because just in this rebellion we are driven to the last extremity of the possibilities open to us as those who have defined ourselves over against God[7]—and so to their *crisis*.[8]

Any sort of relation to a deity is a disturbance, the experience of a question.[9] "Religion is anything but harmony. . . . Innocent westerners . . . may think it is, as long as they can. Here is the abyss, here demons appear (Ivan Karamazov and Luther!)."[10] Religion means sinking into the problematic of human life, until we reach the last human possibility in which we reach out to the unknown God, to the Yes in the No that bounds all our strivings, and find that also our reaching out does not save us.[11] No doubt we embark on religion because we think to find security and fulfillment in it, but the result is the reverse.[12]

In this crisis, the possibility of knowing God in his temporal reflections opens. "In the radical cancellation of historical . . . realities, there appears . . . their true, eternal meaning."[13] All the realities of this world are, as such, caught up in the religious titanism. They are all objects of worship. Just so they are such that their *negation,* despair of their value, discovers them as pointers to the true God. The reference away from itself which one of our idols makes when it fails us, is exactly the authentic concept of that thing as what it really is, God's creature.[14] Every temporal reality is, when known as *only* a temporal reality,[15] an image of the eternal God. In Jesus Christ "humanity, worldly reality, history . . . appear as what they are: only transparencies, images, hints, only relativities to God. . . ."[16] Knowing him, we can know our world as a "world of life, in which nothing . . . temporal . . . consists only in what it is, but also in what it means. . . ."[17]

Thus the play of unity and difference between time and eternity makes yet another flip. Known in its opposition to the eternal, the temporal is the image of the eternal—and so is after all *united* to it. What is imaged is precisely the grace of God, "which cannot be content . . . even before the iron bar which separates . . . the infinite from the finite."[18] In the moment of crisis we are utterly cut off from God, and "the greatest distance between God and man is their true oneness. In that time and eternity . . . are in Jesus unambiguously torn apart, they are also . . . united in God. . . ."[19] The "mere humanity of man and the mere deity of God" are transcended,[20] and the "oneness of this side with the beyond" occurs.[21] For in the eternal God, and therefore in reality, the temporal does not stand over against the eternal as a second independent reality.[22] God's eternity transcends the difference of time and eternity;[23] his eternity is not something cut off from time, but is time's "truth, its origin . . . the cancellation of all relativity and therefore the reality of all relative realities. . . ."[24]

Yet it is essential to remind ourselves that this unity is real only as the critical moment. The oneness of time and eternity behind and above the separation of time and eternity is indeed God's Yes. But we hear it only *as* a No. It is only because God's judgment is so radical, the total denial of meaning to our temporal life, that it binds us to eternity.[25] The "sole positive connection between here and there" is "knowledge of the fundamental separation" between them.[26]

Therefore, within the platonic scheme of time, eternity and the immanent unity of time and eternity, that unity itself is grasped as *history,* fully in the sense of *Isaiah* or *Romans.* For it is not a standing relation between two realities, but rather the *critique* of the one by the other, the denial of the one reality by a freedom so complete as to be able to affirm by the denial; it is the justification of the ungodly. The most compressed possible expression which the *Commentary on Romans* can use for the relation of time and eternity is that it is "a duality which is only posited in being transcended and whose transcending is precisely its positing."[27] Since the negativity of time is the same as its difference from eternity, and since this difference is posited only in its meaning, which is exactly the *oneness* of time and eternity *in eternity,* the relation between time and eternity is an *occurrence with a goal,* a movement from a past to a future. The relation of time and eternity "occurs *for* the second against the first, as a turning . . . *from* the first *to* the second, as a victory of the second over the first."[28] In what we *are,* in the sense of Parmenides' being, we remain always separated from God. It is in the *miracle* of being what we are not yet[29] that we are united with him; the proclamation of our union with him is proclamation of a hope,[30] of a future.[31]

In the *Commentary on Romans* the meeting of time and eternity is in itself a movement to a future. This is the perfected historicizing of platonic religion.

But it is equally the perfect capture of history by eternity. The events which Jeremiah grasped as history were the political and religious events of the day's news, and the future from which he so grasped them was of the same order. But in the *Commentary on*

Romans the critique in which the unity of time and eternity is movement and history is conducted from eternity, so that the occurrence, the movement, is not in time, but of time to eternity—and so *in* eternity. It occurs solely in God.

The divine act of God never becomes what we can know or experience as history.[32] The events by which God's act "makes itself observable within visible history" are mere "empty spaces" in history, which, moreover, are not themselves the act of God, "even when called 'the life of Jesus.' And insofar as this our world is touched in Jesus by the other world, it ceases to be historically visible...."[33] The meaninglessness of our history remains meaningless despite the meaning God finds in it.[34]

In our reality, there is only the old religious man, never the believer[35], and the true church never appears in church history.[36] Rather the saving act of God, the history which is the unity of time and eternity, is their "connection in God."[37] It is "the *actus purus* of an invisible event in God. The oneness of God's will divides itself into duality, in order to prove itself as oneness in overcoming this duality...." And it is essential not to compare this "invisible event in God" with any occurrence of what we know and experience as history.[38] The eternal meaning of what we do in time is God's intention in it and not ours,[39] it is a decision which is made "only in God himself, in God alone."[40]

Thus the sole historical event, in the prophetic sense of "history," is the event of God's eternal deciding, of *predestination*. The doctrine of predestination is the heart of the *Commentary on Romans,* and the most succinct expression of its basic pattern.

The invisible origin of all things is the decree of God before all time. The fall and the redemption are equally determinations of all history, which come finally "from the mystery of divine predestination."[41] Double predestination is the key to the Christian proclamation,[42] and only the God hidden in this mystery is the true God.[43] Nor are we left in any doubt that predestination is an event in that eternity which is *not* time; predestination is a "decree which is made in God *before* all time and so also *before* each moment of time."[44]

The relation between the two sides of double predestination, God's will of reprobation and his will of acceptance, is but another form of the relation we have traced between time and eternity; for the meaning of time, as different from eternity, is rejection, and the meaning of eternity for time is acceptance. In time we are all rejected; in eternity we are all chosen.[45] But our rejection is not for its own sake, and God's decision to accept us in spite of our rejection is not conditional on that rejection. Rather, the contrary is true. Reprobation is the mere presupposition of election, the unavoidable condition of God's will to show *mercy*.[46] In God himself "there is no 'and,' no duality," but only the transcending of reprobation by election. God in his eternity is the God of *election*. But his election is the election of *man* only in the doubleness of reprobation and election.[47] In eternity, God is the God of the elect and in time the God of the rejected;[48] the elect man is in time the rejected, and the rejected is in eternity the elect—the elect man is the invisible rejected man and the rejected man is the visible elect man.[49] But it is election which is the meaning of reprobation and so eternity that is the meaning of time.[50]

The eternal decision of God is thus a *history*. It is a *movement* in God "from time to eternity, from rejection to election . . . ,"[51] a genuine *way* that God travels, with a beginning—rejection, and an end—acceptance.[52] It is an event with a *purpose,* a goal.[53] "The oneness of God's will divides itself into duality, in order to prove itself as oneness in overcoming this duality. . . ."

So far the doctrine of election as the *Commentary on Romans* develops it. What has happened here? We may, from one point of view, regard this doctrine as the triumph, at long last, of the apprehension of reality as history. God himself is *defined* as the God of predestination, as the one who rejects in order to accept, who transcends the past from the future. He is defined *as the event of the justification of the ungodly:* He is defined as transcendence in history. This is an epochal event. Within Christian faith prior to the creation of the Christian religion, no definition of God was needed or wanted. Within the theology of the Christian religion, a definition is needed, and has always been provided otherwise. This is the first time God has been *defined* as history, as the triumph of the future over the past—though as an additional predicate of a God otherwise defined, this note has always been present in Christian theology and could not have failed without that theology ceasing to be Christian.

Moreover, this event in God is the unity of our time with God's eternity. It is thus the unity of our lives with their meaning—so that here the very possibility of our lives having a meaning is in the justification of the ungodly, is in their historicity.

Yet we may equally well regard the doctrine of the *Commentary on Romans* as the final triumph of platonic religion over the believing apprehension of history. That the meeting of Parmenides' two worlds is here a *movement* of the justification of the ungodly, is the final historicizing of platonism. But just so this history between God and us becomes a history in God *alone,* an *eternal* history, a history which *cannot be narrated.* It becomes—and this is the decisive passage in the entire *Commentary on Romans*—a history "of which no history can be narrated, because it occurs . . . eternally."[54]

Therewith our religious devotion to eternity, and our faith as life in history from the future, finally completely immobilize each other—and the inner impossibility of the Christian religion becomes actual. This is the *event* in the *Commentary on Romans*.

On the one hand, the religion of the *Commentary on Romans* could not actually function as religion, for its eternity is not available to us, is not a super-world in which we may seek what we lack in this world. It is not available because its eternity is at the same time its permanent futurity—here is the mark left on it by faith in justification of the ungodly. This *aeternum* is a *"futurum aeternum"*[55] a unity with God which is *"always* not yet arrived . . . , always yet to be awaited,"[56] a salvation to which our relation can only be hope.

There is nothing we can do about the eternity of the *Commentary on Romans;* the possibility of reunion which *God* finds in it "can never become a human possibility."[57] The relation to God is authentic only as his miracle "straight down from above—its historical and psychic side is always its untruth."[58] The subject of the successful relation to God is never I,[59] and the calling I may find in it is never "a step in the development" of my own life.[60] We simply cannot *practice* this religion.

Most particularly, the possibility of *knowing* the eternal disappears. When we use the word "God," we do not know what we are saying.[61] Theology is done in the *Commentary on Romans* as pure negative theology; always it is said what God is not. This is, of course, in the great tradition. But in the tradition of religion the negative predications are *balanced* with positive predications, and both are then taken up into hyperpredications: e.g., "God is love. God is not what men know as love. God is *perfect love."* In the *Commentary on Romans,* positive predications are not balanced against the negative; they are based, with "therefore," upon them. For example: God is "not man, and just therefore . . . the truth . . . of man."[62] Here is a God whom we cannot reach or worship, after whom "man can *only* question and just therefore not even question."[63]

Yet although religion is immobilized, so also is faith. The eternalization of the history between God and man robs faith of its language. The message of faith, the "gospel," is a *narrative*. Surely it is a description of the gospel sufficiently primitive to satisfy everyone, if we say that it is the story of Jesus told as that story from which the hearers may hear their destiny, hear what life is for. For the gospel is the story of Jesus told as the story of the last future, as a message of hope. It says: the story of life-out-of-death and love-out-of-hatred which is enacted in the events of this man's life will be the conclusion of your life also. Thus the gospel is a proclamation of a future hope *with a narrative content*. But in the *Commentary on Romans* it has become an eternal event, of which nothing can be narrated. The doctrine of predestination is the death-blow to religion; but in the *Commentary on Romans* it is the death-blow also to faith's proclamation, for it absorbs the history to which we are called to testify into an eternal now without narrative extension—of which there is then nothing to say.[64]

If there is to be a gospel, then the act of God for which we hope must be an occurrence new and different from what goes before it, and so distinguishable in words from other events. We must be able to give a narrative description which differentiates the future we proclaim from other possible and actual occurrences. But in the *Commentary on Romans* the eternalization of the history to which we testify has made it into a "future . . . , which will never and in no way become time,"[65] so that such a narrative cannot be made: " . . . spoken . . . by men, the new thing of the gospel is nothing new. . . ."[66] The *contents* of our future will never be the resurrection; the contents of our future will always be only "an image of our eternity." The eternal event of resurrection itself is "neither in my past nor in my present nor in my future an event along with other events."[67]

Therefore, "It must not be that we have words and concepts" for the eternal event of salvation, for "then it wouldn't be that event."[68] The proclamation can at best be an "as if" proclamation of God's act,[69] "a hidden proclamation."[70] A consistent policy based on the *Commentary on Romans* would be a portentous silence, which might be religiously impressive, but would mark the cessation of the gospel.[71]

II

Just this point to which the dialectic of the *Commentary on Romans* brings us is surely also the point to which our history has brought us: our religion no longer functions satisfactorily as religion, and the church is no longer able to get the gospel said, to make people hear its talk of Jesus as a welcome message of hope. In this impasse, the God of past history rules alone, rules exactly by his immobility and our answering impotence. Moreover, the course of the history which has brought us to this point matches exactly the course of the dialectics of religion in the *Commentary on Romans*.

It is surely not necessary to plod once again through the melancholy details of the decadence of the Christian religion.[72] On the one hand, the churches maintain their often precarious existence by an almost complete surrender of any attempt to proclaim, to bring a gospel of any sort. The church has, quite evidently, nothing whatever *of its own* to say. The movements that are hailed as budding renewals —the ecumenical movement, the civil rights movement, the calls for political and economic involvement in emerging megalopolitan society—always turn out to be the church belatedly repeating what everyone but the religious had long since said. The task of calling men into, say, the challenge of the great cities, *by* talking of Jesus, and so of speaking a message that would otherwise not be heard, is evidently beyond us. As for the preaching *in* the church, the main trouble is that the particular sort of talking properly called preaching scarcely occurs any longer. The very notion of a gospel, of attempting to narrate Jesus' story as a message of hope to the hearers, simply does not occur to our clergy. The faith has lost its voice—or putting the matter sociologically: "Although the specialized religious institutions have not—entirely—abandoned the traditional Christian rhetoric, that rhetoric increasingly expresses 'ultimate' meanings that have only a tenuous relation to the traditional Christian universe."[73]

But this sellout has purchased no advantage for Christianity. For the civic religiosity which the churches now represent is obviously and increasingly uninteresting to society and to the actual life of individuals. It is uninteresting because it is fraudulent. Our religion is fraudulent because, although the very function of religion is to give meaning to life *as a whole,* it is in contemporary culture restricted to the "private life," i.e., excluded from most of our serious and effective pursuits, which in fact—whatever rhetoric we may use —are governed by norms set by wholly autonomous secular institutions.[74]

III

The breakdown of Christianity is most clearly and directly objectivized in the anti-church which Christianity has brought forth from itself: Marxism. In its critique of religion, Marxism was a protest against that justification of the status quo which is the content of the concept of eternity. Against religion's changeless God, Marxism protested in the name of human freedom, in the name of the future. Its protest was the same as the believer's.

Marxist critique of religion centered in the concept of "alienation." The alienated man seeks the fulfillment he does not find within history—due to the class structure of society—outside of history in eternity.

Feuerbach had already applied the concept to religion; Marxism developed a superior *social* version of his critique. Within the reciprocity of society, man is the creator of his own life, in that the conditions of his life are shaped by his own choice. That is, man is an historical or, in the language of Marx's philosophical tradition, a "conscious" being. Within a class society, the products of the individual's historical activity, at the same time that they mean for him his life as he himself creates it, are not in his control. His historicity therefore means for him that his life is perpetually beyond his reach; he is alienated. Religion is the mode of "consciousness," of being related to future fulfillment, which corresponds to this objective alienation. Marxism was also aware that Christianity is special in this connection; Marxism saw how within Christianity a persistent critique cuts away the middle-beings which in other religions mitigate the difference between time and eternity. For Marxism this meant that in Christianity the alienation of historical activity from its meaning is total, corresponding to the full development of class society in the West.

This analysis is partial, but in its limits quite correct as an analysis of the Christian religion in its historical reality—though the Marxist attempt to say which came first, the religion or the society, was of course idle. And when this analysis functions as a critique, it does indeed seem to strike home. On the convinced Marxist, apologetics based on appeals to his religious needs make no impact. This need not, of course, mean that he has no needs one might wish to call "religious." But he evidently does not need that sort of religion which Christianity has purveyed. He does not need the God of past history. Marxism is also, and even more significantly, able to produce societies in which those who are not Marxists seem able to get along nicely without this religion.

Yet Marxism can by no means be regarded as a triumph of life for the future over timeless eternity. On the contrary, it all too often produced societies which in their actual functioning have been reactionary in the extreme. This is so because Marxism did not overcome the notion of a timeless super-reality, but merely relocated it in a less obvious place, in the notion of the historical process as a whole. The laws which govern history were themselves supposed to be timeless and unaffected by decisions in time—and these laws wholly determine the future. From the brutal and often distasteful realities of revolutionary reality, the Marxist could therefore flee to contemplating the eternal paradise of the classless society. And he could justify absolutely any status quo by its necessity in the eternal plan.

IV

Thus Marxism was the mirror-image and historically appropriate successor of the last and greatest attempt to *save* the Christian religion, Hegelianism. The movement from Hegel to Marx, and from the reasonable state of which Hegel was the apologist to the Marxist revolution, is exactly the movement of the self-cancellation of historical religion as this is taught by the dialectics of the *Commentary on Romans.*

Hegel brought the Christian synthesis or accommodation to its perfection, by *defining* reality as *history.* Reality is defined as essentially a "process," a "course" which the concept of reality runs through contradiction and new resolutions: the unity of reality is not a "changelessly persistent identity," but rather the continuity of a triumphant life-history.[75] "Spirit" is the substance of history, and the substance of spirit is "freedom." [76] Indeed, reality *is* freedom.[77]

Aristotle's question, "What is anything *always,* i.e., so long as it is real?" is given the surprising answer: "open to the future." Hegel's whole way of thinking is set by his determination to be true to the apprehension of reality as history. It is because reality as history brings into being what was not, and so is contradictory in its predicates when seen as a whole, that ordinary reasoning is insufficient, and that Hegel develops a mode of thinking which finds the intelligibility of reality exactly in the *plot* of the drama of contradiction, resolution and new contradiction, i.e., in the plot of history in its freedom and conflicts. Reality is exactly the self-overcoming of contradiction.[78] Throughout his thought Hegel uses the difference of finite and infinite to generate and resolve contradictions, in creating a picture of reality in which every given position of thought and reality is true to itself only in that it overcomes its own fixed and given actuality.[79] The motif of this picture is the justification of the ungodly.

After Hegel, or after the revolutions which he tried to comprehend, we cannot again have the security of an eternal order, either social or metaphysical. Yet this does not mean that life for an open future triumphed in Hegel, for his thought can equally well be understood as the final subjugation of history to the dream of a changeless eternity—a dream now, however, without comfort.

Hegel's "logic" is a *definition* of reality, a definition as freedom, to be sure, but nonetheless a definition, a determination of what *can* happen. The search for the meaning of what happens is understood as the search for the *necessity* of what happens, for a "logical" necessity determined by the transcendental laws of thought, that is, by the nature of an unchanging reality.[80] The fundamental antihistorical drive in Hegel is that all things are understood as the self-development of thought—and that what thought is is not supposed to be changeable in history. "Freedom" itself is thus understood as the superiority to the contingencies of history of a subjectivity which is "free" precisely in that nothing can alter its self-determination, in that it is unchangingly itself.[81] Indeed, the very content of the idea which defines reality is the insight we will achieve at the end of history that nothing is in the end of history which was not in its beginning.[82]

Absolute subjectivity, or "spirit," is the fulfillment of Aristotle's search for God as a perfectly present being. The "logic" is the system of "pure" ideas, i.e., of those which thought has of itself,[83] and so constitutes a description exactly of "the unmoved mover."[84] Hegel's "Spirit" is pure consciousness, pure presence to itself and in itself to all things—the final explication of God as Presence. "Spirit" is cancellation of all finite things in infinity. We may put it so: reality is understood as an *occurrence,* and so historically, but as the occurrence *of* self-identity, the occurrence of Aristotle's God exactly.

The God of Hegel is the perfected realization of the God of *past* history. For history encompassed in a changeless definition of what can be real would be *past* history, a history past in its totality. Reality is history, says Hegel, but means a history in which *all is already decided.*

Perhaps at one point the contrast between Hegel and faith is most apparent. Hegel says: "Thus the Spirit is purely present to itself, and therewith free, for freedom is being with oneself even in the other."[85] The freedom of the justification of the ungodly is precisely the opposite: being with the other even in oneself.

Thus at the same time that Hegel made the old security in the changeless impossible, the dream of eternity at last wholly mastered history. Hegelianism was the perfected synthesis of futurity and eternity, the perfected theology of the Christian religion; but it was also their mutual immobilization. Hegelianism is the perfected theology of the God of past history.

It was not strange, therefore, that Hegelianism so signally failed to survive its creator. Hegel in actual fact developed the religion about an historical event to the same simultaneous perfection and inner impossibility to which its dialectic brings us within the *Commentary on Romans.* The correspondence between Hegel and the development in the *Commentary on Romans* is throughout so perfect that I have not felt it necessary to keep pointing it out.[86] And just as the finished synthesis of life for the future and life for eternity in the *Commentary on Romans* reveals itself as the impossibility of both, so in actual history, only a sort of blink of the eyes, an apprehension of the whole pattern from the other end, was necessary to turn Hegel's defense of the Christian religion into its irrefutable critique. Feuerbach and Marx, and many others, blinked—and that blink is the history we are still living.

V

The end of this history has already come to word many times. Richard Rubenstein has now brought it to words within the theology of an historical religion, in *After Auschwitz*. The inner dialectics of the Jewish and Christian versions of historical religion are of course not quite the same, but here Rubenstein can speak for all.

Rubenstein's rebellion is elementary. "How can Jews believe in an omnipotent, beneficent God after Auschwitz?"[87] A "God of history," a God who has elected Israel to its fate and otherwise controlled what has happened in history, must also have been the author of Auschwitz. Such a God must be denied—"the old God of Jewish patriarchal monotheism" is dead.[88]

It would be easy to rebut Rubenstein. He has not noticed even the abstract possibility of any God of history other than the God of past history, so that the God whose death he announces has in fact been dead since the Babylonian Exile of Israel. The concept of "history" with which he works is one which lacks all reference to the future, and to the meaning of the future for the past. "History" for him is simply what *has* happened.

The prophetic faith in the God of history—which Rubenstein supposes himself to be abandoning—was born out of the Babylonian Exile, a catastrophe of the patriarchal faith in the God of past history even more decisive than Auschwitz. It cannot, therefore, be rebutted by such a catastrophe. Rubenstein has not abandoned the prophetic faith in history; he has not yet arrived at it. It is remarkable that the entire argument of *After Auschwitz* is already in the book of *Ecclesiastes,* the document of a response to the Exile alternative to that of the prophets.[89] Indeed it is odd that Rubenstein should view the situation as somehow different *after* Auschwitz. For if God is to be judged by past history, then the murder of one child is fully as great an obstacle to belief as the murder of six million—as Ivan Karamazov saw. Of proofs of the wickedness of the God of past history there has never been any shortage.

"Historical man, with his Lord of history and his self-estrangement from nature, saw all suffering as the payment of a debt exacted by an angry Master. . . . Earth's joys disappeared with earth's sorrows. Only supermundane terror and guilt were real."[90] But why, if earth's joys and sorrows were replaced by supermundane realities, were there not supermundane joys and sorrows? Why only sorrows? Rubenstein sees the guilt from the past which historical man suffers, but not the justification by the future. He feels the dead hand of the past, but not the resurrecting hand of the future. He hears judgment but not promise. The decisive side of an historical apprehension of reality in the prophetic sense is missing from the object of Rubenstein's polemic. And it is notorious that the ascetic world-denial of which he complains came into the synthesis of historical religion from neither the Old nor the New Testament.

But this rebuttal would be too easy. For whatever may be the future-directed dynamic of the biblical faith in history and however that faith may *also* be preserved within the synthesis of historical religion, the inner logic of that synthesis describes just such a God of past history—and he does in fact stare out at us from both the philosophers and the churches. The God whose will *defines* reality and in *this* way rules history is exactly the tyrant God whom Rubenstein confronts.

The God who repels Rubenstein is not, as he thinks, the God of the prophetic faith of Israel. It is the God of the union of that faith with the God of religious longing for timelessness. And Rubenstein partly sees this. He sees that only in meeting the biblical message does the religious longing for eternity become service of an absolute God, a God who may one day be seen as a tyrant.[91] He does not seem to see that, vice versa, only in meeting the religious dream of an unchangeable reality does the Lord of history become the merciless lord of past history.

But whatever Rubenstein may or may not see of the alternatives, the God he confronts is the inwardly demanded God of historical religion. And in that confrontation he dares the final extremity of revolt against past history: affirmation of God as "Holy Nothingness . . . out of which we have come and to which we shall return."[92] "History comes to a stop" in the "recognition that there is absolutely no way out . . . ,"[93] in the choice of "an absurd . . . cosmos, in which men suffer and die meaninglessly, but still retain a measure of tragic integrity," in the refusal to "see every last human event encased in a pitiless framework of meaning which deprives men of even the consolation that suffering, though inevitable, is not entirely merited or earned."[94] That is to say: "The limitations of finitude can be overcome only when we return to the Nothingness out of which we have been thrust. In this final analysis, omnipotent Nothingness is Lord of all creation."[95]

Or as Barth put it, God is the pure negation of the creature, the cancellation of all being by its not-being. Historical before-and-after is abolished, and every moment is directly related to its meaning—which is its own negation. God is the No in all the ambiguities of life—and the only way out of these to him is death.

The only difference between the *Commentary on Romans* and Rubenstein is, as it were, the evaluative tone. Barth calls us to hear this No as a Yes. But perhaps so does Rubenstein, for he does after all preach, he does call us to listen to the No—and is this not already an affirmation? Be that as it may, in religion such as Rubenstein's, life enacts the final position theoretically reached in the dialectic of the *Commentary on Romans*.

And in both, therefore, the religious quest for mediation between God and man, for a path to eternity, ends in the same way. The ancient church responded to this quest by offering Jesus Christ for the role. At the end of this adventure, Barth told us that the only visibility of invisible eternity is death. Jesus is God's revelation as, and solely as, the enactor of death.[96] Rubenstein, using what has come to be the religious word for the temporal manifestation of the eternal, is blunter: "Death is the Messiah." "There is only one Messiah who redeems us from the irony, the travail and the limitations of human existence. Surely he will come. He is the Angel of Death."[97] "Only death perfects life and ends its problems."[98]

Chapter Three

The Word-Event
in the
Commentary on Romans

I

The content of the modern history of Christendom is the self-cancellation of the religion about history. The event in the *Commentary on Romans* is the occurrence of this epoch as an event inside the theology of the church. This is at once the historical presupposition of all contemporary theology, and a task we have not yet accomplished. It lies behind us, but also before us.

As a *theological* event, the *Commentary on Romans* was what we have lately come to call a "word-event." A word-event is the occurrence that a new way of speaking becomes a part of language, and so also that a reality becomes a factor in human life which was not before. There are no doubt many sides to the word-event in the *Commentary on Romans;* we will trace two (II-III and IV below).

II

In the dialectic we have so laboriously traced, the word "religion" becomes a polemical concept. Within the language of theology it is no longer necessarily a compliment to call a teaching, practice or person "religious." The emergence of even the *possibility* of using "religion" as a theological insult is an immense transformation of the structure of faith's thinking. In its full implications, it is no less than the ending of one form of faith and the beginning of another. Working it out in all of theology and practice is a task on which we have hardly begun.

Looked at in its most general pattern, the process by which "religion" becomes a polemical concept is a case of a rather frequent sort of semantic occurrence. "Religion" in the ordinary language of Europe and America has at last two referents: it is used for "what goes on in churches"; and it is used for "what goes on in temples, churches, mosques, sacred groves, etc." Such uses of a word to designate larger and smaller classes is a common situation, and often leads, as it has here, to reflection on the word-use itself, to an attempt to clarify the relation between the two uses by asking the metaphysical question, "But what *is* religion, really?" It is clear that any proposed answer to this question must itself be a religious assertion of basic importance.

An obvious kind of answer to all questions of this sort is to analyze the narrower use as denoting a subclass of a larger class denoted by the broader use—here, to see Christianity as a species of the genus religion-in-general. The event in the *Commentary on Romans,* and the birth of contemporary theology, was a revolt against this solution. But if this solution is rejected, "religion" must become a polemic concept for Christian faith. If "what goes on in churches" is not a subclass of "what goes on in temples . . . etc.," then it is not differentiated from the larger class by characteristics merely *additional* to those defining *all* religion. The differentiation between the two "religions" must be that "what goes on in churches" is *as* religion no different at all from other religions but that it is also something *other than* and somehow incompatible with religion. If this expresses itself in language, a polemical use of "religion" will arise: "religion" will come to mean that in which "what goes on in churches" is *like* "what goes on in temples," . . . etc., *against* which this something other fights. And this something other will be understood as the specific of Christian faith, and so as the *truth* of faith in contrast to "religion."

In the *Commentary on Romans* itself, "religion" came to mean "the desire which is over all other desires, the desire for the lost immediacy of life" to its meaning.[1] Religion is the attempt to overcome the barrier between us and eternity, the barrier which is real within our experience precisely by our attempt to overcome it. As such, religion is at once our consciousness of the otherness of God and our refusal to abide by it. It is at once the call of God and the lust at the root of all lusts. The linking of these two as facets of one phenomenon is the polemical function of the concept of religion as Barth uses it.

The concept functions polemically so: On the one hand, it is clear that consciousness of the eternal and of its distance from us, and the desire to return to it, does indeed characterize what we have called "religion." It is also clear that the church has understood and undertaken its preaching and life as a religion in this sense. But now we are made to see that this phenomenon is really identical with other phenomena which are clearly opposed to faith and have always been recognized as such. There has always been polemic in the church against "work-righteousness" or the will "to be as God." By way of the kind of concept of religion which is born in the *Commentary on Romans*, this polemic is carried back to levels of thought and life to which it was not previously seen to apply: worship as elevation to God, belief in God as the changeless one, faith itself as a human activity.[2]

A polemic use of "religion" has become a fundamental conceptual structure of all theology since the *Commentary on Romans*, coming into Anglo-Saxon theology largely by way of Dietrich Bonhoeffer's prison letters.[3] It takes nothing from the daring and originality of these letters to say that in this polemic against religion Bonhoeffer mostly puts a name to what Barth had done—especially since Bonhoeffer was aware of this: "Barth was the first theologian . . . to begin the critique of religion. . . ."[4]

In Bonhoeffer's use, the "religious interpretation" of Christian faith is one which is "on the one hand metaphysical, on the other individualistic."[5] By "metaphysics" Bonhoeffer means the positing of a super-reality in which the shortcomings of this life, especially its mortality, are made up. The metaphysical interpretation of Christian faith presents it as a means of access to this reality. God is interpreted as located at the *boundaries* of life,[6] as a positive power who provides the fulfillment of our lives where we cannot.[7]

It is evident that this use of "religion" agrees with Barth's. But Bonhoeffer turns the polemical point of it in a somewhat different direction. Appropriately to the nuances of his formulation, he attacks "methodism," the preaching and piety which lives always at the borders of life, pushing men always to their shortcomings and unfilled needs, and to the final questions posed by death. Bonhoeffer does not deny that Christianity is concerned with border questions. He only claims that it is no more concerned with them than with the questions at the active center of life, and should take up each concern when life brings us to it: "That a man in the arms of his wife should long for the transcendent is, to say the least, a lapse of taste."[8]

"Methodism" can range from a policy of crassly recommending God as the "god in the gaps" to the subtle forms where it can only be tracked down in a basic definition of God in terms of transcendence above our knowledge and creativity. Against this, Bonhoeffer demands a language in which talk of God will occur "not on the borders, but in the middle of life; not in man's weakness, but in his strength; not in connection with death and guilt, but in man's life and goodness. . . ."[9]

This turn of the polemic also makes clear why the conception of faith as an "inward" matter, as an *individual* concern, belongs to the same religious interpretation. To God as the object beyond the border of public expression corresponds the soul as the subject behind the subject of public experience, to the super-object the super-subject.

If we put metaphysics and inwardness together, we get the "salvation of the soul."[10] The "religious interpretation" of faith means commending it as the means of saving the soul. There is no doubt that this is indeed how the Christian religion has understood itself—or that it must stop. For as soon as someone has the audacity to once ask the question: "Do we not really stand under the impression that there are more important things than this question of personal salvation?"[11] we see that there are indeed.

In one important respect, Bonhoeffer's polemic against religion is very different from Barth's. Barth simply declared war on religious Christianity. He did not reflect on the place in history of his act. He did not ask whether there was a special reason why this had to be done *now*. Bonhoeffer, on the other hand, was called to attack the Christian religion exactly by a lively apprehension of his own time as an epoch in history: the history between the gospel and western religion has made religion an anachronism. *Therefore* we must seek an a-religious Christianity. "We are entering a wholly religionless period: as men are now they simply cannot be religious." The "western form of Christianity" has been "merely a preliminary to complete religiouslessness. . . ." And so the question is posed: "How can Christ be lord also of those with no religion? Can there be religionless Christians?"[12]

This historical self-consciousness is undoubtedly necessary if the polemic against religion is to sustain itself. But it led Bonhoeffer to some loss of subtlety. It sometimes seems as though Bonhoeffer expects a world in which religion in any sense will simply have vanished, so that religion as a *problem* for faith is something temporary. "Religionless" Christianity, once achieved, will simply have religion behind it. Barth, on the contrary, saw religion as a permanent problem for faith, and must surely be right.

An epoch in our religious history is undoubtedly occurring. But if the period we are entering has any single character that can be clearly made out, it is pluralism, which means that no one description, such as "religionless," can indicate more than one option out of many that are open. If there is a sense in which "religionless" does characterize our society as a whole it is just in this, that religion is defined by that society as one option among others, and so denied in the claim to universality which is inherent in the Christian religion.

Religion very evidently continues and will continue to be an option chosen by many. But wherever the self-understanding of pluralist society is in full power, either religion is accepted as a system of rhetoric not taken quite seriously, or the rhetoric is accepted seriously but the believer hides his true relation to society from himself, again emptying the rhetoric of point—e.g., Timothy Leary promoting withdrawal from the acquisitive society and eastern asceticism in a mansion donated by "a wealthy LSD enthusiast." The new thing is therefore not that religion is no more an option, but that the religion that is an option is *phony* religion. At the moment, phony religion seems likely to be much more prominent in the mix of our spiritual pluralism than true religionlessness.

To spiritual pluralism, faith must reply with theological pluralism, not merely in the sense of developing alternative systems, as it has always done, but in the sense of pursuing alternative theological enterprises. Barth is surely right that religion is a permanent problem for faith. But he is probably wrong in not at all envisaging the possibility of forms of human self-transcendence other than religion, in his—and Bonhoeffer's—sense of religion. We need both anti- and a-religious theologies.

That religion, in the polemical sense used here, becomes only one option does not mean that those who reject it have no structure of meaning to their existence, have no involvements which, in a broader use than our present polemic use, we might wish to call "religious." Within as many ways of grasping life's meaning or its lack as may be found in pluralist society, the church must learn to speak of Jesus as that meaning. There are many religionless options: we will have to learn to speak of Christ at least in the form of political reflection in the form of articulation of the ethos of science and even of scientific theory itself, and in the form of criticism of the arts. Against the option of phony religion we need not so much religionless as anti-religious theology and piety—the Barthian rather than Bonhoefferian form of the project of theology as critique of religion.

Moreover, there is a sense in which anti-religious theology is basic to all the plural theological projects of faith within a pluralist society. Those believers who undertake to talk *about* their speaking and acting as believers, who undertake to theologize at all, become, thereby, willy-nilly, religious—as Barth has made clear. The theology they need for *themselves* and so as the starting point of all theological projects is anti-religious theology. The project on which the *Commentary on Romans* propels us is the basic project of faith and life in a "post-religious" age.

III

Of these popular theologians who have most recently carried on a specific polemic against religion, Thomas Altizer and Harvey Cox seem to have contributed most to the development of the polemic. Altizer's contribution has been to use the results of the phenomenology of religion in building a polemical concept of religion. One must note that the resultant concept differs in no important respect from Barth's and is indeed rather less sophisticated.[13] Since the phenomenology of religion is a creation of Christian theology and analyzes religious phenomena with categories provided thereby, it perhaps should not be surprising that phenomenological research does not add so much to a theological concept of religion as might have been expected.

Nevertheless, explicitly playing Christian faith against a concept of religion derived from non-Christian religions is undoubtedly a useful thing to do. And Altizer's study of Mircea Eliade[14] has led him to concentrate single-mindedly on one aspect of the common concept of religion, an aspect that does indeed seem decisive for our present task. Religion, says Altizer, seeks "a primordial totality embodying in a unified form all those antinomies that have created an alienated existence."[15] It does, that is, exactly what Barth said. What Altizer rightly insists on is that in religion this means "a *backward* movement to the primordial Totality," "a return to the paradisial Beginning," a "repetition of an original paradise in the present moment. . . ."[16] He rightly discerns that it is this passion that all be as it *was* that is the meaning of "eternity," which is thus "an inactive, or a quiescent Totality." And he rightly finds the difference of faith from religion in that instead of being directed to the past, faith is directed "to a future and final End," so as to be a forward movement in time rather than quiescence achieved in the discovery that time is illusory.[17]

What Altizer scents here is surely the same contrast we have developed from the start. Religion is the return from time to what was before history. Faith is response to a word whose content is exactly denial of this security in how it has always been, and the promise that time and its uncontrollable novelty is good. The religious quest is the enactment of our alienation from the opportunities presented by time. This alienation results from the true apprehension that where we grasp such an opportunity, the fulfillment we find in it is always taken away again by a contrary opportunity in the next moment, and from *fearing* this relativizing of every achieved fulfillment. The gospel, on the other hand, qualifies *achieved* existence as hell, and says of the future, "Fear not."

Harvey Cox gives a sociological version of a diagnosis fundamentally derived from Bonhoeffer. He points to the mutual dependence between a culture's self-understanding and the "shape" and "style" of its social arrangements, and so to the social matrix of the turn to religionlessness or false religion.[18] The social matrix of secularization is identified as metropolis. Metropolis is "a structure of common life" made possible by technology: it is characterized by the immensely increased complexity and deliberate control which technology makes possible. Therefore it is pluralist, and necessarily seeks to deal with its own life by deliberate planning. Just so it is destructive of religion. For religion claims to shape all of life, but where my life is lived in a society determined by a plurality of value-systems, it cannot. And religion adores the sacred just where metropolis drafts a plan to deal with the problem.[19]

Of course, no one item of all this is original with Cox. But it is his tumultuously effective tract that has impressed the social reality of secularization permanently on the theological consciousness. We will not in this book be able to attack this side of our problem as fully as we should—partly because of the limits of our more specific theme and partly because I am not the man to do it. But we must never sink back into supposing that religionlessness is any more a "private matter" than religion or faith—as we might if we let ourselves be guided only by the *Commentary on Romans*.

IV

The second word-event in the *Commentary on Romans* is that "God" became a problematical word within theology. In this dialectic everything that *we* can mean by "God" is unveiled as Not-God, as that which the gospel unveils and opposes. But why and how then do we use the word at all?

From now on, the very possibility of speaking of God will be uncertain within Christianity. Seven years later, Rudolph Bultmann wrote his famous essay "What Is the Meaning of Talk about God?"[20] and this question has remained the preoccupation of his followers and opponents to this day.[21] As for Barth's own subsequent theology, it can in its entirety be seen as an extended attempt to answer Bultmann's question. For a theology in which revelation is the central concept must have the possibility of knowing God as its moving doubt. The entire theological climate of the half-century has been set by the interplay of these two schools; it is in this climate that "atheist" theologies and radical redefinitions of "God" have alike become possible. The meaning of "God" is *the* theological problem of our generation.[22]

Moreover, "God" is a theological problem *because* religion has ceased to be a positive value for faith. For "God" is exactly the link between religion and the gospel.

The gospel promises us the tale of Jesus—which is a story from the past—as our last destiny; in the saying of the gospel, therefore, the past and future occur together. But the unity of past and future is that for which religion seeks in "God" and his eternity. Religion seeks a past which is already all that the future can be, in order to deny the threatening novelty of the future; the gospel promises a future free of the past yet addressed to us as we are, i.e., as we have come to be in the course of the past. Religion and the gospel are thus wholly opposed, but just so in a necessary polemic situation—and precisely by way of the shared and disputed concept of a reality in which past and future are one, a reality which brackets our lives from the future and the past so that within that reality our lives cohere through time as dramatically meaningful stories. In proclaiming what happens with Jesus Christ, faith *must* attack the eternal God. Just so what we have to say about the reality in which we may hope is logically of a piece with religious discourse about God, and just so faith labels its object "God" and itself thereby a religion.

The dispute may be relatively peaceful. Prior to a crisis of Christion religion, "God" may function as the overlap between the gospel and religion. All religion worships an eternal being, it will be said, and so does Christian faith. Thus religion and faith, though different in some ways, are yet continuous.

If Christianity is a species of the genus religion, then the object of faith can itself be apprehended as an eternal God. Faith's necessary polemics will then say merely that other gods are not the real one, though they might have been without contradicting faith's definition of what it means to be God. If faith finds any difficulties with the concept of God which we have apart from the gospel, it will attribute them to incomplete knowledge, now completed by revelation.

But if the gospel and religion turn against each other, if they refuse mutual recognition as species and genus, then "God" becomes a field of struggle. Then faith must ask itself in what sense it has what religion calls a god. It must ask itself this, and so cannot be atheistic. But it must *ask* it—and so acquire the problem of God in a far more radical fashion than before, as a question not merely of what can additionally be said about a God securely identified by the tradition, but of which being we call God and what we mean to say of that being with this word.

Such a crisis is, moreover, a crisis of Christian faith itself. For we come to use "God" in that we try to explicate the unity of future and past in the proclamation of Jesus as our destiny, in that we try to say *how* this figure of the past can be our last future. Thus the doctrine of God states the gospel-character of the gospel; it is the conceptualization of the claim that this piece of ancient history is good news for us now. Where we become uncertain what we mean by "God" we become uncertain in our ability to speak the gospel *as* gospel.

This has all happened, in a different way, once before. In Christianizing Greek religion, the ancient church accepted also the general crisis of antique religion. Christianity captured Greek religion by answering the passion of its day for bridge—entities between eternity and time. But this passion itself sprang from an agonized apprehension of the otherness of eternity from time, an apprehension so ruthless that in its final crisis antique religion offered only the options of despair, fanaticism and apathy. The crisis of religion in which the inner contradiction of Christian religion eventuates is different: in it we lose existential hold of God, whereas in antique religion's inner crisis men lost hold rather of the world. But the *knowledge* of God is equally imperiled in both; and in accepting Greek religion in its time of crisis, Christianity suddenly no longer knew for sure what it meant by "God."

It took two hundred years for the ancient church to work out anew what it meant by "God." *The result of its labors was the doctrine of the Trinity.* The doctrine of the Trinity was born of the meeting between Greek metaphysics and the Gospel, just as its critics have so long insisted. But far from representing a victory of metaphysics over "the simple Gospel," it represents the redefining of what Greek metaphysical religion had meant by "God," in the light of faith's apprehension of its object. The doctrine of the Trinity was the creation, if one will, of a *new ontology of* "God" on the basis of the gospel. The doctrine of the Trinity is the ancient church's victory over the timeless Presence of Greek religion: it was an anti-metaphysical, anti-religious doctrine of God. If the victory had been complete, if the doctrine of the Trinity had become functional throughout the theology and piety of the Christian religion, that religion would perhaps not have been a "synthesis" and would have had no second interior crisis. But this is foolish speculation.[23]

We have, moreover, gotten rather ahead of ourselves. The theological task which the history of Christian religion's self-cancellation and the dialectic of the *Commentary on Romans* alike set us is the doctrine of God. We may divide this task into four sub-problems, which are in varying degree the assignments of the remainder of this book.

There is, first, the explicit question: What is the relation of the one whom believers call "God" to the timeless God of religion? This is the problem of "natural theology," and the critical question throughout Barth's subsequent work.

The philosophically fundamental problem is: How does believing language using "God" work as a language? This is not so much the problem of *what* "God" means as the problem of how it means whatever it means—if anything.[24]

At the center of the present study is the question of the *identity* of God. *Which* being do we mean by "God"? The relation of this question to the polemic against the God of religion is obvious: If not the constant Presence, then what?

We can, moreover, identify God only by using descriptions, by saying things like "God is the one who . . .": e.g., "God is the one who never changes," or "God is the one who made everything." To identify God, we have to decide what logical sort of clauses to use in these descriptions. Therefore the question of God's identity leads straight to the question of his *being,* to the question of what *sort* of entity God is: a thing? an idea? a happening? This question and the second question can only be answered together.

All contemporary attempts to answer any or all of these questions are necessitated at least partly by the crisis of Christian religion. A criterion of every proposed formulation will therefore be: does it sustain the polemic against religion?

Part Two

*God of
and Against
Religion*

Chapter Four

Epochal Possibilities

I

The *Commentary on Romans* represents in theology the end of historical religion. The question is: where do we go from here?

Epigrammatically expressed, historical religion has two possibilities: it can cease to be historical or it can cease to be merely religious. It can abandon its allegiance to the prophetic and apostolic proclamation in the Bible, though probably retaining the Bible as a religious text; or it can transform its relation to the religious quest it accepted from the Greeks into a genuinely polemic relation. It can become a-historical or anti- and a-religious. Rubenstein, meaning by "God" the God of history, put the alternatives neatly: "Dietrich Bonhoeffer has written that our problem is how to speak of God in an age of no religion. I believe that our problem is how to speak of religion in an age of no God."[1]

If it is a matter of being relevant and appropriate to the age born of the death of historical religion, the one alternative is doubtless as likely as the other. It is simply not so that our age is unreceptive to religion. It is unreceptive only to Jewish or Christian religion. Any and every religion not contaminated by a gospel finds ready acceptance; one movement after another reinvents the popular and naturalistic varieties of Hinduism and Buddhism out of sheer need for such a form of experience. We may possibly be headed for the biggest revival of religion yet—in which those churches who most attenuate their religion to a gospel will share. Believers, scientists and creative artists will perhaps smell something phony in this religion. But this will be the hesitation of a minority of outsiders and aristocrats who have always been skeptics and will as always be heeded by few.

Perhaps even this is too rash a prediction. If pluralism should itself become an "ism" and develop its own set of values, and if it should succeed in linking those values to our longing for immortality, we might acquire a genuine new religion. The only thing we can be sure of is that *historical* religion will survive only in fraudulent form.

To such phony historical religion, or genuine or phony unhistorical religion, the gospel will be the alternative it has always been. In the age born of the crisis of its old form as a religion about history, the gospel will assert itself by taking a form uncompromisingly polemic against religion. Such an incarnation of the gospel will be exactly as appropriate and uncongenial, as timely and untimely to its age as other forms of the gospel have been to their ages.

Over against this choice, the *Commentary on Romans* is ambiguous. It is the document of the end of Christian religion; it poses to us the question: faith in a future or the religious quest for assuagement of time? If we pose this question *back to it,* we immediately see that it can be interpreted either way. The book is an attack on Christian religion, but could as well be read as an apology for an unhistorical, unchristian religion as for an anti-religious Christianity.

In the *Commentary on Romans* Christian religion cancels itself at every step, in that the motifs of history as the justification of the ungodly and of eternity as the goal of human self-transcendence are both perfectly achieved, and in perfected synthesis with each other—so that each immobilizes the other. The existence demanded by the *Commentary on Romans* is both unhistorical religion and anti-religious faith, and so neither—and could not be achieved either by human effort or by the grace of God.

The *Commentary on Romans* was a dead end, just as the spiritual epoch which it gives language. "And so always and again we are outside, never inside? Even our freedom in God is a captivity? Yes—insofar as we are the men we are in the world we have, at best, religious men. No—insofar as by a wonder of wonders we are identified with the new man in Christ. . . ."[2] This is right and profoundly Christian, and yet it somehow leaves us hopeless. Always and everywhere is the critical moment, but as God's possibility and not ours, and so unpredictable and unachievable. This is right and Christian; and yet it is not a freeing or moving message, either to religion or to faith. The only thing wrong—but then everything is wrong—is that we cannot *live* under the God of this dialectic; *his* justification of the ungodly is bad news, not gospel.

We cannot live under this God, and not only in the sense in which we indeed ought not to be able to deal with God. We cannot speak or act for this God—for the *way* in which all human deeds are here relativized destroys our ability to distinguish what is to be said from what is not to be said, what is to be done from what is not to be done. We can neither teach all nations of this God nor visit the afflicted in his name. Everything depends on from what vantage-point the justification of the ungodly is proclaimed, and all human distinctions are transcended. Here it is from the vantage-point of abstract eternity—and we are transfixed.

We must not go back on the word of the *Commentary on Romans.* It is a true word, and the presupposition of our theological situation and of any valid theology in that situation. Nor are we to "go beyond" it, for there is no place to go. But if we are to begin to proclaim the gospel of the future, then we must think *what* to say. This thinking does not occur in the *Commentary on Romans,* nor is there any way there to begin it. Or if we are to transform Christianity once and for all into a religion, we must learn the practice thereof. The pure dialectic of time and eternity is an insurpassable projection of such a de-historicized ex-Christian religion. But if we think that dialectic so purely, we will be unable to live it.

When at a dead end, a fresh start is needed. The creative theology of the years since 1922 has been spent in trying to find one. Tracing the history of these attempts would mean writing a history of contemporary theology, which is not our purpose. We will instead discuss only a few very recent theologies—or programs for a theology —chosen for the explicitness of their claims to be the new mode needed after the death of historical religion, not necessarily as the best or most important theological work. We will examine attempts on both the epochal possibilities: religion without gospel (II) and the gospel against religion (III-V). Our question is: have we found a new start?

II

The transformation of Christianity and Judaism into unspoiled religions, viable after the end of historical religion, has been for some time the halfhearted endeavor of the churches and synagogues—to be accomplished by developing the political, social, doctrinal and liturgical life of the communities while emptying these of their previous proclamatory content. This is, of course, rarely admitted, but too often demonstrated to need arguing again here.[3] The thing can be done in the most various ways. There are the harmless self-help societies of liberal religion. There are bodies demanding subscription to every historic dogma, plus a few new "fundamentals," as the ideological framework for a religion of blood and soil. There are "liturgical" movements which "preserve" the historic traditions of the churches to create museums for romantic religiosity. And there are some real new religions.

There is, however, a shortage of *theologians* of this undertaking. Theologians for the most part have been committed—or have thought they ought to be committed—to the "kerygma," to some attempt to think through a Christian message. Their labors have very often contributed to the de-gospelling of the church, but this has not been their intention. Even the "practical" and "churchly" leaders who have presided over the process have had bad consciences in direct proportion to their theological awareness.

To explicitly affirm and deliberately think through the purifying of our religion from its contamination by the promise of the future requires a wrench not easily suffered. It is this that makes *After Auschwitz* such a necessary book. There is, as Rubenstein observes, a way in which Judaism is somewhat less decisively committed to history than is Christianity, which is perhaps why the emergence of an explicitly anti-historical theology occurred in Judaism. But this does not diminish his achievement.

Driven by the medusa God of past history to choose instead the meaninglessness of life in time, to look for no other salvation from time than death and to conceive no other God than Holy Nothingness, Rubenstein does *not* therefore abandon religion, *nor* religion's determination to stop time. Only from our atypical religious tradition would we have expected that he would: the old unspoiled religious traditions know that this is just the point where a man becomes truly and purely religious. Just when we know "that human existence is a tragic and gratuitous absurdity, entirely without meaning save for the meanings and the projects we ourselves actualize and, above all, bracketed in its 'throwness' between two oblivions," we experience "our strongest need for religious community. . . . Even the old religious assurances of redemption and resurrection have decisive meaning for those who are nevertheless undeceived concerning man's fate."[4] Religion is the "futile" but "indispensable" attempt "to make a meaningless life meaningful."[5]

Rubenstein simply does not credit "secular" society's alleged lack of need for religion. "Society will always exhibit characteristic flaws."[6] Surely he is right—there will always be room for religion. Moreover, secular society lacks "a sense of the tragic . . . : that all men are destined to falter and fail. For technical society, failure is an incident . . . leading to the replacement of older units of manpower with newer units. For the human person, failure is of the very essence."[7]

A clear unbeliever in any sense of "belief" which Judaism or Christianity could recognize, Rubenstein clings all the more to "Jewish ritual," to his religion's "priestly rather than prophetic" function.[8] Through this ritual, and the traditional wisdom associated with it, "we come to a knowledge deeper than words of our guilt, our alienation, and our pathetic finitude"[9]—which is exactly what we need to know if we are to achieve the self-created meaning which *is* possible. And we are enabled also to live in our finitude: ". . . each crisis of transition and each seasonal renewal is celebrated and marked within a meaningful community. We know where we are on the road."[10] The religious community allows me to "dramatize, make meaningful, and share the decisive moments of my life."[11]

We recognize already the pattern of all nature-religion, and of the perfecting of nature-religion in the classic religions of India. Rubenstein is well aware that this is his direction: "The end of history is characterized by the return to nature. . . ." And he seeks in nature exactly what religion has always sought there: "to put an end to the development of historical man," "to make a circle out of a process which previous generations had regarded as linear," to restore the rule of natural necessity.[12]

The choice is made clearly: between hope for a future which is ontologically significant for the present, and "tragic acceptance" "that the old world goes on today as it did yesterday, and as it will tomorrow. . . ."[13] Rubenstein is doubtless quite wrong in identifying this choice as a choice between Christianity and Judaism. He is right in identifying it with the division between "gospel" and "law," between the news that the future may be awaited and the demands of the unchanging world. But neither rabbis nor Christian theologians have hitherto supposed that there is only law in Judaism, or only gospel in Christianity.[14]

In the cyclic necessities of nature, and in the religious ritual which repeats them, Rubenstein finds the end of history; he finds, that is, the knowledge of eternity, if only in the form of sad acquiescence in the Nothingness which keeps our temporal strivings from being important and oppressive. The sadness in this knowledge of eternity is brought by recollection of what might have been had not the God of history proved such a monster. Nevertheless, we are not surprised when another God after all appears, when Holy Nothingness proves more than an abstract negative: "We have turned away from the God of history to share the tragic fatalities of the God of nature."[15] With this we move away from the abstractly negative religion of the *Commentary on Romans*.[16]

This resurrection of Baal begins, to be sure, in our experience of absurdity and hopelessness. The "opaque facticity" of the world equally drives us to ask why we are here and prevents us from answering. "Out of this unanswerable question comes our sense of the mystery and the absurdity of existence. Before this Abyss we come to intuit something of the holiness of God."[17] But this experience of the Abyss is also—in the true fashion of all classic religion—experience of the positive "powers and divinities" of earth, and of our vitality as expressions of those powers.[18] And so Rubenstein's emergence out of prophetic faith into pure religion is complete; his theology becomes an affirmation of "Baal, Astarte, and Anath,"[19] of "the life and source of the cosmos" who participates "in nature's vicissitudes and necessities."[20]

That Baal will give what Rubenstein seeks from him is doubtful. In what he calls the "prophetic" religion of history, Rubenstein has evidently found only "law," only demands and condemnations—given the state of American synagogues and churches, he is hardly to be blamed for this. He turns to "priestly" religion, to natural religion purified of prophetic faith in time, to find the consolation and reconciliation the law does not give.[21] But the cruel legalism which he flees came into Judaism and Christianity not from the prophets, but from the synthesis of prophetic faith with the religion of eternity, and in returning to nature-religion he is running into the arms of his enemy. How can he fail to see that "Baal, Astarte, and Anath," embraced by men disillusioned with Christianity or Judaism, define exactly the "mythic" apprehension to which he rightly attributes the death camps?[22] If the establishment of Israel really means the final identification of Jahveh with the Baals, there will be death camps in Israel before long.

Nevertheless, Rubenstein has broken through to one of our genuine alternatives: that we abandon our hope for time, that we contract out of the goal-directed history which we have lived, and seek our happiness in the unchanging conditions of life. That this option will be taken by many can be seen all around us. Drugs may bring even its more exotic forms within reach of all. Rubenstein calls official religion to be wholehearted in transforming itself in this direction. Were his call heeded, forms of Judaism and Christianity could no doubt be developed which would combine wholehearted commitment to pure religious disillusion and bliss with some "values" preserved from the "Judeo-Christian tradition," which would combine life lived wholly for the present moment and its eternity with, perhaps, optimism, this-worldliness, demythologized sexuality and the like. Such a religion should, by its splendid relevance to the spiritual needs of our age, drive from the field all competition such as ersatz Buddhism.

I make the opposite choice. It is consequently hard for me to describe this possibility without a certain touch of irony. Let it be, therefore, explicitly stated: this is one genuine alternative for western religion. It is, for that matter, a genuine heir of the *Commentary on Romans,* if that book is taken for itself and not in the context of Barth's own subsequent work. In this direction we *have* gotten past the dialectical dead end.

III

Of the theologians who have recently become known for seeking the post-religious proclamation of a *gospel,* William Hamilton is most straightforward. Hamilton has simply observed, as a fact to be noted and reckoned with, the death in himself and some others of religious attachment to a supernatural being, to the church, and to the doctrines of the Bible and the Christian tradition as he sees them. But while this observation gives him an "active sense of loss," he has also "an overwhelmingly positive sense of being in and not out . . . ,"[23] and so remains a theologian.

Hamilton interprets this event as Bonhoeffer's coming of age to religionlessness. He defines religion as "any system of thought or action in which God or the gods serve as fulfiller of needs or solver of problems." The root of religion is that "part of the self or . . . of human experience that needs God." Experience no longer necessarily has such an aspect; the religious *a priori* has proved not to be *a priori.* The keyword here is "need": within the modern experience of the world, we can if we like make it without God. There is no longer anything we need done that *only* God can do for us. God is not necessary, he is only an option in a pluralist society. But therewith the whole previous basis of our faith and worship is gone.[24]

Yet Hamilton is in and not out. He is not an atheist. For Hamilton proposes to "wait" for God to return, for it again to become possible to speak of and experience God. It is this waiting which he describes as the contemporary form of Christian existence. This waiting has content. It means on the one hand waiting for the gift of a way of speaking and experiencing God which will not grow out of our need, which will not use God but enjoy him precisely as the one we do not need. It means on the other hand assuming a certain location in the world, turning for the moment from faith to love—evidently Hamilton means little more by "faith" than having strong convictions about God—and pushing "the movement from church to world as far as it can go" so as to "become frankly worldly men."[25]

The world Hamilton has in mind is the "post-modern" world. It is a pluralist, technological world. It is a pragmatic, optimistic and political world. It is, perhaps above all, the world *after* existentialism, a world where the point is less to agonize about existence than to get on with it.[26]

Assuming the location of love in this world is the post-religious equivalent of a christological confession. Jesus is concealed in the neighbor and in the work for justice and beauty in the world, "and the work of the Christian is to strip off the masks of the world to find him" and then "stay with him and do his work." The believer in such work is himself a Christ to his neighbor. Thus waiting in this location is a way to Christ and just so perhaps a way to future new faith in God.[27]

This is clear, simple and immediately helpful. Nor can one help responding to the tone which runs through it. One recognizes the experience that the religion of the establishment is a religion one does not any longer share, and the way in which faith in any God therewith becomes broken and difficult. One recognizes the dissatisfactions with the great theologies of the earlier part of the century, engendered by their failure to alter the actual religion of the churches —though one does sometimes feel that Hamilton's understanding of these theologies is not overly profound. Above all, one recognizes the desire to incorporate the agonizings of existentialism once and for all, and move on to something else, to life in a world of optimism and direct action.

But just this last point leads into the criticism that must be made. For the existence of this "post-modern" world is in considerable doubt. The modern world of existentialism, Freud and Marx does not really seem to be fading away, and where "the new optimism" does appear it often changes almost immediately into a callow sort of amateur mysticism.[28] Hamilton's new optimism is only one possibility among others; the new world contains exactly a pluralism of spiritualities. Hamilton has committed the error to which we suspected Bonhoeffer of tending. He has in much too simple a fashion taken the epoch of the self-cancellation of historical religion for the end of religion altogether and the beginning of simple religionlessness.

As to the beginning of a new post-religious theology, Hamilton simply does not provide much. We must, he says, wait. His advice on where to wait is excellent. But why our waiting should not be an active attempt to *begin* a new language about God is not clear. Hamilton brings us again to the same halt to which the *Commentary on Romans* brought us—and with refreshing lack of dialectics. A fresh start he does not attempt.

IV

Thomas Altizer does not leave us waiting. He has both a gospel and a doctrine of God. Indeed, one has the feeling that after Altizer there could be nothing to wait for, that for him, as for his master Hegel, the only thing that could follow his theology without refuting it would be the beatific vision itself.

Altizer conceives of his task as creating the theological explication of the word brought by the prophets of our time, whom he discovers in Nietzsche and William Blake. His theology bears the stylistic mark of the revelation it explicates; it is ecstatic, mythical and usually non-argumentative. To discuss his thought is, therefore, almost inevitably to falsify it.

We may nevertheless summarize Altizer's positive understanding of Christianity so: the word which first came to full utterance in Jesus, and which Christian theology seeks to follow on its way through history, is unique in the world of religion because it is fully incarnate in its historical appearance, so that it does not call us out of history but into it. It does not call us to a Being beyond its own historical reality. Jesus is not the revelation *of* God; rather "God is Jesus." It is therefore a word that calls us into history, and so a word which closes the past and opens the future.[29]

Therefore this word in its historical actuality can never be bound to its own past forms, but must be apprehended wherever the contingent opening of history to the future occurs. Therefore also the "Jesus" who is the content of this word, who meets us in the challenge of the moment, is not any more the Jesus of the gospel-stories. The "ancient" Jesus is exactly an item of that past from which we are freed.[30]

This position leads inevitably to a question which, although Altizer does not explicitly formulate it, is clearly the moving problem of his subsequent thinking: what is the identity with itself of this word? If the word is absolutely new in every moment, what is the meaning if speaking of *the* word of faith, as if faith were a continuing phenomenon with a single object? Who *is* the Jesus whom we meet in the moment of historical openness; and why speak of "Jesus" at all? Wherein is the God who is this Jesus one God?

The problem, it will be seen, is not unique to Altizer. It is known elsewhere as "the hermeneutical problem."[31] According to Altizer, christology has heretofore dealt with this problem by a past-directed commitment to the ancient Jesus and by very appropriately conceiving the contemporary presence of this Jesus as the supernatural presence of a god. Thus the church has from the very first made a religion out of the anti-religious word of Jesus. Altizer says this now has to cease. Obviously I can only approve both criticism and demand.

Altizer's own solution is no more unique than the problem. His solution is Hegel's. The Christian word, always new in history, is yet identical with itself in that it is fully mediated only by the total historical process as such.³² The word is "progressively incarnate in the actual processes of history."³³ "Jesus" is "the Christian name of the totality of Experience." ("Experience" is Blake's name for history.)³⁴ And God, therefore, *is* the process of history. The goal of the Incarnation is that history shall become "not merely the arena of revelation but the very incarnate Body of God."³⁵ Altizer's solution is explicitly Hegel's: mediation of truth only in the totality of history.

How then is Altizer an atheist and the proclaimer of the death of God? Because the reflection *within* history of God's immanence in its totality, the religious by-product as it were, is the dying of the "primordial" God of religion. This is the God who in his abstract eternity is an *other* being than we. His dying is identical with the exaggeration of his transcendence, whereby he becomes death to all temporal life—and just so himself lifeless and helpless against our unbelief.³⁶ "Religion assumes its most repressive form in the Christian religious tradition, because only here . . . may one find a God of naked and absolutely sovereign power, a God who was evolved out of a reversal of the movement of Spirit into flesh, and . . . becomes abstract, alien, lifeless and alone."³⁷ We recognize immediately the same pattern we have traced repeatedly, limned by Altizer with exceptional dramatic power.

The process of history which is God is his coming to be flesh and so the dying of "transcendent Spirit." Our salvation is that the final emptiness of heteronomous transcendence reveals to us our freedom from heteronomy, and so also reveals the God whom we ourselves are in the totality of our historical life with each other. The object of faith is a God who is the process of our liberation from the tyranny of God's primal transcendent reality.

Thus on the one hand we have the self-realization of the God whose deity is his immanence in and as the totality of history; and on the other the by-product of this history, the death of the transcendent God of Christian religion. We may at first be tempted to ask why Altizer chooses the by-product as the content of his gospel and the object of faith, why he calls himself an atheist rather than, say, a pantheist.³⁸ But reflection will quickly show why he does this, and reveal also his profound intuition of the consequence of contemporary theology. For the word of the wholly immanent God can have no content of its own. It is cut off from every past; indeed, it *is* the occurrence of the cancellation of its own past; therefore it can have no narrative content. It is, in short, *exactly the same thing as the eternal moment of the Commentary on Romans,* and like it can have no other content than its own negative reflection in history.

The event which Altizer describes is exactly that which occurs in the *Commentary on Romans*: the true God occurs as the critical moment; the God of religion dies of his own eternity as this is exaggerated to intolerability by the critique—in the moment—of all religious mediation. The only difference between Altizer and the *Commentary on Romans* is that Altizer proposes this event as the object of faith. The move is ingenious. Is worshipping the dead end itself perhaps the way around it?

I cannot think that it is. The gospel Altizer proclaims can have no source of *content* of its own; it is exactly the language-bereft gospel with which the *Commentary on Romans* leaves us. His only option, therefore, is to create a gospel directly as the negative mirror-image of religion. Since, as Altizer emphasizes, the law of the identity of opposite rules is religion, one would expect this to produce merely an especially intense religiosity. This suspicion is confirmed when we look again at the pattern of Altizer's positive theology. In order to flee from the God of past history, Altizer decrees that the word of the gospel must have no past. But then God can occur only as the total process of history. The difficulty is that the *process* of history is itself, of course, not temporal and not historical. "History as a whole" is a euphemism for eternity. The problem with Altizer is exactly the same as with his master Hegel. Just as with Hegel, the historical unfolding of truth is bracketed by a definition in advance, by an "idea" which, however much it may define reality as history, is itself timeless and historyless. Altizer, like Hegel, can and must always be able to say how history *must* work out.

Thus the worship of the death of God is after all worship of a timeless totality and ground of temporal being. Altizer sees this in a way, but argues that the ground apprehended in the death of God is an *eschatological* totality, which differs from the primal ground of religion in that faith finds its totality in the future while religion finds its totality in the past.[39] Clearly this claim must be most congenial to the bias of this book. But in the framework in which Altizer makes it, it will not work. For the future of which Altizer speaks can in no way be narrated; it is the object of a hope utterly without content. It is, therefore, not so much the future as *futurity*—pure future—future in the abstract. For all the uproar Altizer finally simply repeats Bultmann. As such this future cannot be awaited or hoped for, and is *not* a phenomenon of time. Hope is the expectation of concrete occurrences, and time is the horizon of such expectations. Altizer's "future" is exactly the *"futurum aeternum"* of the *Commentary on Romans*. The primal moment of pure religion and the final moment of pure apocalypticism are the same, are mere alternative forms of eternity.

The gospel of Christ overcomes eternity and promises a future exactly in that it narrates a specific—and therefore past—story, the story of Jesus, as the future for which we may hope. The task posed to theology is how to work this out, how to *narrate* the future without closing it, how to narrate a concrete story of the future *as* a story of how the future is open and unpredictable.

If we are to take with complete seriousness that the Christian word is fully incarnate in history, this must mean *both* that the Christian word does not bind us to any past, but rather frees the future from the past, and that the particular historical occasion of its utterance is that word and cannot be transcended by its own later forms. The eschatological word will always be about "the ancient Jesus."

The task is not impossible, for the story of Jesus is the story of one who gave up his life—i.e., every hold on men based on what they or he *had* been or done—in order to be theirs just as they were. If then he is the future, then the future is free from every determination by the past—and yet is freedom precisely to own what we are and have been. The "unpredictability" of the future is, after all, an ambiguous expression. It might mean the fearful unpredictability of fate, or the blessed unpredictability of human love when it succeeds. If Jesus' story is the story of what is to come to us and come of us, if he is to be the judge, then we know two things about the last future: we know that it is open and unpredictable; and we know of what sort its unpredictability is.

The task is, of course, difficult. But by simply refusing it, and relegating Jesus to the past, Altizer fails to achieve a gospel against religion. The gospel of the death of God flip-flops rather into a realization of religion without gospel. In the end, Altizer's teaching is identical with Rubenstein's.[40]

Nevertheless much can be learned from him. He has grasped the necessity of anti-religious Christianity and the problematical character of the word "God" in so violent and flamboyant a form as to ensure—one hopes—that this will not again be forgotten. And he has attacked the crucial point: the development of a *doctrine of God* fully controlled by the gospel story about events in time and by polemic against religion's dream of timelessness.

His final failure also is instructive, by pointing to the key problem. The gospel is the story of a past event told as the story of our final destiny. This is how believers get involved with a reality appropriately called "God," for the word is used in all religions for the coincidence of past and future. Yet the gospel's meaning for us is precisely freedom of the future from the past. These are not two opposed motifs which it will be necessary to "hold in tension" or something of the sort. The gospel simply *is* a story about the past which does promise an open future. But working this out theologically is another matter, and is the stumbling point for projects of anti- or a-religious theology. The sure way to fail is to cast the gospel's past and future as two "poles"—and inevitably lose hold of one or the other. Rubenstein abandons the future, Altizer the past; but both end in the same situation.

V

A writer from Germany who makes the same claim to epochal appropriateness as the "radical" American theologians is Dorothee Sölle.[41] Like Altizer she speaks of the death of God as "an event which has taken place within the last two centuries of human history."[42] Someone is always dead for someone else; God is dead for those who can neither drop nor answer the question of the meaning of existence, who remain concerned for God yet do not have him.[43] Sölle's attempt is theology in this situation.

Sölle interprets the quest for meaning as the quest for "personal identity."[44] And she proposes that only "representation" enables the achieving of identity.[45] Her analysis of this last concept is essential to her argument and valuable in itself; we must take time to summarize it.

The individual who believes in his identity must believe he is in some sense irreplaceable,[46] yet in the technological world everything teaches us we are interchangeable.[47] The synthesis is in representation.[48] I am only irreplaceable for someone who loves me. Only for such a one is there more to me than what I perform at any given time, so that I am not interchangeable. But this means he sets his hopes on me. To fulfill these hopes, I need *time*. That is to say, I need representation—which is a personal relation in which someone replaces me, but not permanently, and so gives me time.[49] In the search for identity, I need time; otherwise I would already have identity. If I am represented without being substituted for, I gain time.[50] If the search for identity has hope it is because I am "irreplaceable yet representable."[51]

But who represents me? The Christians have said that Christ does. But what can this mean? He *holds our place* open for us, the place of God's free children reponsible for the world; he maintains in us the consciousness of freedom from the powers of the world by being free where we have failed to be and need time to become so.[52] He is free *for* us, i.e., he identifies himself with us, who are not free. "Identification means acceptance without limits . . . , acceptance as a matter of course. . . ." Identification is the act of the *teacher,* who "secures for the growing child the delay it needs."[53] Precisely *in* this representation we find our identity. "Only in and through this identification" by the teacher "with his own botched cause can the pupil learn to identify himself with his own cause. . . . In Christ's representative identification we have identity in non-identity, that is to say, peace with God."[54]

A representative is always representative *before* someone. Christ represents us before God, he holds our place before God while we catch up to it. But by saying "before God" we do not add any content to what we have already said about his representation: "When this representation takes place, God (if not in the direct sense of religious object) is present; and he is being spoken of even if his name is not mentioned."[55] For Christ replaced us but not permanently, he is "provisional"; and "if we add 'to God' we emphasize the provisionality but say nothing new." As our representative, he depends on our affirmation of his work; and "if we say 'dependent on God,' this simply means that Christ is radically surrendered to men." He identifies with us; "if we add 'before God' it amounts to the same thing. . . ."[56]

We are already well into the chief problem of Sölle's attempt. In this theology God is the occurrence of such a radical representation as Christ's, in which we gain for our whole life the time we need to achieve identity and meaning. In itself, this doctrine of representation is a notable contribution; were I now attempting a soteriology, I would appropriate it whole. But the ontological position of the whole discussion is left ambiguous. *When* is the time I need to achieve the identity of my life as a *whole?* Obviously, at the *end* of that life. This doctrine will have content only if we can speak of a last time which is a time after all that we do or could do. We must be able to speak of a "Kingdom of identity"[57] which is a describable specific time and not merely a timeless ideal relative to whatever are the failures of the particular present moment. But does the definition of God we have just been given allow this? Yes, but just barely. We must see whether Sölle's further discussions resolve this.

Christ represents us to God, and just so, represents God to us. In our period of western society, a "direct" religious relation to God, as to a felt presence, is impossible. For some previous functions of the now absent God, those of being a filler of needs and solver of problems, technological society provides a permanent substitute. But society cannot give identity. In this role, Christ represents the absent God. If God had departed and no one had sprung into his role, we would simply drop the question of identity. But Christ holds open the place of the God who has left us, in that in him identity has once attained consciousness, in that he has posed the possibility of identity in such a way that it can never be ignored. "Because Christ produced a new kind of existence in the world, it is impossible ever again to abandon hope."[58]

We cannot solve the question of God's being, in a world where he is no longer a necessary factor. Nor do we need to, for his role is not unfilled. God has changed. He has ceased to be an immediately experienced religious object; his present mode of being is exactly to-be-represented.[59] But we may now ask if this does not simply mean that there isn't any God but Jesus, and that we could as well leave off talking about God. If this were so, it would empty the whole doctrine of Jesus' representation, for he could hardly be supposed to represent us to no one. But Sölle does not intend this. She rejects Altizer's contention; "It would be a mistake to interpret incarnation as God's complete self-emptying into human form."[60] Christ *represents* God, i.e., he provisionally plays God's role. God has not yet "declared himself fully within the world, nor handed over his cause in such a way that he has become superfluous. Identity is still to come...."[61] Jesus' representation of God must be non-identity with God, so as to leave an open future, something to *expect* more than what is—for this is the very point of our quest for identity.[62] God's identity in our history still remains future, and the very function of his representative is to hold this future open for him.[63]

But here Sölle stops. She does not take us further on this promising path. We wait for her to give content to this talk of God's future, to tell us *what* to "expect." But this she refuses to do. Instead, she bends everything back on itself, by identifying Christ's waiting for God to take over with his waiting for *us* to respond to his representation.[64] There is a sense in which this too is right. But it does not suffice to give content to the promise made by Christ's provisionality. Indeed, the only future beyond Christ's representation which Sölle ever mentions is the return of immediate religious certainty.[65] And so Sölle's doctrine of God remains entirely ambiguous between a doctrine of God's own particular future time and a calmer version of Altizer's doctrine.

There are two possibilities of resolving the ambiguity. One would be to stipulate outright that God's future is always simply the next moment, a permanent futurity. This would give a doctrine like Altizer's. The other would be that Jesus holds a *specific* future open, that his story is a promise with *content*. Sölle refuses to do either. But only clearly working out this choice could be the new start of a "theology after the death of God."

We can understand why Sölle is unwilling to make the choice. Either option would be a decisive break with the tradition of dialectical theology, as most clearly represented by the *Commentary on Romans*. Sölle is, and clearly wishes to be, within the tradition of dialectical theology. But just for that reason she does not provide the new start we need.

VI

We have, of course, neither proven nor argued that *no one* has made a new start after the end represented by the *Commentary on Romans*. We have only looked at a few recent theologies which have included a specific claim to epochal appropriateness. Our purpose was both to examine those claims and to get a view of some of the problems in attempting theology after the death of the God of the past.

Our next question must be: where did *Barth* go from the *Commentary on Romans?*

Chapter Five
The Christological Reversal

I

We have examined and rejected several proposals for a new start after the self-defeat of historical religion. In turning back now to Barth and asking where *he* went from this dead end, it cannot but appear that I have set things up for the discovery that Barth has all the answers. I do indeed think that in one very specific way, Barth has made a new start where many more recent and explicit claimants have not. That is, after all, the reason for this book. But let it be said immediately: I do not wish to cry "back to Barth" or, coyly, "forward to Barth." There are very great difficulties indeed in the system he developed in the years after 1930. Some of these are external to the system. Of the two great agents in the death of our traditional religion, the ethos of the natural sciences and the apprehension of reality as history, only the second has made any apparent impact. Some are interior to the system. These are so great that they lead to systematic abstractness, so that it is often impossible to discover on what grounds he justifies his positions. Both exterior and interior difficulties result, I think, from a persisting ambiguity in his talk about "eternity." This will occupy us in the last section, and there I will argue that in one vital sense, Barth has never moved a single step past the *Commentary on Romans*.

But the point in the use of any thinker is not whether one can buy his whole system or not, but what good the labor of understanding him and arguing with him does in one's own enterprise of thinking through the matter at hand. My claim in this book is that Barth's thought can do a very great good for anyone projecting an antireligious understanding of Christian faith—indeed, an indispensable good. Of course, if someone can find the same benefit elsewhere, all is well.

II

Barth could no more remain at the position of the *Commentary on Romans* than we can live in the situation in which its dialectic puts us—certainly not after he was called to theologically responsible posts, where he could no longer merely reiterate what should *not* be said. Indeed, all the "dialectic theologians" found themselves in the same position—and that broke up the clique, for they were united mostly in their negations.

We will not go through the whole history of how Barth found his theological way in the 1920s and '30s.[1] We need only say that around 1930, with the book on Anselm[2] and the important essay "Fate and Idea in Theology,"[3] he mastered his basic intentions and established the definite form of his theologizing. It is the task of this chapter to sketch in a very broad way the fundamental structural innovation which determines Barth's theology after 1930. This will also provide a preliminary summary of that doctrine of God which we will examine more closely in the following chapters.

What is really new and original in the theology of the *Church Dogmatics* and Barth's other post-1930 works has rarely been grasped. Everyone has, of course, noticed an exceptional concentration on Jesus Christ. But to say that Barth's theology is "christocentric" says only that it is *Christian* theology—which is, one trusts, true, but not overly informative. In what sense this observation can become a criticism, as suggested by the label "christomonist," is not clear. If a "christomonist" theology is a non-trinitarian theology, such a theology would indeed be disastrous; but no one could seriously suggest that Barth's was of this sort. It is doubtful who the often-denounced "unitarians of the second article" are supposed to be. If the charge of "christomonism" means simply that someone wishes Barth would talk less about Christ and more about "authenticity," or the death of religion, or the meaning of "God," he will have to show how he proposes to do the one without the other. Our last chapter suggests this may not be so easy.

III

The basic move by which Barth found his way, and which is made in every locus of his theology, is simple and radical. Nineteenth-century theology began by telling the story of man, and then asked what role Christ had in that story. It inquired first into the meaning of life, and second into Christ's assistance in attaining it. Barth simply *reversed the order.* A story of man prior to Christ's story does not occur, he said, and never has occurred. There *is* no human life in itself, and surely no meaning of such a life. Rather, the event of Jesus Christ's life, because it is the central event in the life of the eternal God, is the eternal presupposition of all else that happens.

We are to see the fact of there being anything other than God as itself a great *occurrence,* the meaning of which in God is the self-giving which is the content of Jesus' life. Jesus' existence is the one great event to which all others, from the creation of the world to the blessedness of the saints, are subsidiary. The story is the story of Jesus Christ, and *we and all* creatures occur solely in that we have roles to play in that story.[4]

All men, by virture of their creation, are in one way or another "in Christ," i.e., involved in a history which is fundamentally the story of his life.[5] All the history of the existence of what is other than God, as a whole and in each part and from the battles of nations to someone reading this book, is the reflection and consequence of Jesus Christ's life. It is the detail of the one great happening of Jesus' love for his brothers, which in God's eternal will is the beginning and end of all things.

That there is a reality other than God is his free choice. The *content* of this will is the existence of Jesus Christ, just as his existence was enacted in Palestine, as self-giving to alienated men. "In the beginning with God, i.e., in his decree which precedes the existence, the possibility and reality of all his creatures, the primary element is the decision whose carrying out . . . is Jesus Christ."[6] God's decision to be our God in spite of everything is an "eternal covenant," whose content is Jesus Christ just as he lived and acted in history.[7] The goal of all God's will for a reality other than himself is the life of Jesus Christ as a life for alienated men. All the other works of God are done in order to carry out this decision.[8] The goal of history is Jesus' life for his fellows.

Nor is this eternal decision the mere making of a plan to be carried out later. God's decision is a self-determination, his self-differentiation of what he wills to be from what he wills not to be. God lives in his decision; he *is* his act of deciding.[9] *What* God chose was to occur as God for man in what happens with Jesus Christ. Thus Jesus Christ is the chosen reality of God in his eternal decision. As God's decision, which is God's eternal reality, Jesus of Nazareth occurred in eternity before all time.[10]

If we wish to understand the basis in God of his creation and rule of a reality other than himself, we must look "to where the incarnation, the reality of the divine-human person of Jesus Christ, is before . . . all other reality the intent of God's good pleasure, but where also just this intent . . . , prior to all the reality of the world, is identical with the reality of . . . Jesus Christ. We must look to where the eternal God not only foresees and predetermines this person, but as the presupposition of his revelation in time *is* this person."[11] In the eternal life of God there is a decisive meeting between God and the man Jesus.[12] This "eternal history"[13] is the "principle and essence of all else that happens. . . ."[14]

One possible objection must be considered immediately. By teaching a preexistence of the *man* Jesus Christ in the eternal life of the triune God, is not Barth going off into the wildest sort of religious speculation? Perhaps, but not necessarily. For Barth teaches that the life of Jesus as the life of the one who calls God "Father" is the event of the unity of eternity and time.[15] Thus the eternity of Jesus need not be mythological: it is the human history of Jesus which is eternity, without becoming something other than the temporal event in Palestine.[16] The meaning of Barth's doctrine *can,* at least, be that *the history of Jesus has taken over the place in the structure of reality which "eternity" had in religious Christianity*. The life of the man Jesus in Palestine is the event of "eternity." To speak of its eternity is to say that all other occurrences, as willed by the God who meets the man Jesus as his Son, are the carrying out of the relation between God and man which there occurs.

Doctrines of the metaphysical priority of Christ have appeared before in the history of theology, most notably in the Franciscan schools of high scholasticism. But always before they have been backed up and relativized by the standard teaching of Christian piety, that the event of Christ in its actual historical content as the life of the *crucified* one is God's reaction to a breakdown in his original "plan" for creation. If on this basis it was then also said that "Christ" is the metaphysical basis of all reality, and so also of creation as it would have been had God's "plan" not been disturbed, this "Christ" is a Christ abstracted from his actual historical existence as the rejected and crucified Jesus. Previous doctrines of the metaphysical priority of Christ have meant a constructed "Christ," Christ as he would have been had there been no alienation.

Barth does not perform this abstraction. The story of Jesus Christ which he preaches as the story of all reality whatever is exactly the story of humiliation and suffering enacted in Palestine under Pontius Pilate. It is the man who was the "witness of God's Kingdom," the "Lamb of God who bears the world's sin," a "man in an act of simplest . . . responsibility to God," "Jesus," who is "the man who was in the beginning with God. . . . The entire eternally decided work of God has this man, his existence, as its point." God is "the living God at the beginning of all his ways" just in this, that this "history . . . between God and man occurs" in the bosom of God.[17]

The doctrine that all things are in Christ simply in that they are real might mean transforming "Christ" from the man who lived in Nazareth to a sheerly supernatural being, to an even more than ordinarily suitable object of pure religious devotion. The Franciscan schools only carried Origen's great move one more step. Barth's doctrine of Christ's priority has the opposite meaning: he proclaims the life of the man Jesus, just as it was, as the presupposition of all other reality. Here escape from time and history is shut off for good, for our search for the sense of our lives in time is directed exactly to a temporal event—not merely as its revelation or facilitation, but as its *occurrence*.

Within this basic movement of Barth's theology, the sense of the beginning dialectical attack on the synthesis of religion and faith suddenly becomes unambiguous. Our works and thoughts can never reach God; our faith in religion is false, *not* because we and God are so far apart, but because the attempt to *reach* God rests on the illusory and unbelieving supposition that he has ever left us. The attack on the synthesis of human self-transcendence with the gospel is, in the context of Barth's development, not an attempt to separate them, but a rejection of the whole attempt to bring them together—as if they were, to begin with, apart, as if we began with a life not dependent on Christ and somehow had to get to him.

Not one word of what is said in the *Commentary on Romans* is withdrawn. But where abstract eternity was, Jesus of Nazareth now stands. All human works are relativized quite as radically as before, but from the event of Jesus' existence rather than from the event of the contentless moment of eternity. The predestining God, before whom our works are meaningless and just so gain their meaning, is now Jesus Christ; the decree of predestination is the decision made in his life about us.[18] Indeed, the entire pattern of the dialectic we traced remains quite unaltered in Barth's post-1930 theology. If one went through the *Commentary on Romans* and replaced the tangential intersection of time and eternity with the story narrated by the second article of the Apostles' Creed, he would obtain the theology of the *Church Dogmatics*.

This ingeniously simple move raises problems of its own. It is, for one thing, all too much a mere reversal of the pattern of strictly religious Christianity. But we will discuss the problems later. For now, we simply identify the way which Barth in fact has found around the impasse of the end of the religion of history. We can put it this way: the christological reversal *maintains* the situation created by the dialectic of the religion of history, but as confrontation with Jesus Christ rather than with nothingness, and so as the possibility of faith rather than as the sheer impossibility of being religious.

It is this absolute priority of Jesus' existence, of the life of our brother-man, which is the key to the otherwise puzzling convolutions of the great dogmatic theology which Barth has developed through his years at Göttingen, Bonn and Basel, and recorded in the twelve huge volumes of the *Church Dogmatics*. That one starts with the story of this man, is the key to a thinking which hammers on the sole and absolute majesty of God and the irrelevance of all our works and thoughts to reach him, yet finds anything human an appropriate object of dogmatic reflection. It is the key to a theology which is really one vast doctrine of God, yet involved its creator in the most direct sort of political action. If we forget the priority of Christ in considering any Barthian doctrine we will infallibly turn it into its direct opposite, the kind of isolation of God which people have mislabelled "Barthianism." Barth can insist on the otherness of God because his God is from the beginning one person with the man Jesus; God's otherness is therefore the otherness of one man from another, which is the very condition of mutual involvement.

IV

To put a bit more flesh on this statement of Barth's basic move, we will sketch the way the move works in some of the main topics of theology—though remaining within the bounds of a summary.

We begin with the doctrine of God. If what happens with Jesus in time is the central event in the eternal existence of God, then that existence must be *historical*. God must have a history. God is not a timeless Being; indeed, "The theological concept of eternity must be *freed* from the Babylonian captivity of an abstract opposition to the concept of time."[19] Anticipating what we will develop later: God is not a thing but an *event*. And the event which is God is exactly the event of Jesus' self-giving to his fellows.[20]

Such a God will not provide an object of direct religious devotion. He and the God of religion must dispute the title. Indeed, we may put it so: God is *what happens with Jesus Christ to end religion*. The happening that is God is the happening of Jesus' obedience to his Father in giving himself to us. We call this event "God" not because we recognize him as the long-sought object of our religious quest, but because he condemns this quest as unnecessary—and just and only so fulfills it.

In the doctrine of Creation, Barth teaches that all reality other than God exists to provide the theater and supporting players for the story of Jesus Christ.[21] This purpose is an eternally accomplished reality in God; the true and essential self of any creature is the part it has in this purpose.[22]

Barth turns anthropology on what we have previously supposed to be its head by saying that the incarnation is not the Son of God assuming a "human nature" already defined by *our* lives, but that rather the Son defines human nature by assuming it. Christ freely decides what his life shall be—and *this* decision determines what is human.[23] To be human is by definition to be a fellow of Jesus and involved with him.[24] Our lives occur as events in the meeting between Jesus of Nazareth and his Father; his story is the inclusive plot of which ours are subplots. The true story of our lives, therefore, is the story of our involvement in his history, whether we now so experience our lives or not. What we truly are is what we are as actors in his story.[25]

The doctrine of reconciliation follows. Because we are what we are in Christ and nothing else, the history of death and resurrection in which he becomes just and holy is an ontological transformation of our existence also.[26] And the fulfillment for which we may hope will be the revelation to us of our lives as they have been involved in Christ's self-giving, i.e., as we have truly lived them.

The ethic which must be an integral part of such a theology is necessarily an ethic of *permissions,* the proclamation of the possibilities which are open in that we participate in Christ.[27] The structure of this ethic appears most clearly in Barth's doctrine of the civil community, which is said to form an outer sphere of human fellowship within which the believers' community is an inner sphere. Both have the same center, our basic fellowship with Jesus Christ. The believer's involvement in social and political action is not, therefore, his departure from the realm of Christ's lordship into some alien sphere with different rules. Both civil community and church are preliminary stages to the Kingdom of God, and share the same possibilities. The believer's social involvement must not be an attempt to "Christianize" the social order, or to achieve churchly domination of culture or state. For this attempt assumes that Christ is not already lord of all human community—which is the assumption of unbelief.[28]

V

There is a series of questions raised by all these loci of Barth's mature theology. The historical event of Jesus' existence is, he teaches, the eternal event of the life of the living God. But does this not collapse the distinction of time and eternity, so as to produce a doctrine of purely immanent salvation by the man Jesus, where talk of God is really superfluous?[29] If all other history is merely the detail of the history of Christ, who is God the Son, is there a creation at all, as a reality really distinct from God?[30] If all men are already in Christ by virtue of their creation, what can really *happen* as God's act *in* history to save us?[31] Our real history is claimed to be our involvement in Christ's history, whether we experience this or not. But in what sense can a history we do not experience be *our* history? Do we not simply fall out of this drama, leaving the stage to Jesus by himself?[32] If church and civil community have the same center how does one tell them apart?[33]

In each case, what is feared is the collapse of some *duality* essential to Christian faith and thought. In each case the fear is raised by the vigor of Barth's christological "is." God *is* what happens with Jesus. We *are* Christ's. We *are* what we are in Christ. Christ *is* lord of the civil community. Barth is clearly the last theologian to abolish the difference between Jesus and God, creature and creator, sinner and saint, ourselves and Jesus, church and society. Therefore it must be that his christological "is" does not mean identity. Yet if he were to hedge the "is" in any way, he would end up saying: God is *very like* Jesus. We are Christ's, *if* we do such and such. Christ is *intended* to be lord of the civil community. Then he would merely be repeating standard dishwater protestantism, and would have fallen back to a position well before the *Commentary on Romans*.

At each of these points, Barth requires some way of distinguishing time from eternity, Jesus in Palestine from Jesus in God, us in our own experience from us in Jesus' experience, which will not undo the christological reversal and make time, the historical Jesus and ourselves as we now know ourselves, into realities independent of Christ. At each of these points, Barth in fact uses the same notion, which thus becomes the main structural device of his theology: "image," or "analogy," or "reflection." This is the same notion we have already encountered in the *Commentary on Romans,* and it has exactly the same role as it did there.

Christ, as the man who fulfills God's intentions for man, is "created 'after God'. . . . That is, he exists analogously to God's way of existing. . . ."[34] What he does and says over against us "mirrors and copies" God's act and sentence on us.[35] But this act and sentence of God are the same event as Christ's own eternal occurrence. Thus the same relation of analogy and reflection obtains between Jesus as the man eternally before God, as God's "eternal Son, who is also a son of man," and Jesus as a man in our time and space.[36] The relation between God the Father and God the Son is "repeated and copied in God's eternal covenant with man, as this is revealed . . . in time by the humanity of Jesus." The "being for God of the man Jesus" is the occurrence of this eternal covenant; his "being for his fellow man" "corresponds" to and "resembles" his being for God, and so also "repeats and copies" God's own eternal triune being. That in his being for us Jesus thus copies God's being for us, is the very meaning of his being for God.[37]

Our humanity is essentially co-humanity. Thus it is an *image* of Jesus' life in God for his brothers.[38] The sort of being which man has "is the image of the *meaning* of his being. . . . This imaging determination of man's being . . . *is* his humanity."[39] As images of Jesus, we are, at one remove, images also of God.[40]

Our experience of our own lives is both distinct from and integral to our lives as they are really lived in Christ, in that the content of our experience is our coming to *know* of our true existence in Christ,[41] is our coming to faith. In knowing of our true being in Christ, we *reflect* that being in our experience;[42] the decisive description of faith is therefore that it is the *"analogy"* of Jesus Christ's death and ressurrection.[43]

Finally, both the church and the civil community are communities which reflect Jesus' community with us. The effort of the believer's social involvement will be to promote such social conditions as more adequately reflect the quality of Jesus' fellowship with us, to polish the mirror as it were.[44]

VI

Barth thus retains in the heart of his thinking a pattern of thought which runs through the entire theological tradition: the pattern represented by "analogy" or "image." We are sent back to Parmenides.

There were two parts to Parmenides' revelation. The one is the word of true changeless being; the other an account of the world of our temporal experience. The goddess' revelation included an account of the world of time, in order to warn Parmenides against it. To do this the account had to be *true*—but truth lies only in the word of eternal being. A true account of the false world can only be created by taking at every point the exact antithesis of the word of true being; and just so will be an account which corresponds point by point to that word of true being. "I will describe for you the world of oppositions, as it corresponds to the true reality in all points."[45] The world of our temporal experience is at once the antithesis of eternal being and corresponds to it; it is eternity's mirror-image.

Parmenides did not reflect thematically on this analogy of time and eternity, and so did not describe its nature. Plato did, and his doctrine determined the following tradition. He drew his categories from the language of artisanship: the artisan "imitates" a "paradigm" and so creates an artifact which is the "image" of the imitated reality. Eternity is the paradigm, the world of time the image which imitates this paradigm.[46]

This language provided for Plato a solution of his fundamental problem, the relation of time to eternity. Only eternity is truly real: if temporal occurrences are in any way real, they must therefore in that same way be eternal. Yet they are temporal exactly in that they are *not* eternal. This paradox seems resolved in the peculiar reality of the image: the statue, for example, both *is* the woman of which it is an imitation and *is not* a woman. An image has its meaning only in the other reality which is its paradigm. It is something and not nothing—but is something only for its paradigm.

It is important to note also that *analogy* and *dialectic* are in no way opposing phenomena. They are two sides of the same phenomenon. The *correspondence* of the two parts of Parmenides' revelation is exactly that of perfectly fitting *antitheses*. In Plato, it is the same: "image" is a way of grasping the relation between realities, eternity and time, which have been defined by their opposition to each other. The way from time to eternity is the dialectic; looked at from the other end, from eternity, this same way between the two is grasped by calling time the image of eternity. Given the model, the statue is its image. Given the image, we may think our way to the model by dialectic.

Plato thus specifies the correspondence between time and eternity as *resemblance*. The analogy is that which obtains between two entities whose characteristics are compared and found to be the same in some ways though not in others—as the statue and the model have the same visible form though not the same origin, stuff, or even tactile form.

It is Plato's notion of resemblance between an image and its paradigm which has come down through the entire philosophical and theological tradition as the content in all talk of the analogy of time to eternity. In the *Commentary on Romans* the platonic pattern is received without variation, though its original function is frozen. We must now ask if and wherein Barth's use of this pattern of thought changes in his positive theology.

God is Jesus Christ—he is other than Jesus Christ. The world is redeemed—and lost. We are in Christ—we are not in Christ. Barth sees in analogous predication a stuttering but unavoidable way of saying both sides of such pairs at once, as we must if theology is to be possible.[47] "If God is what he is quite *otherwise* in himself than in his work, so that the relation between what he is in himself and what he is in his work is only a relation of *resemblance,* nevertheless . . . in himself and in his work he is *no other*"[48]—i.e., God's reality in his work, the creature, is analogous to his reality in himself.

It is only a stuttering attempt, for the creature is not partly like God and partly unlike him, but wholly like God and wholly unlike him.[49] Exactly as in the *Commentary on Romans,* this *analogy* of eternity to time is the other side of the *dialectic* of time and eternity.[50] In this, Barth's analogy, both early and late, but continues the pattern of the whole tradition.[51] The attempt to speak of God by means of analogies with the creature can never be successfully concluded. The hiddenness of God is always not only behind but before it.[52] Rather, our knowledge of God by analogy succeeds just when we confess its failure, and so succeeds only by the justification of the ungodly.[53] Particular analogies are always true only in the *future.*[54] Here, too, the dialectic is a movement to a goal.[55]

The formal structure of Barth's later doctrine of analogy does not, therefore, differ from that of the *Commentary on Romans* or of the tradition.[56] Barth's later doctrine differs only—but this is a large "only"—in that analogy and dialectic both now become *christology*.

Barth's fundamental objection to the classical doctrine of the analogy of God and the world is that as the correspondence between them it puts being-in-general where Jesus Christ belongs.[57] In the classical doctrine of analogy, the fundamental resemblance between God and creatures is that God is Being and creatures are beings. The classical doctrine does not say—as Barth sometimes supposes[58]—that God and creatures resemble each other in that both share in Being. It says that creatures resemble God, in that creatures are beings and so share in the Being which he does not share in but rather is. Nevertheless, the resemblance between God and creatures is posited by Being-as-such, by both God and creatures possessing whatever characteristics anything must have in order to be anything at all: intelligibility, value, unity and beauty. Barth replaces Being with the life of Jesus Christ. The creatures' likeness to God is not mediated by the changeless reality of what all things must be in order to be at all; it is mediated by the event of the existence of Jesus Christ. God's reality is, by his choice, the occurrence of the life of this person; our lives are incidents in his life—and *so* we creatures are analogous to God. For there to be either analogy or dialectic, there must indeed be a common term of God and the creature. In Barth's mature theology, this is Jesus Christ: "As the reality of God is *his* reality, so is the reality of man originally *his* reality."[59]

Indeed, the creature who is analogous to God is not the creature in general, but *this* creature, Jesus. Other creatures are analogous to *him*.[60] It is important also to remember that "Jesus Christ" does not intend a supernatural cosmic being of some sort, but the events of Jesus' life, death and resurrection for his alienated fellows, just as these occurred in time and space. So we repeat: the dialectic of the *Commentary on Romans* is not reversed by the christological move, nor is the situation to which it brought us abandoned. Rather, the analogy and dialectic which were in mutual necessity the content of the *Commentary on Romans* have both become *christology*.

In the creature itself, there is no resemblance to God. But the creature is not in itself. For we exist as reflectors of the occurrence of Jesus Christ; and the meaning of the occurrence of Jesus Christ is exactly the grace which redeems us from what we are in ourselves. Thus we, too, are images of God, who *is* this occurrence of grace. Here is exactly the pattern of the *Commentary on Romans,* with "Jesus Christ" where "the moment" used to be.

The event of eternity, and of eternity's union with time, is no longer specifiable only by a play of abstractions, it is an event which can be *narrated*. Jesus Christ's story is the story of "the critical moment." The *christological* analogy and the *christological* dialectic make possible a choice of the things we might abstractly say of God,[61] and so give faith its language again. We have a *particular story* to tell about eternity.

Chapter Six

Against Religious Theology

I

Barth is now in position decisively to work out the difference between faith and religion. He is in a position to describe the reality and possibility of faith's cognition of God with every step of the analysis controlled by determination to sustain the critique of religion. This is done most conveniently where he comes to grips with "natural theology."

"Natural theology" has meant many things in the history of theology. It is essential at the very beginning to indicate what *Barth* means by it, lest our prior expectations lead us astray. By "natural theology" Barth means the reflecting about God which occurs in the course of our religious quest. For Barth's use of the notion, it is irrelevant what the immediate source of an opinion about God may be. It may be derived speculatively, communicated by the Buddha, or read straight from the Bible; this does not settle whether it is natural or revealed. The question is rather: to what enterprise of human life does holding some idea about God belong? The attack on natural theology does not, therefore, mean that Barth has classified our opinions about God into two groups by source—nature and revelation—and decreed that all in one group are necessarily false or otherwise suspect. Since all our thinking about God is part of our religious quest, all our theologizing is inevitably natural theology. The question is whether it is only that.[1]

Barth begins by assuming, and making explicit that he assumes, that we do in fact know God—not that we know "a" God, but that we know as God the particular being of whom the Christian gospel speaks. He does not, therefore, begin with the question whether it is possible to know God, but rather with the question how we are to explain the fact that we do know God.

Already we see the control of anti-religious polemic. For were we to begin with the question of *whether* we can know God, we would be asking whether a being appropriately called "God" can also be knowable. "God" in our question would have to mean an entity satisfying such-and-such criteria for being so classified. The question would thus be one posed in the course of the religious quest for such a being. Our question must, therefore, not be whether entities appropriately called "God" could also be of the sort that are knowable; but rather, what is involved in the situation that we do know the Father of Jesus Christ as God. We must not start with the need to choose the "real" God from the class of beings candidate for the position, but start rather with our knowledge of Jesus Christ and inquire into what we can mean by saying that we know God in that we know him.[2]

This means that we must begin with a surprising assertion: God's revelation means that he has made himself our *object;* we as subjects have God as an object. He is just there as one of the objects of our knowledge—and that is where we have to start.[3] This reverses the procedure of natural theology. As the expression in thought of our religious self-transcending, natural theology always reasons *from* something there that is not God, *to* a "ground" or "primary cause" or "telos" beyond—or behind or below or inside—that something that is there. The God of religion is by definition not our object.

The assertion of God's objectivity is a direct challenge to nearly all theology since the beginning of the nineteenth century, which has unanimously insisted on the nonobjectivity of God. Barth denies all conceptions of our knowledge of God as a "nonobjectifying knowledge which tries to leave behind the distinction of knower and known."[4] In knowing God, we distinguish between ourselves and God, and relate ourselves to God, as we do with any object of our experience.[5] The motive behind the doctrine of God's nonobjectivity has been the belief that to treat something as an object is to detach it from myself, and so to be myself *detached* from it, that it is to put it out there away from me, and so to adopt a neutral, take-it-or-leave-it stance toward it. This negative evaluation of "objectification" lies deep in modern philosophy and theology. Nor is it simply false; clearly the striving for objective knowledge influenced as little as possible by our hopes or commitments *may* be the attempt to secure ourselves from any existential challenges which the other-than-we may pose.

But the activity of objectifying cognition may also be just the opposite of such a flight into oneself. Precisely the otherness, the out-thereness, of an *object* ought to break me out of myself and compel me to be determined in some part of my life by a reality which I do not control. Objectifying cognition may be, and is when authentic, itself a highly charged particular mode of existential involvement.

Developing an analysis of the positive human reality of authentic objectifying, and using it in a theological understanding of the sciences, is an urgent theological task. Barth has not embarked on it. But he does use such an understanding of objectivity in elucidating our knowledge of God. To have an object is to have to attend to an other-than-me, and so to be challenged to be other than I am—and this is exactly our appropriate relation to God: "In faith the same thing doubtless happens as always happens when . . . man's subjectivity is opened for an objectivity and insofar is newly grounded and determined."[6]

God is, of course, a different sort of object than chairs or galaxies. The same opening of the subject which happens over against all objects "happens in faith quite otherwise."[7] This difference is the truth in the doctrine of God's nonobjectivity—which Barth never really acknowledges. The ordinary priority is reversed: to know *this* object is to know that I exist as a subject only insofar as he has made himself my object.[8] Knowledge of this object is essentially obedience.[9] Moreover, it is true that with all other objects, to know them as objects is in some sense to "see through" them, and so to dominate them. Here we encounter the object we cannot see through; we encounter *mystery*. This does not mean that our knowledge is vague or "mysterious." We know God clearly—but what we know is in part that our attempt to see through everything is at an end.[10]

Therefore, our objective knowledge of God is "indirect." God is our object, but "clothed . . . under another object distinct from himself."[11] What we have before us is an object other than God, the humanity of Jesus with the historical continuations of the witness thereto in Israel and the church.[12] In this object we know God; that is, between us and this object there occurs that particular opening to an other-than-we which is knowledge of God.[13]

II

But now we are back with the problem of natural theology. For the question cannot be suppressed: how can we know the object Jesus in this way? And Barth agrees: the question of the knowability of God, of the possibility of knowing him, must be asked—though not until now. Now it arises in the form: how is it possible for us to know Jesus as the one in whom *God* is there for us?[14]

It is just at this point that many who, like Barth and perhaps persuaded by him, have refused to start with a natural theology, have still insisted that one must be introduced. I should confess that I belong with them, and indicate briefly why. Surely the possibility of knowing Jesus as God presupposes that the word "God" is already given in language. This further presupposes that we have already had occasion to use it, and that those previous occasions and the present occasion of confrontation with Jesus are not so unrelated as to make sheer equivocation out of the use of the word in both cases. The relation, as I have already claimed, must indeed be a polemical one: the rules for speaking of Jesus as God are set by polemic against all that has been earlier known as God.[15] But the relation does obtain.

Barth makes, and must make, a quite different and completely characteristic move. He makes his answer to the question of the knowability of God part of his doctrine of God itself. As *triune*, God is eternally and essentially knowable. He is knowable, moreover, as an object, and as *this* object Jesus Christ.

"As the triune God, God is an object first and before all to himself."[16] The Father knows the Son, and the Son the Father, as *other* than himself, and so objectively.[17] This objectivity of God to himself is in fact and by God's choice—though it might have been otherwise—the same event as the confrontation between the Father and the man Jesus. Thus the "primary objectivity" of God to himself is the same event as the "being for God of the man Jesus." And Jesus' humanity for us is in turn the image of his being for God.[18] Thus the subject-object relation between us and the man Jesus reflects the subject-object relation between God the Father and God the Son—and so it is that in the opening of our subjectivity over against Jesus there occurs that opening of our subjectivity which is knowledge of God.

God is therefore intrinsically knowable. He is the truth, the root of all truth. And he is knowable and the truth because he is triune. In that God is triune he is open to himself. In that same openness he is open to us as the man Jesus. Therefore, truth is a possibility. "For this is the origin and concept of all truth, that God is not hidden to himself but open. Truth is openness. In that God is open to himself, the Father to the Son and the Son to the Father, through the Holy Spirit, and in that he is lord of all things, all things are open to him. . . ."[19]

We come here to a first instance of Barth's constitutive use of the doctrine of the Trinity throughout theology. Using, and not merely asserting, the doctrine of the Trinity is one of the fundamental features of his theology, to which we will be brought repeatedly.

If God is eternally and essentially knowable, it might seem that there were no more problems to be faced, that knowing God is the ordinary thing. On the one hand, we might, on the grounds of the absolute priority of Christ, suppose that all knowledge of God is knowledge of the true God, however gained. But Barth will not say this, for he teaches the ontological priority not of a general principle of divine immanence but of Jesus of Nazareth. We might then go to the other extreme and suppose that only the specifically Christian knowledge of God which derives historically from Jesus is true knowledge of God. But Barth will not say this either—though he often in other contexts uses such forms of words—because of his doctrine of the priority of Christ. Therefore the matter must become yet more dialectical.

God in his eternal reality is essentially knowable. There is, therefore, nothing in itself remarkable about knowing God. What is remarkable is that *we* can know God. For insofar as any knowledge of God we may have is *ours,* it is unavoidably the absolutizing and "projection on infinity" of our own reality.[20] Barth's description and estimate of our religious knowledge of God has not varied from the *Commentary on Romans.* Nor has his determination to keep it clear that "also our . . . theological knowledge of God, the movement of thought which is in all due form concerned with the triune God, and is led and controlled by the Bible and dogma, has this natural . . . side."[21]

If our knowledge of God has another side, if it is not only—as it always also is—the projection of our religious flight from time, but is also knowledge of the object God, this is a miracle. That is, it is not in any way the achievement of our religious quest. In Jesus Christ, God *gives* "our knowledge of God its object."[22] He *chooses* to be the object of that activity we call knowing God, an activity which apart from this choice would be merely our self-glorification.[23]

III

The possibility of speaking of God rests, therefore, in a "take-over" of our language with its objectifying patterns of grammar and its concepts for describing objects. "Theology and the church, and the Bible itself, speak no other language than that shaped formally and materially by the conditions . . . of the world . . . : the language in which man, as he in fact is . . . , tries to come to terms with the world as it confronts him and as he sees it and is able to understand it. . . ."[24] This human enterprise does not have in itself the potentiality of extending to God, but God has chosen to be our object and so commanded us to speak of him.[25]

Thus perhaps we speak of God as "triune," as "one being in three hypostases." And perhaps we go on to say that God is "self-related" in himself somewhat like "mind," "memory" and "will" are self-related in the human spirit. Such talk seeks to "*interpret*" God's being. We interpret God's being in that we speak of him *as* such-and-such: *as* one being, or three hypostases, or loving, etc. So God acquires "shape" in our language; these interpretations, if justified, *describe* him.[26]

But, says Barth, such talk is in itself unprotected from being mere "illustration" of God's being. We "illustrate" God when we proceed by first finding in our language certain patterns of reality, and then saying perhaps God is like this. In so doing we rely on the ability of our speaking to be about God, and just so deny him.[27] In fact, all our talk of God is illustration; the hope is that it is not only this, that it is also interpretation.

We can interpret God's being, and not merely illustrate it, only because God has already interpreted himself to himself in our language, and we merely follow his interpretation. His revelation in Jesus Christ is his self-interpretation *as* all that we can say truly of Christ. We pick up earlier points and combine: in his Son who is Jesus, God knows himself *as* a particular describable form,[28] as such-and-such worldly realities, as all that Jesus is. This act of self interpretation as Jesus *is* the revelation of God; our interpretation follows—and just so is not mere illustrating. God truly is all that we, following his self-interpretation, say he is.[29]

Again we have arrived at the doctrine of the Trinity, this time as Barth's solution to the problem of theological language. His explicit solution is, of course, the doctrine of *analogy*.[30] We can see how he must adopt this doctrine: Jesus as the man we know is the *image* of God's Son. Thus God's self-interpretation in our language about Jesus, and our following interpretation, are analogical speech; we can speak meaningfully and truly about God only in analogies of the creature, as we have earlier seen the analogical structuring of all created reality to God. But it is the doctrine of the Trinity that interprets the real possibility of such analogous speech about God.

"Analogy" is, after all, a nearly empty concept. In itself, it merely repeats the difficulty: God and man must be understood as at once alike and unlike. But the question is how? If we merely say that we can talk about God in words meaning creaturely characteristics because creatures are analogous to God, and say no more, this is the same sort of explanation as those of medieval medicine that fever results from "feverish humours." If one does say more, it is this that is the real proposed solution.

Thus Barth and many traditional theologians share the concept of analogy. Yet in the old doctrine Barth once found an invention of anti-Christ. Barth attempted to distinguish *formally* his doctrine from traditional doctrines: his is an "analogy of faith," the traditional doctrine is an "analogy of being."[31] But this attempt is unsuccessful. It is nevertheless easy to see why Barth has to oppose the traditional concept of an analogy of being—only the reason does not lie in any formal character of the concept, but in something more that is said, in what the traditional doctrine goes on to say materially about "being."

Creatures are said to resemble God in that he is their creator. God must have had a purpose in creating; that purpose must be to share with other beings his own perfection, otherwise God would be seeking to realize a value external to himself, and not be God.[32] Thus creatures must somehow be like the Creator. As the creator, God is cause of the very being of creatures, and it is in this that they fundamentally resemble him.[33] The fact that a creature *is* whatever it is is its fundamental resemblance to God.

The primary analogous name of God is, therefore, "Being."[34] But if all that could be said of God were that he is "Being" nothing would have been said about God. For "being" is the word that applies to everything that is, just because it is; applied therefore to any particular being it tells us by itself nothing whatever about it. If all that we say about God were meaningful only by way of an analogy of being, and if nothing could be said further to specify "being," all our statements about God would be vacuous. The traditional doctrine of analogy avoids vacuity in its talk of God only by what it goes on to say materially about "being": that "goodness," "truth" and "unity" are convertible with it,[35] i.e., that if a thing is anything at all, it has a definable unity, and in that unity has value and can be known. On this basis, if we can say of God that he is Being, we can deductively go on to say that he is Goodness, Truth and Unity. And it is this that is the content of our talk of God.

It is this material doctrine about Being that Barth must reject. For it amounts to the claim that all beings, and so also we, by virtue merely of our existence and independently of what happens with Jesus, possess the value and truth of our lives in our own personal unity. It amounts to the claim that in the substantial unity of what we already are we possess the truth and goal of what we are, that in what we already are we have the future. The doctrine of Being which makes the traditional understanding of religious language work is exactly the Parmenidean doctrine of Being, with all its religious titanism. Therefore, the traditional understanding of religious language must be rejected by any theology which tries to maintain a polemic relation to religion.

Whether Barth's own doctrine of analogy is completely purified of religious titanism is a problem we will have to discuss.[36] But for the present, the point is that he replaces the doctrine of Being and its convertibility with value by the doctrine of the Trinity. Analogy by itself is an empty notion. It functions as an understanding of theological language only when something more is said. In Barth's mature thought, this something more is the doctrine of the Trinity.

God is in himself a word, a word to and about himself. God the Son is in God's eternal will a creature, Jesus. God's word to himself is, therefore, a word by, about and to a creature; it is an *utterance in our language*. Therefore Barth can say: "We have with our . . . words no claim on him that he must be their object. But he has indeed . . . a claim on us . . . and our words, to be their first, last and proper object." For insofar as our words have God's creation, his creation in Christ, for their object, "God knows about himself in them."[37]

As *our* speaking, what we have to say about God does not achieve him. Only by his free will does he make himself our object.[38] God is at once unlike and like what we say of him; in our repetition of his self-interpretation he is at once hidden and revealed.[39] It is this duality of hiding and revealing for which Barth uses "analogy"; and this duality, too, is a piece of trinitarian theology.

The *self-revealing* of the hidden God is the "root" of the doctrine of the self-repetition of the Father in the Son. The self-revealing *of the hidden God* is the root of the continuing distinction of the Father from the Son.[40] The doctrine of analogy, which seeks to grasp both at once, *is but a form of the doctrine of the Spirit.*

IV

Barth is at last in position to attack natural theology. The *Commentary on Romans* is often thought of as the great attack on natural theology. It is not. Only in his post-1930 theology does Barth identify his target in this way. Indeed, the whole *Commentary on Romans* could very well be taken as a grandiose piece of natural theology. For what, after all, is the "critical moment"? It is the moment of the shipwreck of the religious quest, the moment when our pursuit of the eternal *condemns itself*. But this moment, too, is a moment of the religious quest and its cognitive aspect a piece of natural theology. Negative religion and negative natural theology are still religion and natural theology—as Barth, of course, well knew.

The knowledge which constitutes the critical moment would be more than natural theology only if it were a response to a reality not given in that present moment itself, only if God were also outside of the present crisis. But this is exactly what is not possible with so ruthless an identification of eternity and the future as is made by the *Commentary on Romans*. And so our own despair of our religious efforts is—dialectically to be sure, but nevertheless—knowledge of God.[41]

In the *Church Dogmatics,* this ambiguity is overcome by the christological content which the dialectic acquires. And now the challenge of natural theology is met with an explicit attack. We do, indeed, says Barth, have knowledge of all sorts of *lords, causes, reconcilers* and *redeemers*.[42] There is neither need nor possibility of denying this. We can indeed set up a series of, e.g., "causes," and "project the series to infinity." And there is nothing to prevent us from designating "the point where we tire of the series with the vocable 'God' or 'Creator.' . . ."[43] When we do this sort of thing, what is underway is "man's attempt, by means of certain answers to the riddle of himself and his world, to come to terms with himself and his world . . . , in the belief that he should take the supposed goal of his answers or perhaps the supposed origin of his questions for . . . his God. This attempt is of course possible and possible of accomplishment."[44] But what so comes to be called God is an idol—which man does indeed know naturally.[45]

The true God, however, is known exactly when all our assertions formed in this way—and all our assertions about God are formed in this way—are contradicted,[46] and not by the immanent failure of the enterprise but by a contradictory message.[47] The true God is known exactly when the whole enterprise is shown to be perverse, by the pure contingent facticity of God's being there before us as an object, so as to obviate this projecting of our objective experience beyond itself into nothingness.

Now also the polemic can extend to the kind of religion and natural theology which could be read from the *Commentary on Romans*. For even if man's attempt to master his life must end with despair of the attempt, even if the absolute which this quest discovers is only a great question mark, "why should not this question mark be unmasked as the most idolatrous idol yet, and this despair . . . as the most desperate form of man's fight against the real God?"[48] Existentialist or atheistic religion is no less religion, and existentialist or atheistic theology no less religion's theology. God is exactly the condemner of the whole enterprise, however it may in a particular case end.

V

But we are still not at rest. For having been assured of the knowability of God, we are, according to Barth, faced with the fact that nevertheless we do not know him. This fact raises the question of *our* ability to know the intrinsically knowable God.[49]

The conditions of our knowing God in Christ are *need* of God's grace in Christ, *knowledge* of our need of the availability of the needed grace, and *willingness* to accept it.[50] These conditions are fulfillable and fulfilled—but in contingent fact they are so fulfilled and only so fulfilled that thereby we oppose rather than grasp the true grace of God. Our need of God's grace in fact consists exactly in our ability to hide our need from ourselves. We can know of our neediness, but our knowledge is the kind Eve got: we can know ourselves to be publicans and just so be pharisees. We can very well will to live by grace, but the grace *we will* to live by is only a new variety of religion.[51]

Man is not *in himself* ready to know God, not even "the man who has been addressed by the preaching and sacraments of the church and so finally by the word of God itself, not even believing man...."[52] For man will not live by grace. "He will believe in grace. He will assert that he feels it and rejoices in it. He will praise it, perhaps teach it and defend it. And he will do all this sincerely. But he will not in all this live from grace, but from his belief in it, or his zeal for it, or his knowledge of it, or his willingness to accept it...."[53]

Natural theology, therefore, is any theology insofar as it is the theology of man as such, insofar as we abstract from the possibility that God, by interpreting himself as Jesus Christ, has *chosen* some of our theology to be true theology. Our natural theologizing is our interpretation to ourselves of our possibility and necessity of coming to terms with our own life, also and even especially when we find that possibility in God's revelation.[54] We cannot desist from this.[55] But the one thing we must not do is to insist that this inevitable theologizing of ours carries its success in itself, that the knowability of God can be "made intelligible as a predicate of man," that we can point out in our lives how it is possible for us to know God.[56]

But what then of our knowledge of God—with the reality of which we began? Surely man must be able to know God, if it is true that man does know him? To be sure. But the whole fault of natural theology is that it looks at the wrong man in trying to understand man's ability to know God. It looks at man in himself, who, whatever might have been, is in fact not ready to know God. It should have looked at the man Jesus Christ.[57]

God the Son is ready to know the Father. God the Son is this man Jesus. Therefore *this* man is open to the knowledge of God. And it is in him and not in ourselves that we find our true selves—and so find ourselves open to the knowledge of God.[58] Again, the doctrine of the Trinity is the key.

In this trinitarian framework, the christological knot is tied up. Every path of natural theology is roped off. Jesus Christ is God known to man; and Jesus Christ, we now are told, is the man who can know God. Man's knowledge of God occurs between the "two natures" of Christ. Again Barth makes the same move he has made at every point: the dialectic of hiding and revelation, seen from the other end as image or analogy,[59] is exactly the same as that of the *Commentary on Romans,* only that it has become christology.

The assertion that we know God only in Christ could very well be merely pious or obscurantist. It is intelligible only against the basic move of Barth's theology. He has described our very existence as participation in Jesus' life. We participate in Jesus' life in and through our knowledge of it. If, then, the content of Jesus' life is exactly that he knows God, we share in Jesus' knowledge of God as we know Jesus—and knowing Jesus is our true reality. Our interpretation of God, controlled by the story of Jesus, is controlled by God's interpretation of himself.

The knowledge which Jesus has of God, the idea he has of him and the assertions he makes about him, are human. They share all the problematic we have traced. But in the perfect union of God and man in Christ, his knowledge is perfect obedience and perfect faith, and so is perfectly open to reflect God's knowledge of himself. This readiness of Jesus to know God *is* our readiness to know God, in which we participate by our faith in him. We *believe* that that enterprise of seeking to know God to which we are called and in which we are determined by Jesus Christ, is knowledge of God, as we believe that our lives are lived in his.[60] In that we believe in Jesus we believe that his knowledge is adequate, and so we believe that ours is also. In that we are involved in a theological enterprise inaugurated by his words and deeds, we believe that our theology is not vacuous.[61]

VI

The final assault can now be launched on natural theology. Natural theology is the theology of man's need of God, knowledge of and willingness to accept him—in its factual qualification as man's closure against God. It is the theology of man's religion.[62] "The vitality of natural theology is the vitality of man as such."[63] There is therefore no possibility of man as such desisting from it. Nor is there any point in attacking it on the assumption that man as such can be dissuaded from it.[64]

The only difficulty with natural theology is that this "man as such" does not exist: "The presupposed independent existence of a man-as-such is . . . an illusion. . . ."[65] Christ, as the eternal meeting of God and his creature, *is* man. We are men only as those who are coming to know him and thereby are playing roles in his human life. We are only what we are as those involved in his open existence for God.

The attempt to act as if this were not so, as if we existed independently of the existence of Jesus Christ, is an illusion. It is the illusion which is the content of our fallenness. Natural theology is the attempt to handle our knowledge of God—*however* we got it and however correct our opinions may be—as if it were authentic knowledge independently of Christ's knowledge of God. It is thus the self-explication of our fallenness, of our attempt not to be what we in fact are. This attempt cannot succeed, for we are what by God's will we are. Christ is *eternally* man. The last judgment to be made on natural theology is that it is the futile self-explication of an illusion.[66]

There is therefore no need to attack this enterprise as such; there is nothing real to attack. Nor can one seek to forbid natural theology to the man caught in this illusion—who is all of us.

"He is not at all in a position to allow this to be forbidden. That would attack his very existence."[67] But there is, nevertheless, one thing "which cannot be conceded to natural theology: that it could have any legitimate function in the *church*."[68] The final verdict is that faithful theology must simply let "the undertaking of natural theology lie as something already rejected," must simply *"ignore it."*[69] The final assault is the discovery that no assault is needed. The theology of religion need not be overcome, it is always already overcome.

VII

Barth's admirable consistency cannot be denied. This elaborate and subtle doctrine of the knowledge of God is a perfect application—and the only possible application—of the christological reversal to theological epistemology. The *method* which founded theology in our religious capacity has been consistently contradicted, perhaps for the first time in the history of the faith. The way is indeed open to a post-religious doctrine of God. The very assumption that we must open the way to a doctrine of God by general methodological reflections has been overcome; here is a theologcial epistemology which is itself based on a doctrine of God. And it is only this *order* that really overcomes the fundamental religious notion: that we must find our way *to* God.

Not every doctrine of God could stand at this point in reflection. Such consistent rejection of the religious way to knowledge of God is enabled only by a particular doctrine of God—the trinitarian doctrine. We will see that Barth develops the doctrine of the Trinity as an explication of the Christian concept of revelation. His argument will be if God is the one whom we can and must come to know in the *way* in which Christian faith claims to know God, then he is triune. We are already deep in this argument. The God who makes himself our object precisely in order to obviate our religiosity is the triune God. Therefore the alternative to the synthesis of religion and faith, of eternity and the future, is not some other procedure on our part, perhaps a method of paradoxes; it is quite simply a different God than the one posited by this enterprise. The doctrine of the Trinity merely states what makes this God different. The difference between faith and religion is that faith worships a triune God.

But we are well ahead of ourselves. And it would not do to pass on without noting that Barth's doctrine, for all its consistency, has its problems. The most serious is undoubtedly raised by the question: ought faithful theology really simply ignore natural theology? That is, can faithful theology win the dispute over the concept of God by abandoning it? It is hard to see how this could be so. After all, even the counsel that one must ignore natural theology is a kind of involvement with it, and this counsel is a necessary part of Barth's theologizing. His entire doctrine of the knowledge of God, and the trinitarian doctrine of God on which it is based, is developed under the control of the intention to avoid natural theology. Had this intention not been repeatedly effective at the points where Barth had to make theological choices, his doctrine of the knowledge of God would have been very different, and his doctrine of God not necessarily trinitarian. Barth's entire theology does in fact have the critique of religion as a criterion.

Repeatedly we have noted that at the points in the chain of reflection where it seemed Barth must engage those religious concerns in which we come to use "God," he instead turns back into the doctrine of God itself. We may well think we should applaud and emulate Barth's move itself, and yet think we should also take up the apologetic discussion he avoids. "Also," of course, is the word Barth most abhors in theology. In all expressions of the form

"God *and* . . ." he smells the old religious supposition of a separation of God and our lives and the old religious quest for their reunion.

The question is whether Barth has not substituted a pervasive *ambiguity* for the "and" he refuses to admit. He refuses to have anything to do with natural theology, but then makes this refusal itself the chief criterion of his theological choices. The consequence is that the relation of what Barth says of our lives as they are in God, to what we know and experience of our lives, shifts and shimmers. One moment Barth's entire theology seems to be the first wholly existential theology; the next moment the whole thing seems a dream having nothing to do with us.

I will suggest in the last part of this book that this ambiguity results from Barth's retention, now within a christological and trinitarian theology, of an analogy-principle which has its proper home in quite a different sort of theology. After all, "analogous" is in a way just another word for "ambiguous," and to say that we and God are united by "analogies" *may* only be to say that our relation is ambiguous, that he both does and doesn't have to do with us.

These remarks are again anticipations. For now, let us take the ambiguity from the good side—or from what I choose to regard as the good side—and go on to examine Barth's anti-religious doctrine of a triune God on its own terms.

Part Three
God Who
Happens

Chapter Seven
The Doctrine of the Trinity

I

In two ways Barth's development of the doctrine of the Trinity is the proposal of an anti-religious God, a God after the God of past history. First, Barth arrives at the assertion that God is triune, and at a doctrine of what it means to say this, by at every step persisting in the question: what must be true of God if he is not the God of religion and its natural theology? He does not, of course, ask the question in this abstract form, in which it could merely lead back to a negative religiosity. For Barth, after the *Commentary on Romans,* religion is obviated not by its own inner development, but by the occurrence among us of God as the knowable object Jesus, so as to make the religious quest vain. Therefore he asks the anti-religious question in its concrete form: what must be true of God if he reveals himself in the particular object Jesus?

The doctrine of the Trinity emerges out of a two-sided determination to maintain polemic against religion and to speak concretely of God—a determination both sides of which are made necessary and possible by what the Scripture says about Jesus. The doctrine of the Trinity states which being is God, if God is the one present in Jesus and so other than the God of religion. It answers the question: in which God do you believe, if what happens with Jesus compels you to believe in God, yet will not let you believe in the God of religion? The doctrine of the Trinity results from attempting to stipulate what would be required in an antireligious doctrine of God.

Second, the particular form which Barth gives the doctrine, and even more the way in which he thereafter uses it, fundamentally transforms the whole notion of "God." God comes to be understood not as a transcendent thing but as a transcendent happening, and his transcendence therefore understood not as his timelessness but as his radical temporality. Discourse about God is philosophically determined not by considerations of what it would mean to escape time, but by working out the phenomenology of time itself—which must mean, of one particular temporal event, for "time itself" would be just another euphemism for eternity. The doctrine of the Trinity identifies God not as the definition of the eternalized time of the past, but as the lord from the future.

It may seem bizarre to point to Barth's doctrine of the *Trinity* as his great move into the future of theology, past the death of the God of past time. The doctrine of the Trinity is nothing new. It is in fact the very oldest item in our entire burden of inherited dogma, and has been taught through the whole period of religious Christianity. It is, moreover, one of our most clearly moribund inheritances from the past, moribund to the point where bishops can go about denying it without so much as needing first to inform themselves about what it says. In the piety even of most traditional churches and believers, it is safe to say that the triune character of God plays no role at all.

This is reflected also in theology, where it has long been forgotten what might be the point of the doctrine for the church's proclamation and action. The options have been to ignore or eliminate the doctrine; repeat the traditional formulations without giving them any necessary function in the whole body of theological reflection; or make up some new point for the old doctrine, since it is there. This last move is, of course, quite justified in itself. If the doctrine is true, then it is quite appropriate to explore its implications also along lines other than those which originally led to its formulation. But the decisive question still has to be: why should we teach the triunity of God at all?

I must therefore admit: the morbidity of the trinitarian doctrine may mean that the history of the gospel has passed it by. Yet a quite different interpretation of the historical situation is possible: that the doctrine of the Trinity was born of the churches' overcoming of just such a crisis as the present one; that it has since represented the continued virulence even within religious Christianity of the God who justifies the ungodly; and that its present incapacity is the main symptom of the churches' utter capitulation to degospelized or phony religion. Perhaps the doctrine of the Trinity has not yet had its moment; perhaps it has waited for just the present crisis. Fully establishing so sweeping an historical thesis is too large an undertaking for its place in this book; and the thesis may well be the kind that cannot be conclusively established at all. But we will have at least to make the thesis plausible by a quick look at the origins of the trinitarian dogma.

It is, of course, not just *Barth's* doctrine of the Trinity that is the effectively anti-religious identification of God. If it is only Barth's new formulations that are anti-religious, then it is misleading to call his doctrine a doctrine of the Trinity. It must be the church's ancient doctrine of the Trinity that has always been anti-religious, unless Barth's entire enterprise is to be condemned by his own understanding of his task as a church theologian. What then is new with Barth? What is new is that by his *interpretation* of the doctrine he has made us aware of its anti-religious character—and so made it effective. The trinitarian dogma becomes in his *interpretation* a new proposal for the post- and anti-religious understanding of God. For Barth's is an interpretation in the full sense; it is a creative appropriation of the past for the future. His location, use, and much of his application of the old dogma are indeed new, and these are the new anti-religious proposal.

II

The mere position of the trinitarian doctrine in the *Church Dogmatics* is itself arresting and important. It appears at the very beginning, as part of the doctrine of revelation. It appears as prolegomena, as part of the discussion of how and why we are called and able to theologize at all.

Barth puts the doctrine of the Trinity at the very beginning of theology in order to have it clear from the start that we are not talking about the class of entities called, by some criteria or other, "God," but about the particular being revealed in Jesus Christ— as God. He puts the Trinity in the prolegomena, in the discussion of revelation, to make it clear that we are not discussing a general idea of "revelation," of what *a priori* it would mean were a god to reveal himself, but the particular event of God's revelation in Jesus. Before we begin anything else, we must settle whose revelation we are analyzing.[1] We must ask who God is *before* we ask whether he is or what he is. And we must also ask who God is before we ask how we come to know him.[2]

The "question which the doctrine of the Trinity is to answer" is, therefore, "Who is God?"[3] The function of the doctrine is to *identify* which being we are going to be talking about in our theologizing. If we say that God is revealed in Jesus, we raise the question *who* is God, or perhaps the question *which* God is revealed in Jesus. The doctrine of the Trinity is an answer. Its logical function is thus closely related to that of a proper name. To the question of who God is, or which God we mean, believers might respond with "Jahve." And according to Barth "the doctrine of the Trinity is nothing ... but an explanatory confirmation of this name."[4] "Explanatory confirmation" is not, perhaps, a very helpful or well-thought-through expression. We must try to work out for ourselves what Barth might reasonably have intended with it.

If I say "Jones is ill," and you do not know whom I mean by "Jones," my attempt to identify a particular thing by this proper name will succeed only if I am able to respond, "Jones is the fellow who studied math, married Nancy Smith ..." etc. I will pile up such "who ..." clauses, such *descriptions,* until identification succeeds, and you know which entity is named by "Jones." In general, proper names work only if there are descriptions available to back them up, so that such a response is possible when needed. Moreover, each introduction of such a description implies a truth-claim. "The fellow who married Nancy Smith" identifies Jones only if "Jones married Nancy Smith" is true.[5]

I suggest that Barth provides the doctrine of the Trinity as a set of descriptions to back up the name "God." One side of Barth's point about theology's sources and priorities is that we must use "God" as a proper rather than a common name. This does not mean that there will be no concept or "idea" of God, but only that the concept will be of the type appropriate to a proper name: the sum of the descriptions used to back up the identifying force of the name, together with whatever other propositions can be derived from those descriptions. In Barth, the set of identifying descriptions is the doctrine of the Trinity. Then there follows an analysis of what sort of reality must be attributed to God if he is triune.[6] These two sets of statements make Barth's concept of God. His doctrine of God is then completed by a discussion of what material proportions about God so conceived can in fact be asserted, on the basis of the events which reveal him.[7]

One could say that all Barth has done is reverse the usual order of the two doctrines of the nature of God and the trinity of God. But this exchange has radical consequences. For a not-yet-trinitarian doctrine of the nature of God can be discussed first only if we think we are able to identify God without reference to his relation to Jesus Christ. The set of descriptions we use will depend on corresponding items we know or claim to know of God: if, for example, we identify God as the one "who is eternal" we must know that God is eternal. If we identify God before speaking of Christ, this knowledge will have to be knowledge gained by the religious quest; it will have to be knowledge of the God of religion—for there is no other sort of knowledge of God if we are to abstract from his self-objectifying in Jesus Christ.

Any concept of God has as its definitive starting point the assertions which correspond to the descriptions used to identify God. Therefore the traditional order of the parts of the doctrine of God, by itself and quite apart from any material assertions, makes it inevitable that we will have a basically religious conception of God. Merely reversing the order does not, of course, guarantee overcoming this—that will depend on how a relocated doctrine of the Trinity is developed and used. But it makes it possible.

Whatever we may eventually come to say about a particular thing, the "concept" of that being is basically determined by the descriptions which identify which thing we mean to be talking about. It is, that is to say, what we *begin* with that is all-important. We may very well wish to say both that God is "the one who raised Jesus from the dead" and "the one who is omniscient," but the concept of God and, indeed, the force of both descriptions depend on which we say first, on which serves to identify him.

The fundamental identifying description of God is, according to Barth, that God is the one *"who has revealed* himself in Jesus Christ." The doctrine of the Trinity is but an interpretation and analysis of this expression; it is an explication of the Christian concept of revelation: "We arrive at the doctrine of the Trinity by no other way than by way of an analysis of the concept of revelation."[8] This does not mean by way of an analysis of a general concept of "revelation" but by an analysis of the particular way in which the Scripture speaks of the particular event Jesus Christ as the revelation of God: ". . . we find the revelation so attested in Scripture that the understanding of revelation we acquire in attending to this testimony . . . must be exactly the doctrine of the Trinity."[9] We may put it so: the scriptural witness to the particular revelation which Scripture claims to occur poses certain questions to us which, when we try to answer them, lead to the trinitarian doctrine.[10] If what happened with Jesus is "revelation," then we have a triune God.

How does the biblical claim about revelation lead to the doctrine of the Trinity? The scriptural witness to revelation poses the question: *who* is revealed? It poses it in that it insists on being understood from its subject, and not from our religious concern for revelation. And it elicits the answer: *God* reveals himself. But the revelation of

God insists also on being taken seriously as *revelation,* and therefore poses also the question: what does he do to reveal himself? and the question: what does this act accomplish? The answer to any of these three questions is at the same time the answer to the other two: the answer to all three is *"God." "God* reveals himself. He reveals himself *through himself.* He reveals *himself."*[11] The agent is God. What happens is God. And what is accomplished is God present among us. If the first question is answered with an appropriate answer, so are the second and third questions. Yet until the second and third questions are so answered, any answer to the first remains ambiguous. And so for all possible combinations. For we do not know who has revealed himself as God apart from the fact and manner of the event of this revelation, nor apart from what this revelation means for its recipients. Nor do we know the fact of his revelation, or its meaning, apart from knowing who reveals himself.[12]

Moreover, the question of who is God is *completely* answered also by the answers to the questions of what happens as revelation or of what happens to the recipients: *God* happens as revelation, and thereby *God* happens to us. There is no shading of the answer: it is not that the event of revelation is the life of someone rather like God, or that what this revelation produces is God-like behavior by us. "This God is precisely not only himself, but also his act of self-revealing. . . . He is not only himself, but what he creates among men. . . . It is God himself, in intact oneness the very same God, who according to the biblical understanding of the revelation is the God who reveals *and* the event of the revelation *and* its work among men."[13]

The key point in this analysis is obviously why our answers to the second and third questions must repeat the answer to the first. They must do so because otherwise the door will open to religion and its natural theology. If the revelation is in any way different from the God who is revealed, then our knowledge of God is the result of our concluding back to God from the revelational data at hand, of our projecting an image given in revelation back into infinity. Our knowledge of God is then the fruit of our religious quest, it is natural theology whatever its content. God is sought by us *by way of* the revealer, and is the terminus of our quest—and we are back again with religion. If, therefore, God so reveals himself as to put an end to our religious titanism, we may know that we are to give the same answer to the second and third questions as to the first.

He does so reveal himself. He so reveals himself as to make impossible any attempt to get behind the agency and activity of the revelation, any attempt to be ourselves the agents of the knowledge of God, or to *use* the revelation as the clues for our search. Also as revelation and work of revelation, God remains and asserts himself as the subject of revelation. He remains "Thou," never the "it" or "He" *with* which we might operate.[14]

That is, God reveals himself as the *Lord*. In this sentence, Barth says, we can summarize the whole biblical witness to revelation. And *therefore* we must give the same answer to each of the three questions he poses us by revealing himself. As God's revelation is attested in Scripture, it is an instance from which we have no appeal, a basis for our lives "which has no sort of higher or deeper basis over or behind it. . . . Its reality and its truth rest on no superior reality and truth. . . ." Thus we cannot accept—or reject—the revelation on the basis of some other instance—and just so God halts our religious quest and so encounters us in his revelation as Lord.[15]

God reveals himself as Lord, i.e., as the one who is free to be *our* God and who is our God, i.e.. who is able to *reveal* himself and does reveal himself. Therefore "God reveals himself as Lord" is "an analytical sentence"; what God reveals himself as, is exactly as the one who is able to reveal himself.[16] "The distinction between form and content cannot be applied to the biblical conception of revelation." Exactly this identity of form and content is the lordship of God in his revelation. We affirm this identity of form and content by giving the same answer to the three questions the revelation puts to us. "God reveals himself as Lord," is "the root of the doctrine of the Trinity."[17]

We can get the same result in another way. Were the answer to question two or three in any way different from the answer to question one, God-in-his-revelation would be only partly God and so one or another semi-divinity, whether a depotentiated God or an apotheosized man. There would be "levels in God's deity." Such a revelation would evoke the middle realm between God and man which is the sphere of religion. But the biblical revelation is exactly the clearing-out of this realm. Therefore we can respond to the biblical revelation only by giving up all notions of degrees, of more and less between God in himself and God in his revelation.[18] There are really only three options: either God does not reveal himself, or revelation occurs on the religious bridges between God himself and us, or God's revelation *is* God himself. But it is the entire religious conception of an heirarchy of bridge-beings between us and God which the biblically attested revelation requires us to repudiate. Therefore if we are obedient to this revelation, we confess the one and unaltered God as Revealer, Revelation and Work of Revelation.

Yet we cannot reduce the three questions to one, we cannot

eliminate the need to give our one answer to the questioning of revelation three times in three ways. "It does not appear possible, and no attempt is made in the Bible, to dissolve the unity of God . . . and his revelation and his revealedness into an undifferentiated sameness, to lift the boundaries which separate the three forms of his deity in his revelation by reducing them to a synthetic fourth and proper reality."[19] We must abide by the three questions for exactly the same reason we must answer each of them with the same answer. If God as revealer and God as revelation and God as revealedness are "really all the same," then the true God is the "divine essence" which lies *behind* what will now be regarded as mere forms of God—and again we are embarked on the religious search for God behind his revelation. Then the structure of God's revealing act is not taken seriously, and all our knowledge of God is natural theology only.[20] Also at this point it is God's lordship, his sole agency in his own work of revelation, that is at stake. Or what is the same thing, it is his veto of our religion that is at stake.

III

We must now look at the more developed form of Barth's argument that the biblical witness to revelation does indeed pose exactly these three questions, and require as our answer that we affirm a self-distinction in God. Barth develops each aspect of the trinitarian revelation in turn, beginning with the one we have so far referred to as the second.

"Revelation means in the Bible the self-unveiling to man of the God who essentially cannot be unveiled to man." This self-uncovering is real as the content of a certain series of historical events, which are for us the center of the event of revelation. God makes himself present, known and meaningful to us. He takes up a particular place in our historical existence, and makes himself the object of our perception, thought and language. He puts us in a position to address him.[21]

Just so, God acquires a specific *form* in history and in our experience and language. He acquires form in what is other than himself. "It is neither impossible for him nor unworthy of him to be in his revelation his own double. . . ." This is the event of the unveiling of the one who cannot be unveiled and so is not a "natural" continuity, but rather a new *occurrence*—also for God. That God takes form among us is a *step* which he takes, and this step "means: something new in God, God's distinguishing himself from himself, a being of God in a mode of being . . . which is other than his first, hidden mode of being—a mode of being in which he can be-for-us."[22]

Then Barth makes the move: "He who reveals himself here as God, *can* reveal himself . . .: it is appropriate for him to distinguish himself from himself, i.e., to be God hiddenly and in himself and at the same time to be God in another way, in a revealed way, in the form of something other than himself—to be God *again* a second time."[23] From the historical occurrence of a revelation of God among us, we move to the God who is in himself able to be God also in what is other than himself.

The move from analysis of the biblical concept of revelation to assertions about God himself is legitimized by a principle which is omnipresent in Barth's theology: that where actuality is there must its possibility also be—that if God has in fact revealed himself, then God must be in himself such that he *can* reveal himself. As an ontological principle, this principle may seem to hover between obfuscation and utter triviality. But in Barth's thinking the principle is only shorthand for the whole polemic against religion: we are not, by searching for a God more sublime or more worthy of religious devotion than the God who encounters us in our history, to deny God-in-himself the potentialities seemingly realized in the revelation. We are not to say that although God meets us as a figure of our history, it is unworthy of God to become other than himself, that although we meet God living in time, he himself is timeless.

Thus this power of God to distinguish himself from himself is "a first confirmation of our proposition: God reveals himself as Lord." The lordship which is revealed is exactly that God can become other than himself, can become an historical figure. It is "exactly God's freedom to distinguish himself from himself, to become other than himself and still remain the same—yes, to be the one self-identical God exactly therein, that he so deeply . . . distinguishes himself from himself that he is not only God the Father but . . . God the Son. . . ."[24] *What* God reveals about himself is exactly that he is free, as the God who is absolutely lordly, absolutely above us, to be *our* God, i.e., to reveal himself.

But: revelation also means in the Bible the self-unveiling to man of *the God who essentially cannot be unveiled to man.* To move to another aspect of the witness to revelation, Barth needs only to change the accent. "It belongs to God's essence, that he cannot be unveiled to man. But note well: this belongs exactly to his *revealed* essence."[25] Revelation is a miracle; it is the revelation that teaches us this. Also in the form which he takes in our history, God is *free* to reveal himself or not to reveal himself. Revelation is and remains his free act; he remains in full free control of the event of revelation, also in that he takes form in a reality other than himself.[26]

This means that "the form itself . . . does not take the place of God. It is not the form that reveals, speaks . . . comforts . . . but God *in* the form. Therefore even in that God takes on form, no middle-thing results, no third between God and man, no reality different from God which would be as such the subject of the revelation."[27] Again, the control over the course of reflection is anti-religious polemic. The revelation *is* exactly God's becoming our object to put an end to the quest for religious mediation. Any description of the revelation which implied that in the revelation there arose mediating almost-Gods is therefore false—and its contradiction is true: that God so gives himself into otherness as to remain absolutely himself.[28]

Barth makes the target of polemic explicit: "The 'beautiful Lord Jesus' of mysticism, the 'Saviour' of pietism, Jesus the teacher and humanitarian of the Enlightenment, Jesus the essence of elevated humanity in Schleiermacher, Jesus as the embodiment of the idea of religion in Hegel and his followers, Jesus as a religious personality in the manner of Carlyle. . . ." In all these cases the humanity of Jesus *in itself* and in its own power and self-identity reveals God.[29] In all these cases, a divinely infiltrated or elevated man is the revelation, a figure in whom the line between God and man is blurred. But the revelation in Scripture is exactly the refutation of all such blurring. Therefore we must so speak of revelation as to make clear that no divinized creatures result, that God in his revelation remains the one self-identical God he was. Barth argues that an attack on the various versions of Jesus-the-elevated-man leads to the doctrine of the Trinity—and is supported by the fact that the modern versions of this figure arose from an attempt to evade the trinitarian dogma.

Again it is the anti-religious principle that we must always conclude from actuality to possibility that dictates the move: God is in himself one who can thus remain himself precisely in becoming other than himself. It is characteristic of God himself that in being God "once more again and wholly otherwise" he can remain wholly himself. Precisely this *freedom from*—and so also for—his own revelation is, from this other side, the lordship which is the content of his self-revelation. It is the lordship of the *Father,* who is "God as the free origin and free power of his being God also in the Son."[30]

Third: "Revelation means in the Bible the self-unveiling *to man* of the God who essentially cannot be unveiled to man." It is an *"historical"* occurrence in the sense that it is "a concrete relation to concrete individual men." Whatever problems may be introduced for us by the circumstance that the witnesses of the revelation did not have our idea of historical fact, the witnesses intended to narrate a stretch of our history. Revelation is not a timeless dialectic of veiling and unveiling in a God above time, it must be narrated in one breath with Cyrus and Pontius Pilate.[31]

It is the contingency of the revelation which the biblical witness to revelation here insists on. Exactly as something which occurs to particular men in particular situations, revelation is not our creation, is out of our control as no general idea or universal principle would be. There is no higher principle beyond the pure facticity of the revelation; it happened and *might not* have happened, and must simply be registered. There is no disposition to revelation, and none is needed. The dialectic of unveiling and veiling in God is not deducible from any general principles or constants of experience; it can only be confessed that it has in fact occurred.[32]

This too is the *lordship* of God in his revelation.[33] And here again the move is the same: "That God *can* do this . . . , that he can not only assume form, and not only remain free in this form, but in this form and freedom become the God of this man and this man—this is the third meaning of his lordship in his revelation. . . ."[34]

IV

The formal pattern by which the assertion of the triune being of God emerges is always the same: the move from the formal structure of the event of revelation to the content of what is revealed, or rather, the refusal to separate form and content at all. What God reveals about himself is that he is Lord; that he is Lord means that he is the God who can reveal himself in the way in which the Bible testifies that a revelation has occurred. *What* is revealed is exactly that revelation occurs and therefore *can* occur.

It may seem that a revelation so structured must be empty of all content, that this reasoning is circular or infinitely regressive in the most vicious possible way. It may seem that this notion of lordship is vacuous, so that nothing is in fact revealed about God, except that he is whatever he is. But God's lordship means that he can be and is *our* God, that he allows us to pray to him, that the promise of God-with-us is fulfilled and the threat of alienation and meaninglessness overcome.

That the content of revelation is merely the fact and possibility of a revelation occurring, with the formal structure which Scripture attributes to revelation, does not empty the revelation of content. For "the formal structure of the event of revelation" means the formal structure of a particular historical event: Jesus Christ. The formal structure of the event of revelation is the pattern of existence enacted in the life of Jesus of Nazareth, as that life came to be proclaimed as revelation: the pattern of a life that gave itself, its past, up to God and the other man, and was, just as such self-giving, given into the future. That what God reveals about himself is that he can reveal himself, means concretely that God occurs in a life *so patterned*.

The structure of the event of revelation, which is the being of God, is very far indeed from being a mere empty formalism. It is the *plot* of Jesus' history which is the plot of God's being. It is the structure of our history with God in Jesus, *just as* it has been and is enacted, that compels us to confess God as triune—the structure of our history with God even and exactly as a history of alienation and redemption. It is because the revelation is God's "lordship in the midst of our enmity to him" that it cannot be "the work of a superman or half-god."[35] It is because alienation lies between creation and redemption that we cannot identify God's lordship in the one with his lordship in the other.[36] Only in the sign of *death* to our possibilities is the lordship of God as the Father revealed.[37] Were God's revelation not the revelation of alienation and its overcoming, of death and resurrection, we would not be called to confess God as triune!

Barth's doctrine of the Trinity identifies God as the one whose being is the occurrence for and among us of the history of death and resurrection in Jesus—just as it in fact occurs. It is in this concrete meaning that the doctrine will function throughout Barth's theology.

The principle that what God reveals about himself is that he can reveal himself, which is the heart of Barth's whole development of a trinitarian identification of God, has a double anti-religious function. On the one side, it cuts off that sort of relation between God and Jesus Christ which would make Jesus' personality, the psychological and biographical facts about him, the indication of what God is like. It is only the ontological pattern of his life, the mode of existence he enacts—partly in and by his biography, to be sure—which is the revelation of God. This is the positive meaning of the haunting emptiness which indeed lies at the heart of the trinitarian identification of God. What God reveals about himself is that he can and does involve himself with us in the *way* in which God and man are involved in the proclaimed story of Jesus. If, for example, we speak of "Jesus' love" as the revelation of God's love, this principle prohibits us from thinking of some set of historically ascertainable facts about how Jesus felt about people, and requires us instead to think the second article of the Apostles' Creed, the pattern enacted by Jesus of a life wholly free from itself for the other—however he may have felt about them. We are instructed to take the plot—and the plot only—of this existence as the plot of God's existence.

This instruction is important in view of the circumstance that we do not in fact know much about Jesus' biography or psychology, about whether, for example, he had a loving personality. More to the center for Barth is concern that we shall not confuse hero-worship of Jesus with worship of God. Nor are these two unrelated: the "quests" for the historical Jesus have often been driven by the hope of discovering a man of such elevated humanity as to bring us painlessly to "the divine."[38] Thus Barth's whole pattern of thought, the pattern by which he derives the necessity of speaking in a trinitarian fashion of God, is simply the anti-religious dialectic of the *Commentary on Romans,* in full and unweakened sway. But this dialectic has now become an account of what happens with Christ, rather than of the immanent failure of religion—and so used leads straight to the doctrine of the Trinity.

On the other side, the principle that what God reveals about himself is that he can reveal himself, is the same as the principle that we move always from actuality to possibility. On this side it prohibits us from searching for anything in God other than what is revealed. For here the lordship which is the being of God is so defined that it is just the fact of the revelation in Christ, so that if we know *that* God seeks us in Christ, i.e., if this revelation has come to us at all, we know *all there is to know* about God. If we ask what permits us so to define God's lordship, Barth will say that obedience to the Bible's particular witness to revelation requires us to do so. Nor does this understanding of God in his revelation mean that God's mystery is abolished, so that knowing him is an easy task. For to know of God that he can reveal himself is to know him as the Father, and so to know that we shall never have hold of him, never see through the mystery of how God can be our God, never be at an end of the task of witness to his revelation.[39]

Finally, there is another possible objection, which is worth raising because the answer to it will lead an important step deeper into Barth's doctrine of God, or into what we should gain from that doctrine. One might ask whether the accusation that Barth's idea of the lordship of God is empty is really answered by pointing to its meaning that God is our God. Is this not also, in itself, empty? Could it not as well be a curse as a blessing that God is with us, if he is evil and not good? Or a matter of indifference, if he is indifferent? That is, do we not need to know something *other* than that God can be revealed to us before we know anything material about him?

The reply to this is that to know that God can be with us is to know *both* that he can become other than himself and that he can nevertheless remain himself in this alienation. Which is to say, it is to know that one who is utterly free from us is utterly with us. To know this *is* to know a good thing. Indeed, it is to know *the* good thing, that we have a fellowship which is at once disinterested and indestructible. If God is with us as the free God then he is good to us.

"We may . . . well remember that to have time for one another, is really the essence of all the good that a man can do for another."[40]

And now we must observe what has happened in this reply. The goodness of God has been understood not as an attribute of a substance God, but as the structure of an occurring situation. And this does, after all, fit with the implication of the whole argument: God's deity is the formal structure of an event; it is the plot of his life which we may know from the revelation; what God reveals about himself is what he can do; and this is all there is to know of God. We are well on the way into the fundamental transformation of our understanding of the being of God—and of what it means for anything to be —which occurs when we make the doctrine of the Trinity the identification of God. "God's being is in becoming."[41]

V

We do not yet have Barth's particular doctrine of the Trinity before us. We have the problem to which his doctrine is a proposed answer: "the oneness and differentiation of God in his revelation as attested in Scripture. . . ."[42] And we have the "root" of the answer: the possibility of summarizing the biblical testimony to revelation in the sentence, "God reveals himself as Lord."[43] According to Barth, every explicit doctrine of the Trinity develops from this root in the attempt to answer this problem. In the biblical witness to revelation we find "the three moments of unveiling, veiling and communication; or form, freedom and historicity; or Easter, Good Friday and Pentecost; or Father, Son and Spirit. . . ."[44] A doctrine of the Trinity is an attempt to deal with this circumstance.

The doctrine is the front line of the struggle to keep the identification of God unambiguous—to keep the identifying descriptions of God from being provided by some concern foreign to faith. A doctrine's success in this is the criterion of its adequacy.

We may sum up the entire previous discussion so: the doctrine of the Trinity has the function of making it clear that as "Father, Son and Spirit, God is *our* God antecedently in himself."[45] God's *relatedness* to an other than himself is part of what he is in himself. Therefore we need not fear that God is "really" other than he is in his revealed reality as God for us. We are freed from the religious quest for God behind his being-for-us, for there *is no* God who is not yet God-for-us. The criterion of the adequacy of a doctrine of the Trinity is its success in this attack on religion.

Barth's treatment begins, characteristically, with the *unity* of God, with "Oneness in Threeness." The distinction of Father, Son and Spirit in God by no means puts his oneness in question. On the contrary, the unity of God's being consists precisely in this threeness of "hypostases." For God's being, his deity or divine nature, is what we have called his lordship, and we have seen that it is exactly in and by the distinction of the three in God that he is Lord, that he is the *only* Lord.[46] God's act of possessing his one deity is the same act as his act of distinguishing himself from himself as Father and Son in the Spirit.

The last sentence shows how we are driven to use categories of action and event in paraphrasing Barth's doctrine, even at the rare points where he himself does not directly use such categories. This also fits the key category which Barth introduces to explicate the assertion that God's oneness is exactly his triple self-differentiation; the category of "repetition." One sentence states his position so concisely it will be best simply to quote it: "The name of Father, Son and Spirit says that God is the one God in a triple repetition, and in such a way that this repetition itself is grounded in his deity, i.e., in such a way that . . . only in this repetition is he the one God. . . ." Only in this repetiton is God the "Thou" who can never be evaded or spoken past—and this inescapability of his personhood is his deity or lordship.[47] God repeats himself—and that he does so is what we mean by calling him the one and only God.

It is the anti-trinitarians who have endangered the confession of God's oneness. The very function of the doctrine of the Trinity is to maintain God's oneness against these threats. Natural theology seeks the oneness of God as the oneness of eternity's indifference to the multiplicities of time. Anti-trinitarianism in Christianity invariably results from finding the self-differentiation of God in the witness to revelation, affirming his oneness as a postulate of natural theology, and then desperately and hopelessly trying to reconcile the two. Just this duality of conceptions of deity is the true threat to the unity of God, which the doctrine of the Trinity combats.

If we once set out to reconcile a religious and metaphysical concept of God's static oneness with the biblical witness to the gift of the Spirit in knowledge of the Son, we will be driven, says Barth, to "modalism" or "subordinationism." Modalism simply does not take the revelation seriously; the real God is static oneness somewhere and somehow behind the history of the Son and the Spirit. If, on the other hand, the attempt is made to take the testimony to the Son and the Spirit seriously, yet still insist that God "himself" is statically one, the Son and the Spirit will have to be described as God, yet not God "himself." They will be middle-beings, almost-Gods. If we are nevertheless told to *treat* them as God, to seek God in this revelation, we are in the full power of polytheism. The doctrine of the Trinity is directed *against* this polytheism.[48]

Barth is clearly on the right line. The "oneness" of God is, after all, a most ambiguous expression. It could mean the identification of God as the real unity in and behind the apparent multiplicity of the events of life and of the world we live in—as typically in Indian religion. It could mean God's moral isolation—as in Islam. It could mean a theoretical postulate to balance the many gods of practical religion—as in the popular piety of all times. It could identify God as the being who satisfies our demand upon being, that it not alter in time—as in the antique religion of our culture. It is no good speaking of the "oneness of God," and perhaps defending it against "trinitarian perversions," until we have settled what we mean to say of God by calling him "one." It is just this that the doctrine of the Trinity intends to do.

The oneness of the triune God is, says Barth, neither "singleness nor aloneness."[49] The relatedness in which he can be and is our God is not foreign to him. His oneness is exactly that of one person over against another—and what the doctrine of the Trinity says is that he does not need us to be thus personally related.[50] Just so the doctrine of the Trinity defends God's personal oneness against the suggestion that only together with the creature is his deity enacted.

God is one *so,* that his oneness is not established by separation from another. Rather, his act of being the one God is an act which, to be the act it is, is three times *repeated.* A personal being is a person, and is the particular person he is, in and by the life of communion in which he lives. God in his threefold repetition of himself lives *as* communion for himself, and so is independently the personal God—which is exactly his oneness. He is one not as a solitary monad, but as a person living of himself. For the threeness in God, Barth prefers "three modes of being"[51] to "three persons." What is meant by "person" in contemporary language is appropriate rather to the *one* nature of God. It was, moreover, never a very convenient word for the purpose.[52] God is the one God in the mode of the Father. He is the one God in the mode of the Son. He is the one God in the mode of the Spirit.[53] The "one God is three times God in a different way." He is so God, that none of the three ways of being God is dispensable or interchangeable—if he is to be the one God he is.[54]

The formulations are neat, but do they mean anything? Only if we see with Barth that God is not a substance with a fixed set of attributes, but rather a *deed.* The formulae work only if "is" in "God is God" is a transitive verb. It is not so much that God *is* deity, as that he *does* deity. His deity is exactly his lordship. God does his godhead, his divine nature. And he does it three times. He *repeats* himself: God can be repeated without change and yet in real repetition only if God is a happening rather than a something. The repetition is the structure of the event which God is.

God does God three times, each time in a special way. He does it *three* times and in *these* three ways, to be the particular God he is and not some other. Each "hypostasis" is a repetition in a particular way of the act of being God—an act which is itself accomplished only as this precise repetition.

Turning to the distinctions between the three modes of being in God, Barth says we cannot establish them by parceling out roles derived directly from the threefoldedness of God in his revelation—so as to identify Father, Son and Spirit as Revealer, Revelation and Revealedness, or Creator, Redeemer and Fulfiller. This would indeed compromise the oneness of God. Creating, redeeming and fulfilling are all acts of the one God, and so with all the triplicities of God in his revelation. The difference of God's three modes in his revelation is the reason why we must believe that the one God is three different modes of being also in himself. But it does not *define* the threeness which God has in himself.[55]

Rather, the three modes of being of God in himself are to be understood "from their special *relations*—from their special *genetic* relations—to each other."[56] The *content* of God's self-distinction in his revelation cannot be directly used to characterize his self-distinction in himself. But we can so use the *fact* of this self-distinction, i.e., the *formal* character of the relations within a concept-triplet such as Revealer, Revelation and Revealedness, or Creator, Redeemer and Fulfiller. In each such case there is an Origin, and an Originated, and an originated Origination.[57]

The threeness of the one God subsists in these *relations*. In "the act in which God is God, there occurs first a pure Origin, and then two Goings-out, . . . the second of which . . . derives from the Origin and at the same time from the first Going-out. God is . . . God, in that he has these relations to himself. He is his own forthbringer and he is, in two ways, . . . what he brings forth. He possesses himself as Father, i.e., as pure Giver; as Son, i.e., as Receiver and Giver; as Spirit, i.e., as pure Receiver."[58]

Thus Barth adopts the medieval formula: the three in God are "relations subsisting in God," they are the relations of paternity, filiation and procession. The three in God are "modes of being, *consisting* in their relations to each other."[59] God is not first the Father, who then begets the Son—begetting the Son *is* the Father. And so for each of the modes of being. Each of them is—let us now put it so as to show the meaning of all this—being for the others, with nothing held back.

The doctrine of subsisting relations, and of God as the occurrence of these relations, is manifest nonsense, if we insist that an act must always be the act of something that is not an act. But why do we insist on this? I suggest that this "natural" ontology is only a projection on reality of the pattern of our alienated existence: the "I" that persists *behind* and aloof from my acts is precisely what I *hold back* from my fellows. It could be that far from representing my true being, this "I" represents what I lack of myself. God has no such lack.[60] He is what he does for the other. God is the occurrence of relation.[61]

But why do we thus struggle to speak of God's oneness and difference *in himself,* in distinction from his oneness and difference in his revelation? Was not the whole point of the doctrine of the Trinity to overcome this distinction?

As Barth uses the old distinction between the immanent and dispensational Trinity, between God's "essence" and his "working," it does not mean a distinction between two sets of facts: "God's working *is* God's essence as the essence of the one . . . who is Revealer, Revelation and Revealedness. . . ."[62] The point of saying that God is in himself Father, Son and Spirit is exactly to make clear that God is triune in himself as he is among us. But we say it a second time, as this purely formal description of modes of being in God's immanent self, in order to confess God's *freedom* in his work of revelation,[63] to say that he *could have been* the very same triune God, Father, Son and Spirit, otherwise than as self-revelation to us, otherwise than in Creation, Reconciliation and Redemption.

God is not in fact otherwise Father, Son and Spirit than as Revealer, Revelation and Revealedness, or Creator, Reconciler and Redeemer. He could have been otherwise God, but in his free choice is not. But this freedom *is* God's being, and therefore we confess the immanent Trinity which God would be in himself, even were he not working among us. "Father," "Son" and "Spirit" are the name for the triune, that is, communicating, occurrence of freedom which is God.

The freely chosen fact nevertheless remains the fact: God is not otherwise the triune God than in his triune work among us. The triune occurrence of Veiling, Unveiling and Unveiledness, or Easter, Good Friday and Pentecost, *is* the triune occurrence of God. Therefore we are permitted to conceive of God himself as this describable occurrence, and not merely as the event-structure of Origin and Originateds. We are permitted to call the Father himself our Creator, the Revealer, the one who raised Jesus. We are permitted to call the Son our Reconciler, and the Spirit our Comforter. For such knowledge and talk of God, Barth borrows another traditional term: "appropriation."[64]

"Appropriation" means assigning to one mode of God in himself one trinitarian aspect of his work among us, even though we know that all aspects of his work among us are the work of God in all his modes. It is, e.g., to address the Father as "Creator," even though creation is the work of the one triune God.[65] We make such attributions by following those same formal analogies which led us to speak of God's immanent Trinity in the first place. Thus within the Trinity of Creator, Reconciler and Redeemer, "Creator" has the place of origin, so that we appropriate it to the Father.[66] Only by such appropriating can we speak meaningfully of God in himself at all: even "Father, Son and Spirit" carries meaning beyond the abstract scheme of Origin and Originateds and commends itself to us for just that reason.[67]

But what permits us to make such "appropriations"? Barth's explicit discussion is not very helpful,[68] but in the whole context of his theology the answer is clear.[69] God's revelation, i.e., his occurrence among us as Creator, Reconciler and Redeemer—or any of the other "dispensational" Trinities—is his *self-interpretation* to us. He interprets his triune reality as the trinity of our Creation, Reconciliation and Redemption. Our "appropriating" is our interpretation of God, an interpretation which merely follows his. Moreover, we have seen that self-interpretation, being himself as something other than him-himself, *is* the being of God. Thus God's self-interpretation in his work among us is his reality also for himself, it is his interpretation also *to himself* of what he is. *God understands himself as what he is among us.* Therefore our appropriating is possible. It is analogous because God's self-interpretation is, as we have seen, itself analogous.

And so we are back at the beginning. God is what he does among us. All the complicated subtleties of Barth's developed doctrine of the Trinity say this one thing at all the different places where it might be forgotten.

VI

Is this how the doctrine of the Trinity actually came into the church? It is again time to look back to the ancient world.

At the beginning of Christian reflection about God, we find people whose claim to know God and to be able to speak about him is determined by several factors. First, the one whom they call God was not himself problematic for them. He was securely identified by one or another tradition, quite prior to the call to faith in Christ. For some, God was identified as the God of Abraham, Isaac and Jacob; for others as the highest One in whom all beings are intelligible; for others as the Savior in whose eternally recurring death and rebirth we may come to share by knowledge or cultic initiation. But in one way or another he was always already identified by tradition *before* any particular experiences or new beginnings of the believers.

But there was also the *new* thing that had happened: the coming of a person whose acts and words canceled all previous bets on God, so that it was now no longer possible to speak of God except in sentences that also were about this Jesus. Moreover, what is now said about God—the same God already given by the tradition—is always antithetical to what had been said before. Jesus himself set the pattern: "You have heard that it was said to you of old, but I say to you . . ." Paul preached a message that was "foolishness" over against all previous talk of God, and John called men to be born again. Such antitheses but expressed the pattern enacted in Jesus' existence for God and his fellows: the *contradiction* of the God of the past and the God of the Kingdom was enacted in his crucifixion. And just this contradiction was proclaimed as the last future, as the reality of God-for-us-at-the-end.

Finally, their apprehension of God was determined by a corresponding new sort of religious experience, the experience of "the Spirit." Life in the Spirit is very evidently a variety of religious experience; in the primitive church, all the familiar phenomena of antique religion appeared. Yet somehow the feeling of standing between God and mere humanity, of having climbed decisive steps on the hierarchy of being, which had always made religious experience self-verifying, was exactly what was here repelled. This "Spirit" refused to amalgamate with his possessors, but remained always ahead of them, always the power of the future against whom they were defined by what they were *not* yet. This "Spirit" was not his possessor's transcendence above time: along with giving tongues of angels and visions of heaven, he set them to the tasks of time, to visiting the sick and managing church property. Such a "Spirit" was Eros, yet not Eros; he was Eros, yet God-*himself* and not man.

Christian reflection about God was, as it remains, the attempt to deal in thought with this situation. So long as the traditionally identified God was Jahweh, the God of Abraham and Isaac, there does not seem to have been much difficulty. However scandalous the claims about Christ and the Spirit may have been to Judaism, those who once accepted these claims found no difficulty with the inherited understanding of what it means to be God. Insofar as they needed to think Jesus' relation to God, they simply used whatever religious or philosophical pictures and concepts came to hand. Nothing that we could regard as a satisfactory identification or concept of God resulted, but on the basis of the Old Testament traditions none was felt as needed.[70]

This eclectic procedure continued through the first incorporations of the "hellenistic" world, of the general antique religious tradition of what it means to be God. But here the results were often disastrous. Believers tried to identify God from the tradition of antique religion, and then to say about this God what the new happening with Jesus compelled them to say. They produced by this means some of the most implausible and spiritually damaging religious conceptions ever made by man.

Where deity was understood as changelessness, if freedom from the past was nevertheless asserted, this could only be done by denying the reality of the past. Freedom was inevitably understood as the past's irrelevance and unreality over against the true God. This sometimes meant that the reality of the present world, with its contents given by the past, was denied. It sometimes meant that two gods, one for the past and one for the future, had to be posited, either primally or by way of a mythological derivation of the one from the other. In either case, license was provided for a religiosity which supposed itself freed from the concrete tasks and choices posed by the past for the present moment, free to dwell in the anticipation of heaven.

Moreover, the religious notion of a middle realm of intermediary beings between God and men appropriated what believers had to say about Christ and the Spirit. The entrance of such lively figures into the kingdom of Eros, enjoying such positive commitment by their devotees, gave the whole realm a rebirth of vigor. The immediate impact of Christianity on antique religion was a recrudescence of mythology.

Those whom we have come to call "the Fathers" fought this paganizing of the gospel—which was also, of course, the vulgarizing of paganism. But they did not at first take decisive hold of the *theological* task: to rethink what could be meant by "God." They fought instead with mere negations of the false consequences drawn by the "heretics," backing up their negations with authority and tradition.

The Fathers did not truly get down to the task until compelled to by confrontation with ancient philosophy, or rather, with the subtle and sophisticated blending of philosophy and cult which was the rather overripe fruit of late antiquity. This brings us to Alexandria in Egypt and to the beginning of the third century after Christ. In appropriating the heritage of ancient philosophy, the church appropriated its central question: what is the definition of reality? and what is then the definition of God, who is the being who perfectly fulfills the definition of reality? what do we say of God, when we say that he is God?

As soon as this question was posed, most of the pictures in which

Christians had tried to think at once of God, Christ and the experience of the Spirit failed utterly. Especially in the eastern part of the empire, where most of this thinking was done, one pattern of thought soon ruled alone: the Alexandrian vision of an hierarchically structured reality.

In the years around the beginning of the third century, the thinkers we call the "middle Platonists" prepared an infinitely thought-through conception of an hierarchy of being, which came to equal fruition in pagan "neoplatonism" and the Christian theology of Origen and his disciples. At the top is God, who is "above being"; at the bottom is pure matter, which is below being; and descending and again returning from the one to the other there is the great procession of levels of being: from God's Mind, which alone simply *is* what is, through all other beings, which are what they are in that they reflect, at one remove or many, the intent of God's Mind.

There was, of course, no pure philosophy in Alexandria. Alexandria enlivened its philosophical conceptions with mythological pictures drawn from its fantastic cultic life, and deepened its cultic apprehensions with philosophical reflection. One such cultic picture, integrated into the hierarchal vision of reality, provided the possibility of understanding God together with the Christ and the Spirit: the Jewish conception of the hierarchy of angels, here identified with the hierarchy of mediating levels of being between God and man. In this vision, the mediating beings were *persons,* beings to whom petition and praise could be addressed. And at the top of the hierarchy were the two great "advocate"-angels, who have the ear of God.

These advocates, said Origen, are the Son and the Spirit: the first and second personal mediators between God and man, so near to Godhead in the hierarchy of being as to be themselves God for all lower beings. Therewith the Alexandrians created the first doctrine of a Trinity, of three distinguishable beings who together are the one God-in-his-relation to all other beings.[71]

Once a doctrine of a Trinity was formulated, all other ways of thinking of God in relation to Christ and the Spirit were passé. Thus the first doctrine of a Trinity was born as the integration of Christ and the Spirit into what may well be the most perfectly religious apprehension of reality ever realized. Indeed, the beginning of a doctrine of the Trinity was but one part of that creation of the Christian religion which we earlier discussed.

Yet this religious trinitarian doctrine is not yet the doctrine which became dogma, the main mark of which is exactly that it repudiates the description of the Christ and the Spirit as almost God, as one step down on a hierarchy of being. The church's doctrine of the Trinity was born of a struggle for dominance between the religious vision of Origen's doctrine and the new thing in Jesus which that vision had taken into itself. Religion lost this battle—though it won the war—and the final form of the doctrine of the Trinity represents that defeat. The church's doctrine of the Trinity is not, therefore, an a-religious doctrine, it is an anti-religious doctrine. It was born of the *self-critique* of religious Christianity; it is the result of polemic against a perfected religious identification and conception of the Christian God.

Religion's bid for mastery over Christ and the Spirit was the movement we call "Arianism." The Arians defined God's being as changelessness. Therefore, they said, the Son cannot be God in the full sense, for the Son became man, suffered and died. The temporality of the Son is the bar to his deity. The Son is almost-God. Thus the Arians bluntly assimilated the Son and the Spirit to the daemons of religion's middle realm. They did what Origen had done, but without his subtle ambiguities. The reaction they provoked created the churchly doctrine of the Trinity.

If we look at the whole process, we can say that what happened was that by way of Origen's religious trinitarianism and the controversy it provoked with older pictures of Christ and the Spirit, the gospel's claim that God is there for us in a being other than himself was built into the very conception of God. Once reflection on the gospel has achieved this, it could turn against the whole religious vision by which it had achieved it. It could turn and debunk the religious ascent to God, and the hierarchy of being it traverses; for once it is grasped that God-himself *is* God-for-us, we see that there is no distance to God to be transcended, that the religious ascent is vain.

This polemical turn, and so the churchly doctrine of the Trinity, was accomplished by the great "Cappadocian fathers" toward the end of the fourth century. The polemic is at its height in the treatise *Against Eunomius* of Gregory of Nyssa.

Gregory has one decisive argument why the Son—and the Spirit—must be God in exactly the same sense as the Father. The Arians make the Son a "God without being God by nature." But treating as God what is not God, is exactly what the gospel frees us from.[72]

If, "in order to preserve for the Father that part of deity which is supposed not to be communicable to the Son," we deny that the Son is fully God,[73] we have a clear choice to make. We may then "abolish his worship altogether," in order not to worship another God than the true one.[74] But this would "cancel the evangelical proclamation;" that is, deny its decisiveness for our knowledge of God.[75] And this would be to deny the new event and return to Judaism;[76] it would be to "deny the God of the Christians"![77] For God cannot be thought as Christians know him except *with* the new thing of the proclamation of the Son, and the worship of the Son which responds to it.

Or, if we do not revert from specifically Christian faith in God, if "the wonder of the Gospel" drives us too strongly to seek our salvation in Christ,[78] we will worship a being who is not God by nature. We will give the title "God" to one other than the true God,[79] to one who since he is not God must be a creature.[80] This is idolatry: Arianism calls us to worship "God," and when we respond presents us a creature of God for our worship.[81] It is just as much idolatry when we call the divinized creature "Christ" as when we call it "Baal" or "Dagon."[82]

It is also polytheism. If Father, Son and Spirit are all in some sense "God," yet differ essentially from each other, then there is a plurality of Gods.[83] The charge is explicit: the Arians are fallen to "the superstition of polytheism."[84]

Gregory's grasp of the issue is amazing. What he fears in Arianism is that it blurs the line between Creator and creature, that in this created Christ "they treat created and uncreated reality as of equal honor." Once this is done, there is no way to prevent the "predicate of divinity from spreading through all creation"—which is, he observes, exactly what has happened in late antique religion.[85] He sees that this posit of a continuous spectrum of semi-divinity is made by platonism[86] and by gnosticism.[87] He sees that it is of this mixed demonic being that the idols are images.[88] He even sees that in his worship of divinized creation religious man worships, at bottom, himself.[89]

In his polemic against Arianism, Gregory comes at last flatly to deny the entire principle of hierarchical participation in divinity.[90] He comes, that is, to deny the central concept and experience of all antique religion—to deny Socrates, Plato and the philosophical Eros, but equally to deny Pan, Baal, and the Mother. He denies this principle, moreover, not only in the pagan world, but also and especially when it bears the name of Christ. For the gospel, "truth is distinguished only from error, and God from what is not God. . . ."[91] There are no degrees of God. The divine nature is singular, "coherent with itself and indivisible, not admitting of degrees."[92] And just therefore we must teach that the three modes of being in God are all fully the one God.

The very notion of religious transcendence is rejected as the way to knowledge of God. Gregory quotes Eunomius: "The mind of those who have believed in the Lord transcends all sensible and intelligible being, and does not stop even at the generation of the Son, but goes beyond to seek eternal life in . . . the First Being." This, says Gregory, is exactly what the believer does *not* do. This would make our ascent and not God's revelation decisive, it would make the preaching of Christ, baptism and faith pointless.[93] The God whom we seek speculatively, by using Christ as a starting point to be transcended, is *not* the Father of Christian faith.[94] If Christ is, like Eros, between God and man, himself drawn upward to God by what he lacks, then he lacks what we lack, and "faith is vain, the proclamation empty and hope without object. . . . Why should we be baptized into Christ, if he has not his own power of goodness . . . ?"[95]

It is, finally, an entirely different concept of God which here stands against Arian religion. In the doctrine of the Trinity, Gregory has learned so to think of God that God's being and goodness are *constituted* by the reality of Christ and the Spirit: to think of God without any one of the three modes of being would be to think of God without "the fact or concept of either goodness or deity. . . ."[96]

The doctrine of the Trinity has incorporated relatedness and temporal potency into the very notion of God. Eunomius argued that the Son's relatedness to us shows that he could not be fully God. Gregory simply denies the principle.[97] Eunomius argued that the Son could not be of the same nature as the Father, because the Father could not become incarnate or be crucified, while the Son could. The Cross would be unworthy of God *himself*. But just this act of atonement is for Gregory the very proof of God's graceful power.[98] The temporal work of mercy is no bar to deity, and transcends all considerations of what would or would not be appropriate to God's "nature."[99] Gregory charges that the effect of Eunomius' doctrine would be to isolate the Father from the work of salvation. Gregory was right—except that this was Eunomius' *intention*. What Eunomius says in order to save the deity of the Father, empties it for Gregory.[100] For Gregory, the "sign of the Cross" is exactly the paradigm which God gives of his hidden might in all things.[101]

In God so conceived, there is no difference between his willing to be something and his being it by nature. The Father wills the Son's existence, yet the Son's existence is necessary to the being of God.[102] The Father and the Son are one by their "free choice"; they are one "by nature"; and these two unities "amount to the same."[103] God's nature *is* what he wills. And just therefore God is—against all Greek thought whatsoever—"infinite."[104] That is, no changeless essence sets boundaries for what God can be. Therefore also his nature is not definable—including not by "infinite."[105] An entity can be defined because some of the things that it is, it *always* is; because it is in some ways immune to the future. God's being is not of this sort.

In one remarkable passage, Gregory goes beyond all that he says elsewhere, and penetrates to the very heart of the conflict between the Arians and himself, and between religion and the gospel. To God's infinitude, he says, there are two parts: that he is limited by no beginning and limited by no end. These we express by calling God "ungenerated" and "endless." The Arians illegitimately separate the two and define God's being by its having no beginnings, making his endlessness a mere consequence. But if such an illegitimate separation were to be made, it would be better, says Gregory, to define God's being by his having no end, rather than by his having no beginning. It would be better to define God by his insurpassable futurity, rather than by his insurpassable pastness. Let them find God in what is hoped for, rather than in what is stale and old. An eschatological doctrine of God's being beckons: "What is awaited has substance through hope."[106]

From this new conception of God's being, a new anti-religious ontology emerges. The ontology of late antiquity had as its key operating principle the idea of degrees of being, the idea that there are sorts of entities distinguished from each other by being more or less real, by reflecting God's nature at fewer or more removes. The main function of the principle was to serve religious mediation between man and God. Gregory denies the whole principle. So far as "being" is concerned, a thing either is or is not, and that is all. There can be no more or less in likeness to God, for God is infinite.[107]

Eunomius shows how he can speak of degrees of being, when he calls "being" a "value-predicate." If "being" is a "value-predicate" then it can indeed have degrees, for clearly it is possible to compare relative values on a given scale: one man may be more honest than a second, yet less honest than a third. Gregory is indignant at the notion that being is a value: "Whoever thought such a thing?" he asks.[108] Now of course the entire ancient world thought just such a thing. The central faith of Greek thought was that whatever is, is in some way or other good, beautiful and intelligible; so that "being" can be used as shorthand for "in some way valuable." It is this principle which gives content to classical talk about "being": when the "being" of a thing is asserted and weighed, it is that thing's relation to its purpose, and to the final purpose of all reality, that is being stipulated.

Gregory's incredulous rejection of this kind of thinking shows how fundamentally his way of grasping the world has been transformed by the gospel. The Greek faith about Being is the faith that what we already *are* is our justification and purpose. This faith is exactly what the gospel seeks to free us from.

Thus the whole ontological scheme is redone by Gregory. There are no degrees of being. There are different sorts of being, distinguished not by degree but simply by difference. The antique distinction of visible and invisible being is retained. But antiquity's identification of this difference with that between divine and mortal being is broken. It was this identification which located man, with his invisible soul and visible body, between divinity and mortality and defined him as a religious being. Instead, Gregory draws a line *within* invisible being between the Creator and created being.[109]

The line between Creator and creation is for Gregory the fundamental ontological distinction, and the presupposition of all his arguments against the Arians.[110] This dichotomy is exactly what is not and cannot be supposed by religion. And it is used for exactly the same anti-religious polemic as Barth's similar dichotomies. The triune God is wholly on the one side of the line, we on the other. The Son and the Spirit are *not* midway between,[111] nor is our soul. And therefore we are dependent on God's action, not on our self-transcendence.

The parallel between Gregory's and Barth's derivations of the doctrine of the Trinity is perfect. Both are confronted with a perfected state of *religious* Christianity. Both are driven to attack this religiosity by the need to speak concretely of God in connection with what happens with Jesus Christ. In both cases, this two-sided determination to speak concretely of God-as-given-in-Christ and to carry through an anti-religious polemic leads necessarily to the doctrine of the one God who is equally God as three hypostases, and to a consequent fundamental rethinking of what it means to be God.

VII

The ancient doctrine of the Trinity did not then, however, overthrow religious Christianity. The time for an explicitly and theologically anti-religious gospel was not yet. The doctrine of the Trinity meant that the anti-religious thrust of the gospel remained alive within the general structure of the synthesis of religion and faith. In the Arian controversy the ancient church clearly saw the need of a particular skirmish with religion, and won it. But it did not see that there was a continuing war. The doctrine of the Trinity was simply set alongside another doctrine of God's being derived in wholly religious ways. Nor did the trinitarian understanding of God really penetrate the whole body of Christian thinking. Inside the doctrine of the Trinity, a new identification of God was made. But the whole doctrine was then assigned a place in a structure of thought that was religious, where the very structure had already identified God as the changeless guarantor against the future.[112]

These limits can be seen in Gregory. When he uses the notion of God's infinity in the argument for the Trinity, its meaning is that no timeless definition can capture the active God whose nature is what he wills. But when he steps outside the trinitarian argument, he automatically identifies God's infinity with changelessness and timelessness.[113] The triune God as such is identified as that "nature" which is self-sufficient and eternal, in the sense of being before both space and time.[114] And in the argument for this identification, Christ and the Spirit play no role at all. Nothing is said which could not have been said by any platonist.

Within the synthesis of Christian religion, the fourth-century doctrine of the Trinity saved the gospel from being simply absorbed by religion. It did not spring the synthesis. Nor could it have.

We need not commit ourselves to a Hegelian idea of history to say that every great age of the church has a theological task reserved for it: its particular insight to achieve into how to say the gospel. Whether our age is epochal we cannot of course, know. But if it is not, we should leave it to posterity to discover this. If we have an epochal task, it is to affirm the full significance of the doctrine of the Trinity. It is to carry through the attack on religion's understanding of what it means to be God, at last.

Chapter Eight
God's Being in Time

I

If "God" is a proper name, the concept of God will, we suggested, have two parts. First will be the descriptions we have ready to back up the identifying force of the name. For any particular, all the identifying descriptions will have a common logical pattern, such as one of these: ". . . is the one who . . . ," or ". . . is what happens when . . . ," or ". . . is the idea of . . ." Second will be reflection on the type of descriptions in fact used. Of a particular whose descriptions fit the third example above, we would say that it had "intentional" being, and was neither (taking the other examples) a person nor an event. Such reflection is ontological reflection; it talks about what *sort* of reality a particular thing has. It is possible to use a proper name well, yet be mistaken here. In such cases, ontological reflection will become polemic and even revisionary. Then we will say things like: "People think 'Communism' is a sort of force. It isn't; the word is only a label for a merely genetically connected group of political and economic phenomena."

What sort of entity is God? Barth asks: "What does 'God is' mean? What or who 'is' God?"[1] The question is: "What makes God God? What is his essence?" What is his "being"?[2] The questions are ambiguous. They could be interpreted as requests for the *identification* of God, i.e., as the question to which the doctrine of the Trinity responds. But the kind of answers Barth proposes shows that he is proceeding to the second part of a concept of God.

The question, for all its abstruse appearance, is a simple and necessary one. It is the inevitable question of a crisis of religion, and therefore *our* question: "What do you mean, 'God'? What, for example, is the object of this strange behavior you call 'praying'? You act like you were talking to a man or to some other thing equipped to receive sound signals, but we see no such thing there. What do you mean, 'God'? Where is he? Out there? Up there? In there? If he is just *here* with us, why don't we see or hear anything in addition to what we see and hear anyway? Is he identical with everything here? Or with certain relations between things here? Then why invent an extra word, 'God'?"

The *Christian religion* provided an answer, an answer which was satisfactory only because the question had not become urgent: "God is an invisible, timelessly present, something-analogous-to-a person." Religion provided all of this answer through the words "analogous-to"; Christian faith provided "a person" as a specific characteristic. As long as the Christian religion functioned as the spiritual tradition of the West, the answer worked. If it was said that "Jesus reveals God," the statement could be disputed, but there was no problem with what was to be affirmed or denied. "God is" was affirmed by some and denied by others, and just so understood.

The Christian religion has become a field of battle, and thereby this answer has become implausible. The images which attach to talk about a supernatural something rather like a man have become offensive, but without the images the talk may altogether lack content. It is all very well for defenders of "theism" to point out that no one ever really meant a thing like a man out there somewhere, and against overly childish polemics against religion it is proper to do so. But the question still has to be answered what one *did* mean. If we pare away the images is anything really left? In the crisis of the Christian religion, the old answer will not do—and especially not in its technically sophisticated and intellectually admirable forms, such as that God is "pure Spirit," or the "Primal Cause" or temporally and spatially "transcendent Substance." Nor is it to the point to insist that the old answer *used* to be a good one.[3]

A believing and anti-religious answer will be found by ontological reflection on the set of descriptions which identify God as the one revealed in Jesus. The doctrine of the Trinity is Barth's proposal for such an identification. Therefore he answers the question about God's sort of reality by asking what sort of being God must have to be triune. His discussion will be an "interpretation of the triune being of God as the Father and the Son in the unity of the . . . Spirit."[4] "All the remainder . . . of the doctrine of God . . . we will build on this presupposition, the trinity of God."[5]

It was, indeed, impossible to discuss the doctrine of the Trinity in the previous chapter without getting well into this kind of reflection. The decisive statements have already been made. Let us summarize once more before continuing. First, the being of God is the being-for-each other of three modes of being in God—modes of being which are not static structures somehow imposed *on* God's being, but rather such that each of them only becomes what it is in its active relations to the others. God is this becoming. Second, God is in that he repeats himself. Just so he is an event, rather than a semi-thing. His self-repetition is not a static duplication—as of a thing. It is living self-repetition. God *is* this self-repetition. Third, living self-repetition is *interpretation*. God interprets himself, to us and to himself, in living as Jesus with us. This act of interpretation *is* God.[6]

II

Therefore Barth's first proposition about God is, as expected: God is an event, a happening.

He is an event which cannot be transcended, which is inescapable in all temporal dimensions. He is never something that has happened and so is over and done with. Yet neither is he only in our present, but always has already happened. And again he is purely future, the not-yet we await. Because there is no way past the temporality of God's action, there is no static "essence" of God behind God's act. "In that we seek and find God in his revelation, we cannot get beyond God's action to an actionless God . . . , because there simply is nothing over and beyond the divine action. . . . With respect to God's being, the word 'event' is the last word. . . ." The act and event in question is the revelation.[7] God *is* the event of what happens with Jesus.

The self-identity of a thing is given by what does not change about it. My desk remains my desk just so long as I can recognize it as "essentially" unchanged since yesterday. Where God is conceived as analogous to a thing, his self-identity as God is dependent on his *not* changing, on an essence transcendent to any acts he condescends to. And then, since God cannot be conceived of as *un*essentially anything at all, he is barred altogether from change. It is this straitjacket from which Barth has liberated our idea of God.

Yet we may nevertheless feel compelled to come back to the

worry: how can we describe God as an *event*, and yet still continue to speak of him as "he," as if he were a substance? As if he were an agent or sufferer *of* events? It is time to deal with this.

The difference between an event and a substance is given by the discontinuity of time. What we mean by a substance—a thing or a person or an organization or whatever—is the something that we posit to provide the continuity of a series of successive and so temporally separated events. *As* distinct from what I do, "I" am a "something we know not what" that bridges the temporal discontinuities of the various things I do. But precisely the absence of such discontinuities is what distinguishes God from us—and therefore the dichotomy between an event and its agent or sufferer does not apply to God. Why then not drop such words as "he" altogether when talking of God? Because then it would seem that we recognized the applicability of the dichotomy to God, and put God on the one side as against the other.

Back to Barth. God is *an* event; he is not the general principle of eventness or something of the sort.[8] The temptation is strong to lapse back from the insight gained and understand God as "the dynamic" of change, or something else abstract. Bultmann called God "the insecurity of the future." This is a fundamental breakthrough—in one way more radical than Barth's. But often Bultmann seems to mean that God is the futurity of the future, the future*ness* of events. This is a lapse, for also abstract futurity is a futureless essence. God is a *particular* event.

According to Barth, the event that is God is a particular event because it is the origin and goal of all others. But it is also particular in the simpler—and here more important—sense that it is this event and not that,[9] as Waterloo was not Austerlitz. If we were now to ask: *which* event? Barth's answer would be: what happens with Jesus, or: the triune event. But in our present discussion we presuppose this identification, and ask instead: *how* particular? To this question Barth answers: God is a *free* event.

God is, of course, free in the sense that what God does is not decided for him by others. But this freedom from others is merely the reflection of God's freedom in himself. God's freedom in himself means that there are no presuppositions for the fact *that* God occurs or for *what* he is in his occurrence.[10]

God's freedom is that of a *subject,* of a *person.* God's freedom means that he is always "I" in his action, never "it" or even "he." This is the difference between God and other "persons." Other persons are always—precisely in the relations by which they are persons at all—also "he" and "it." Other persons are subjects of the relations by which they are persons, but are at the same time observers and passive objects in those same relations. God is never other than the active and deciding agent. God is the person whose personhood suffers no infringements, not even infringements arising from himself.[11]

That is, God is the subject who determines his own nature. My freedom as a subject is limited by my nature, with which I begin and which I did not choose and cannot alter. I am limited by my humanity and by my particular characteristics, by objective factors chief among which are the facts about me. God is not so limited, for he himself determines what his nature shall be. He himself determines what sort of being he is.[12]

This does not mean that God has no nature—so as to be abstract, contentless freedom, "pure Spirit." God's freedom is decision *about* something, about a concrete describable event.[13] God is indissoluble unity of concrete reality and absolute freedom, of being this particular describable being and freedom from all determination by what is already given. God is "the I that knows itself and wills itself, the I that posits itself and distinguishes itself...."[14] God moves himself.[15]

Therefore the final formulation is that the act of being God is a *decision*. God's being "is his own, conscious, willed and accomplished decision."[16] Here is Barth's final ontological classification of God's being. God is the free event, independent even of his own nature yet nonetheless having a nature, because he decides to be and to be what he is.

The content of this decision is *love,* his free relatedness to us. That love is decided means that it is the free love of one who in no way owes his love. God, therefore, is the one who loves freely.[17] And therewith we are back with the doctrine of the Trinity, with the one who is related to us and free in that relatedness.

III

He is "primal history": "the pattern of action in which God, by God, we may therefore say, has *history*. Or rather, he is a history. virtue of the decision of his free love, wills to be and is God." This history cannot be separated from the Christian concept of God.[18] We saw that in Barth's definition of history,[19] temporal self-transcendence and communion are the characteristic phenomena of history. It is God's being that originally provides both motifs.

God has *time*.[20] In him, there is "beginning, middle and end." God's eternity, understood from his revelation rather than from our dissatisfaction with time, does not mean that he is timeless. It means that what he begins and ends are not cut off from each other, cannot conflict with each other, are not beyond his present. God does not lose his past or have to wait for his future. What God leaves behind and what he projects before are wholly present in his act, *as* what is no more to be and what is to be. Eternity is the "simultaneous possession of life" in its differentiated movement away from what is left behind and toward what is to be.[21] The trinitarian nature of this understanding of God's eternity is already apparent.

The whole argument has the pattern familiar from the development of the doctrine of the Trinity. Time is the form of God's life with and for us.[22] In Jesus Christ, God "takes time," and in the most radical way: he becomes temporal, he makes our time the form of his eternity.[23] In Christ, God's presence is a temporal present, with a temporal past and future, in the very simple sense that it can be remembered and awaited.[24] Then comes the familiar move: since God's eternity "became time" since God without ceasing to be the eternal God took time and made time his own, we must confess that he *could* do this[25] God has this possibility, this readiness for time, in *himself*—in that he is triune.[26]

The Father begets, the Son is begotten and the Spirit proceeds; here is movement, here is "before and after," here is God "again and yet again." God's Trinity is an "order" in God, an order of *succession*. That God is eternal means that the temporality of the three relations which are God occurs as the oneness of God.[27] God's eternity is the unity of Father, Son and Spirit; the three modes in their temporality are the one God,[28] so that past, present and future do not fall apart. God's eternity means that in him are origin, movement and goal; past, present and future; "not yet," "now" and "no more"; potentiality and actuality; whence and whither—and that between them there is no contradiction.[29]

The parallel to the argument of the doctrine of the Trinity is completed with a form of the doctrine of "appropriation": in that God takes the form of creation, time, to be the form of his eternity, the temporality of his work in time is *his* temporality. As Creator, Reconciler, and Redeemer, God *"has been, is* now and *will be,"* in the ordinary sense of this language. We can look back in time to God, look forward in time to God, and just so experience God as a present reality.[30] God's eternity in himself is the precondition, the possibility, of his temporality with us.[31] We may say: God's eternity is in fact his temporal unsurpassability in past and future. He might have been otherwise eternal, but has chosen to be so.

What has happened here is that the whole argument of the trinitarian identification of God has been repeated in a different form. And thus the doctrine of the Trinity is discovered to say that God's being is achieved temporal self-transcendence. God is the one who for the future leaves the past behind, without the past becoming a set of fixed conditions for his future, and without the future emptying the present.

God's being can therefore be defined as "pure duration."[32] This pure duration is the oneness of God's past, present and future,[33] which nevertheless does not cancel the difference between past, present and future, because it is the oneness of the act in which God is past and future to himself.[34] God *is* the before and after of all being.[35]

God in himself is the possibility of there being time, of occurrences with a before and an after, with a departure and a goal. He is this possibility because he has for himself departure and goal, and so can be departure and goal for other beings.[36] If we occur, it is because he has chosen to be origin and purpose also for beings other than himself—which decision is itself God's choice of purpose for himself and so the act of his achieved temporality.

God is the possibility of our temporality. If we occur, he is our temporality: God "has time for us . . . , he himself *is time* for us."[37] That is, his occurrence as achieved temporal self-transcendence gives the structure of origin and goal which is our temporality. The fact that we can now live *for* something, and do so as the persons our past has made us, is the same fact as that God is.

God is history because he is time, and because he is *communion*. "In that and before God creates . . . fellowship with us, he wills and accomplishes it in himself. In himself . . . he does not wish to be alone, but is the Father, the Son and the Holy Spirit; and therefore is alive in being with and for and in another—in himself. The unbroken unity of his personal being, knowing and willing is at the same time conferring, deciding and acting—not in solitariness but in fellowship."[38] We must see the concreteness which the vision of God's inner communion acquires when Barth puts aside abstraction and lets the "appropriations" operate: "God is eternally alive in himself, i.e., God *is* in that he *acts* in his inner relations as Father, Son and Holy Spirit, in that he wills himself and knows himself, in that he loves, in that he uses his sovereign freedom in affirming himself and busying himself." God "confronts" himself.[39]

IV

And this brings us back to Jesus Christ. The confrontation in God is in actuality—whatever might have been—that between Jesus and his Father. Lest all this specification of God become only the metaphysical speculation and natural theology which it also is, we must return explicitly to the language about Jesus with which it all began.

The confrontation and communion which is the trinitarian life of God is the confrontation between the Father and his Son who is Jesus of Nazareth. God might have lived otherwise, but has chosen so to live, and this choice is his life. The "covenant" between this man and the Father is the reality in God of his will to be God for us and to have us as his own;[40] it is a covenant with the Son who is man and so at once God's covenant with the man Jesus and his covenant with himself about men.[41]

Here is the focus of Barth's doctrine of the pre-existence of the man Jesus. On the one hand there is God's eternal communion with himself, on the other hand his communion in time with us; and as the unity in God's freedom of the two there is his fellowship with his eternal Son who is Jesus.[42] The Father and the Son in the unity of the Spirit will that the Son shall live for his Father as the man Jesus[43]—and in God's achieved temporality this choice of what is to be is already the reality thereof.[44]

What then of this eternity of God? It must also finally be a fact about Jesus. God gives us time, and is time for us—in that what happens with Jesus gives us a past and a future. "In that eternity takes the form . . . of a temporal 'now,' " there is a "center" of time, so that time therewith also has "its meaning backwards and forwards, its content, its whence and whither—so as just so to acquire also a meaningful present."[45]

What happens with Jesus is, by virtue of its particular structure of death and resurrection, an event which we may and must both remember and await—and both absolutely, so that we remember him as antecedent to all our story and await his as the conclusion. From the time that God takes for us, we "look back to" the time we spend otherwise occupied, our "own" time, "as lost time, i.e., as the basically already past time of the old age, which is now still real only by its passing away." Yet insofar as this time is nevertheless still our time, our business in this time can only be to wait for God's time.[46] Just so we have true past and true future,[47] and just and only so we have time.[48]

This fact about Jesus *is* the eternity of God. *"He, Jesus,* was in the beginning with God. . . . That is why we do not need to project things into eternity: eternity is this time. . . ."[49]

We have retraced our steps to the central assertion. God is a decision. If we now again ask *what* decision, the answer is: the decision about us that is made in the confrontation between the man Jesus and his "Father." "In the beginning with God was this one, Jesus Christ. Just this is the predestination."[50]

The "decree of predestination" made in God about us is in fact identical with the decision in which God chooses to be God.[51] What God chooses is to be God *as* Jesus Christ.[52] The choice is the choice of the triune God in his concrete aliveness: "In the beginning was the choice of the Father. . . , to give his Son. . . . In the beginning was the choice of the Son, to obey this command. . . . In the beginning was the decree of the Holy Spirit, that the oneness of . . . the Father and the Son . . . should only become the more lordly through this covenant with man. . . ."[53]

As the chosen man, Jesus Christ is the object of this choice. As the obedient Son, he is its subject.[54] His existence is therefore identical with the occurrence of this choice in the inner-trinitarian life of God. Jesus Christ "was at the beginning of . . . all God's acts with a reality other than himself. Jesus Christ was God's choice about this reality."[55] To understand God's reality for us, we must think of "the *concrete* decree of salvation made in the bosom of the triune God . . . , of the Johannine Logos who, identical with Jesus, was in the beginning with God. . . ." The divine choice is "the decision which falls at the beginning of all relation between God and reality other than himself, whose subject is the triune God—and . . . so also the Son—and whose object is the Son in his determination as man. . . ."[56]

Jesus Christ, the man Jesus as the occurrence which gives us time, "is the God who chooses. . . . In no depths of deity will we meet any other." Jesus does not merely *reveal* God's choice about us, he "reveals our election as accomplished through himself, through his will as the will of God. He tells us that precisely *he* chooses us."[57]

Jesus Christ is also the chosen man. His life is the "occurrence, that God wills and posits another than himself as his creature." All other creatures than this one are chosen "in" him—which, according to Barth, means that we are chosen in that Jesus historically chooses us.[58] "That man Jesus is *the* chosen of God. Whomever God chooses . . . , he chooses in his person, through his will and choice."[59]

Thus the innertrinitarian community and temporality is concrete as the choice of the Son: to be obedient to the Father's choice that he shall live as man for men.[60] And since what is decided is exactly that the Son shall live as man for men, his act of obedience *is* his act of revealing this choice to the others chosen. In his existence, the eternal triune decision therefore "becomes directly the promise which occurs in time of our own election, it becomes calling, challenge to faith, promise that . . . we are God's children. . . ."[61] In fact—though it might have been otherwise—the Son's obedience is identical with "the prayer in which Jesus gives God's hard will the right against his own. . . ."[62]

V

We could very well make some startling interpretations of this identification of God and doctrine of his being. Let us provisionally do so.

Does Barth mean that the decision which falls in the life of the man Jesus *is* the decree of God and so *is* the being of God? In every life, something is settled. In Jesus' speech, action and destiny over against his "Father" and us, it is the nature of our relation to that "Father" that is settled. What is decided is that we do have such a Father. The occurrence of this settlement is what is meant by "God." The making of the decision that fell in the life of Jesus is the occurrence, the reality of God; God is the decision that happens with Jesus Christ. Is this what Barth means?

We can carry such questions through the whole preceding statement of Barth's doctrine. Jesus is the "Son," the second mode of God's being. Moreover, he is *always* so; there is no time before the reality of the Incarnation. God might have been the Son other than as Jesus, but in fact is not. Moreover, God *is* the mutuality of Father, Son and Spirit. Does this mean that God is the relation between Jesus, the invisible "Father" to which he went in death, and those for whom he went? Is God what happens between this unveiled man, the Veiled one to whom he lives, and the seekers for unveiledness for whom he lives?

And what of God's eternity? Does Barth mean that eternity is the temporal unsurpassability of what temporally has happened and will happen with Jesus?

It is sure that Barth does mean: the reality within which we all do our work and have our dreams is the one great event of the life together of God and man, i.e., the life of Jesus Christ. At the center of this event is the personal existence of Jesus, of what went on in Palestine. Surrounding it are the circles of those whom this man took as his brothers by living *for* them as man. But it is in *God* that we do our work and dream our dreams. Therefore the being of God is this event—in its particular temporality. Barth has abolished the notion of the timeless being of God by putting the historical event of Jesus' existence for his Father and his brothers in the place formerly occupied by timelessness.

We are tempted to go on to say: God is what happened with Jesus of Nazareth in Israel, grasped as the event whose contents articulate the structure of our time. If we ask after our origin, the gospel proposes the will which occurred as this self-giving. If we ask after our destiny, the gospel promises full participation in his act of mutuality before a Father. Here are the only possible past and future which by their concrete content could never be evaded or surpassed. If and only if these promises are true, we may live temporally, called just as we are, as the past has made us, to be ready for each other and the newness each of us brings the other, called to the future. *That* we may so live is the occurrence of God.[63]

We want to say this is what Barth means. But does he? As soon as the question is put, we see the answer must be "Yes and No." He says all this—ambiguously. And the ambiguity is neither unintentional nor the result of inconsistency. He says it all—but *"analogously."*

We have gone as far as we can go within the limits of this part of the book. And there is one more piece of Barth's doctrine we should examine briefly before going on.

VI

We will not even outline what Barth says about the attributes of God.[64] Our concern is what he says about the whole idea of God's having attributes, and with the *way* he develops his propositions.

The doctrine has always been something of an embarrassment. No theology has been able to refrain from saying of God that he is wise, and loving, and here with us, and the like—i.e., from predicating attributes of him. Yet within the theology of the Christian religion, it has always been felt unworthy of God to attribute to him a plurality of characteristics. The feeling runs through the whole history of theology, that doing this is an accommodation to our temporality, in which succession introduces plurality, whereas God "really" is timeless, knows no succession, and so is not really describable in this way. Sometimes the accommodation is thought to be made by God, sometimes by us. In the latter case, our whole description of God becomes a necessary fiction.

Yet making statements of the form "God is . . ." can be avoided only by falling altogether silent. It will not do to say that with God we have a pure "I-Thou" relation, so that our utterances are not propositions *about* him, but rather addresses *to* him. For if I am to address Smith the carpenter, I must know that this a person and not a chair, that he is Smith and not de Gaulle, that he is a carpenter and not a plumber, and so on. All this knowledge is essential to the very existence of an "I-Thou" relation, and is perfectly ordinary third-person knowledge, which can be stated as a set of attributive propositions about Smith. The case is no different with God. If I am to pray, praise, preach, bless, and all the rest of it, I must also be able to theologize, in the dry and straightforward way of describing him: I will have to say he is such-and-such and is not such-and-such. And then I will have to explicate and defend my propositions. That is, I will have to develop a doctrine of God's attributes.

We are not surprised when Barth attributes theology's traditional hesitancy about the doctrine of attributes to a basic conception of God derived elsewhere than from revelation. [65] If God is the religious projection into infinity of our dissatisfaction with time, then the more complete the abstraction from our temporality, the more perfect the conception of God. But the more complete the abstraction from our temporality, the less we are able to say *about* God without embarrassment.

But in Barth's anti-religious doctrine of God's being, God is not abstracted from temporality. God *lives* his being. Our knowledge of him is therefore a matter of following the way he goes, of tracing after a history. Our knowledge is therefore discursive, it is a *succession* of apprehensions. And this is not because we are incapable of the simultaneously complete grasp which traditional theology thinks would be the proper knowledge of God: it is because God is in fact a life, so that this is the proper and inevitable way of knowing him.[66]

It is true that God is fully present in each thing that he does. Thus Barth can take over the scholastic maxim that all the attributes of God are one. But this maxim has often been used to mean that the plurality of God's characteristics is only apparent, that the reality of God is a—to us—incomprehensible unity behind his perfections. Barth uses the maxim the other way around: each of God's attributes is a materially complete and adequate description of him. If we understand, e.g., that "God is holy," we know all there is to know about him. Each true proposition about God is a new and in itself complete answer to the question of what God is like. We need a succession of answers because the question is repeated. It is repeated because God is a life and a history, so that the question he puts to us is repeatedly put anew and differently.[67]

It would, of course, be possible to attend to the plurality of God's attributes in such a way as to miss their unity. This happens when we take some quality or other—such as "love"—as antecedently known to be godly, and therefore apply it to God. If we then encounter more than one such quality in the world, we end with a collection of divine potencies. Against this we must say that all the plurality of God's attributes is but the richness of the life of the one living God. There is nothing godly about love-as-such, only about the God who in fact shows himself to be loving.[68]

It is hardly necessary to remark on the way in which also this development is controlled by negation of the religious way of knowing God. We are told not to seek God behind the attributes in which he interprets himself to us. Each of them is true, and the whole truth about God. Nor on the other hand is any of the predicates of our language godly in itself. Barth himself points to the parallel between this doctrine of the plurality and unity of God's attributes and his doctrine of the Trinity.[69]

An additional embarrassment has always been how to get started making such a list. There is something fantastic in sitting down with a pencil and paper and asking: well, shall we say that God is "loving, kind and just," or "merciful, wrathful and holy," or what?

In this matter Barth is really "systematic" in a narrow sense. His actual list of divine attributes is a sort of Renaissance building: each determinant of God's being grows out of and leads to all the others, and the whole is deliberately and perfectly symmetrical. Barth claims that it is inevitable that this doctrine will develop as an exercise in concept building and balancing—but the structure of this building must be under the control of its object.[70] What Barth says must be done to keep his particular system under the control of its object brings us to the last—and for piety most decisive—of the points at which anti-religion polemic controls his doctrine of God.

The traditional scheme is to develop God's attributes in two parallel series, one of God's "absolute" attributes, the other of his "relative" attributes. Barth approves this scheme, and identifies one set as the attributes of God's *freedom,* the other as the attributes of God's *love.*[71]

The structure of the system of attributes, says Barth, must reflect the relation of freedom and love in the life of God. The endlessly dovetailing structure which Barth creates to do this is a work of art, but reproducing it is not our concern. What we should note is the way in which this structure endlessly insists on a certain *order*: first the attributes of God's love, then those of his freedom.

This, as Barth insists, is the reverse of the usual order, which took the absolute attributes of God first, then discussed the attributes of his relation to us. We know what Barth will say to this: "The basic error of the ancient church's doctrine of God is reflected in this order: first God's essence in general, then his Trinity. . . ."[72] God in himself is understood without building on the fact of his relatedness to us. Just so God becomes altogether the product of our religious self-transcendence.

VII

Of the Christian God, the first and last thing to be said is: "As Father, Son and Spirit, God is our God . . . antecedently" in himself.[73] Thinking this through is Barth's revolution in the concept of God— the revolution which sets before us the only developed candidate for a doctrine of God after the death of the God of past history.

Part Four

The God of Future History

Chapter Nine
Ambiguities

I

It is now widely recognized that the notion of timeless Being is inappropriate to believing knowledge of God. Determination to conceive God in terms of temporal potency, change and freedom is by no means limited to Barth—though it elsewhere often goes no further than expression of the determination. There are, however, two movements in this direction which deserve attention. One is the attempt within Roman Catholic theology to "dehellenize" the faith; the other is the widespread attempt to rework theology on the basis of a new metaphysics, the metaphysics of "process." We will discuss each of these movements in the person of a popular and highly visible protagonist: Leslie Dewart (II-III), and Schubert Ogden (IV-VI).

II

Leslie Dewart, in *The Future of Belief,* demands what we will all applaud, the "resolution of the . . . problem of which the Reformation was an unfortunately abortive issue, namely the integration of Christian belief with the post-medieval stage of human development."[1] It may be that the work is not so far behind-hand as he supposes—his remarks on Protestant theology are embarrassing—but that the victory is yet to be won is a thesis also of the present study.

Christian theism, Dewart argues, is *relative* theism. It does not affirm "God" unconditionally. It affirms only a particular God.[2] "The impression seems fairly widespread that for Christianity belief in God means most basically a sincere conviction that somewhere there exists a Supreme Being . . . whose principal properties are omnipotence, omniscience, and infinity. The implication seems to be that the Christian faith believes in exactly the same God as any intelligent and well-disposed non-Christian might well believe in . . . and that what is peculiar to Christian belief is revealed and begins hereafter. . . ."[3] This impression must be banished, both because it is false and because the contemporary experience of the reality of man must dethrone such "absolute theism."[4] The congruence of this starting point with ours is obvious.

Dewart claims that what is now necessary is the "dehellenizing" of Christianity, the overcoming of the ideals of "immortality, stability, and impassability" which Christianity adopted in its necessary —but now passé—adoption of the "Greek cultural form."[5] The *Christian* God is, against the Greek experience, a God to whom eternity is, far from a necessary divine attribute, a highly unbecoming one. He is a God whose "self-communication to us implies the self-communication of himself to himself. . . ,"[6] who *is* "subsistent self-communication."[7] The Christian God is not transcendent by abstraction from time, he is transcendent in the way that another who communicates himself is transcendent.[8] Just so he is the only truly transcendent God.

All this is congenial to the claims we have been making. And the correspondence goes further, to the affirmation of God's Trinity as the necessary starting point of our reflection on God: the basis of "New Testament theism" is not "the unicity of God (monotheism) but the self-communicating procession of God (trinitarianism). The doctrine of God of the New Testament does not begin with the oneness of God, to which the concept of the three-persons-in-one is added by way of modification. It begins with the procession of God."[9]

Dewart's critique of the classical doctrine of God repeats Barth's. The doctrine of the Trinity, he says, was fitted into a general conceptual scheme which made God's Trinity appear a revealed "property" of a "divine nature" otherwise defined.[10] And the Greek ontology was accepted, which compels us to conceive God as a definable essence.[11] Dewart's claim is that now the time is due and overdue to go beyond the synthesis with Greek metaphysics and seek an understanding of "the presence and reality" of a God who "would be wholly and exclusively the Christian God."[12]

His fundamental proposal is that we must stop conceiving of God under the category of "being." God is neither a being, nor is he

Being.¹³ A being is that-which-is-something or other specifiable, which has a definable essence. The Greek metaphysics has Parmenides' equation of reality and intelligibility at its heart, enshrined in the notion of *being*. But if we deny the principle, so that "reality is not assumed to be constituted" by its "relation to mind," then it no longer follows that only "beings," i.e., definable somethings, are real. Reality is only "as a matter of fact" definable, for what in fact exists will have a past, and be definable by that past—and so "be conceived as being." All creatures are beings. And all beings, since they are determined by their past, are creatures. But beings need not be the whole of reality. God is not a creature, and so must not be conceived as being, as defined by an essence. He can nonetheless be real, if the Parmenidean equation is once broken.¹⁴

This extraordinarily compressed argument, of which my statement was not a summary, but rather an expansion and attempted partial explication, is curiously ambiguous. It would be most naturally interpreted as straight neoplatonism: God is beyond being and intelligibility, because he is timeless and has no history. Far from overcoming "hellenism," such a position would repristinate its purest form. Augustine modified hellenism by calling God Being-itself, in order to make possible some sort of active relation between God and the things of time. Dewart seems to revert even from that modification. And there is one central point where it is certain that Dewart is indeed bound to hellenism: he is so used to thinking in its terms that he simply identifies intelligibility with the kind of *definability* which an "essence" has. It does not seem to occur to him that there might be other sorts of knowing besides defining and deducing from definitions. If God is not to be eternally defined by his past, he must, Dewart supposes, not be intelligible at all: "If God is not a being, then he is not an object of thought, and has no definition, essence, or meaning as a thing-in-itself."¹⁵

The ambiguity persists when Dewart says what God is, if he is not being. He is a *presence*.¹⁶ The term itself could very well mean the neoplatonic God beyond being, who is pure *present* without past or future, and just so present to all being. But here Dewart's intentions are clarified by other remarks. The kind of presence he has in mind is an event of communication: as when you and I speak, so as to be present to each other. Christians experience God "as self-communicating and thus as present to man. . . ."¹⁷ It is therefore possible to summarize Dewart's position so: God is not analogous to a thing-with-attributes, he is an event of communication. Such a summary undoubtedly represents his basic intention, and states a position obviously akin to that of Barth and this book.

According to Dewart, two benefits follow from so conceiving God.

First, we are freed from the problem of "the existence of God." "Christians should thus find it logical to reason that if essence is proper to the being of creatures, then God has no essence, and therefore is not a being. And if God is not a being . . . , then he does not exist." What requires our reflection is not whether the essence "deity" is exemplified in a God-being, but "whether, in what sense, in what way, and with what consequences God is present."[18] To this we simply assent.

Second, we are rid of the need for a doctrine of "analogical" speech about God. Dewart claims, without much evidence, that calling our assertions about God "analogical" has merely been a way of admitting that we are using a conceptual schema inappropriate to the reality about which we want to talk, while evading the consequence that we should seek a different one.[19] This is obviously a gross misinterpretation of the tradition: the notion of analogy is an essential part of ancient religious ontology itself, whether used by Christians or not. Nevertheless, there is something in Dewart's charges—and we will have some questions along this very line to put also to Barth.

Yet although Dewart makes what we can interpret as the right basic formal moves, the consequences which he then draws from them renew the ambiguity. God, we hear, does "not have meaning in-and-for-himself." He can only give himself "meaning for us." Meaning is always *for* someone. God therefore can have meaning for us, but not for himself, for were he to *give* himself meaning he would have a history and so be a being.[20]

It is a little hard to know what Dewart is claiming here, but apparently it is that had not God created us, he would not have "meaning," for example, the meaning "love." Would he then occur at all? Here is a dilemma. If we say no, then God occurs only in his relations to us—and since our experience of God is always our religious quest, God's transcendence to our religion is lost. If we say yes, then God-in-himself vanishes behind his revealed meanings such as "love," and we are abandoned wholly to religion. Only a doctrine which insists that God would be, for the example, love even though he did not love us, i.e., only a seriously trinitarian doctrine, can sustain the polemic against "hellenism."

And the ambiguity deepens. In discussing the concept of God's "omnipotence," Dewart suggests: "The question we might ask ourselves . . . is not this: what are the possibilities open to a being, God (who . . . lacks by definition all limitations), for acting upon other beings . . . ? The question is rather: what can . . . happen, once God and man enter into personal relations?" Since God is not a being, "his relation to being cannot be understood in terms of action and passion."[21] God's omnipotence should properly be conceived as "the radical openness of history—an openness which not even man's freedom can annihilate...."[22]

This could be fine stuff—but what Dewart turns out to mean by it is that "unless we make it be, the Kingdom of God shall never come,"[23] that "there is no divine decree that assures the inevitability ... of ... the ultimate success of man."[24] This is to say there is no gospel, no promise of the future in spite of the past, in spite of what we in any conceivable moment will already be. The anti-hellenic gospel is the promise that history's freedom will triumph *in spite of* what *we* bring to pass. Dewart's denial leaves open only the road into the past of our achievements. The test of whether the assertion that God is not a being is genuinely an attack on antique timelessness, or is itself a piece of hellenism, is that it *not* issue in statements like those of Dewart.

Again, there is a brilliant revision of the notion of God's "eternity"; "God is *temporal* in the same way that man is, namely in the sense that he makes time ... (but) unlike man, as he makes time God does not make himself; what he makes is being." But immediately our hopes are disappointed; and we read that "God's temporality does not consist in a self-projection out of the past toward the open possibilities of the future ... , it consists of his being present to ... history."[25] What is the difference between such a presence to history in general and as a whole, and hellenic timelessness?

To take one more point, Dewart perceives that if God is not a Supreme Being, the fundamental attitude of worship should not be abasement. Worship should not be the enactment of mere relations of superiority-inferiority,[26] should not be the "rendering of homage."[27] This is a freeing and wide-reaching insight. But what comes of it for Dewart is that worship is essentially *wordless* communion with a wordless presence.[28] But this means that our relation to God requires no gospel. The Greeks, at their best, worshipped just in this way.

III

We must finally say that all Dewart's talk of God lacks particular content. There is no gospel, no specific set of promises, which promises God to us. We agree that God is not a being; he is a communication. But for Dewart he is not any particular communication. We are not surprised when Dewart concludes his book with a denial that "God" is a proper name,[29] and suggests that in our religious discourse it would be best to substitute silence for identifying references to God,[30] in the very best late-antique tradition. Dewart has made all the right formal moves in rethinking the idea of God—but he has made them in abstraction from the particular story of Jesus. By this means he will achieve only purified religion.

To overcome "hellenism" and its dream of timelessness it will not do to say merely that worship is communicating; it is *what* is communicated, a particular story with its particular temporal structure, that transforms worship from cultic homage. If God's temporality is the temporality of *death* and *resurrection,* then he does indeed project himself toward a future—and just so overcomes our dream of timelessness. It will not do merely to say in the abstract that God's omnipotence is the openness of history to man; we must say very concretely that God is omnipotent as the self-abandonment of the Cross, that it is because he so perfectly accepts all our action upon him that his presence is ineradicable.

Just what, after all, *is* this "presence" which is God's reality? Dewart does not further identify it than to say that "in the presence of myself to myself I find that over and above my own agency . . . there is a presence which reveals me to myself in a supererogatory and gratuitous way. . . ."[31] But by itself, this identification is obviously quite empty. For merely *that* Dewart experiences a presence in himself is of no help to me; and even if I am able to make an analogous report of my own experience, we have no way of knowing whether these "presences" are the same presence. Unless these presences can be described, and so perhaps identified, we have no grounds for common worship, for self-transcendence, for the shared specific hope that makes time possible.

At bottom, Dewart is trying to do the same thing as much of protestant theology has been attempting for a century, to understand our relation to God as a pure "I-Thou" relation—as self-communicating presence—which needs no third person knowledge *about* the one encountered. He shares the failure of that attempt. If I meet God it is simply a necessary part of the meeting that I know that I am confronted with a person and not a galaxy, and that this person is whatever "God" means. All this knowledge is and must be descriptive knowledge of the most ordinary sort, statable in proportions testable by anyone. A *pure* presence, in no way describable in shared language, would be exactly the undifferentiated, motionless Presence-above-time of pure hellenic religion.

Despite all talk about God as self-communication and about God's temporality, what comes of Dewart's insight that God is not being is what we feared at the beginning: reversion to unspoiled hellenic religion. We must therefore make one fundamental amendment: God indeed is not a being, he is transcendent to being—but he is the transcendence *of* a being, of this being Jesus. In his self-communication as the Trinity, God includes a being, he is the Son who is the man Jesus. He is also the Father who is transcendent to all being. And only *as* the mutuality of these two, i.e., as the Spirit, is he God.

Therefore also, God does have meaning for himself. He means for himself all that Jesus means for us. And if it follows that he is a creature, we have no cause to deny this: he is in one mode of being the creature Jesus, and does have a past history. By reference to this being and his history, we can concretely and particularly identify the presence of God, so as to be able to worship a God other than the abstract Presence of hellenic religion. The narrative of this being's story is the gospel, the specific promises which are the content of our talk and experience of God.

Dewart's repristination of hellenism is the paradoxical result of setting out to overcome our heritage of hellenic religion by pure philosophical reflection, by an effort of mind which, in its abstraction from the event of God's objectivity as Jesus, must itself be a religious quest. God-as-event is not a possible object of natural theology. Only God as *the* event Jesus is the God who happens rather than exists. Only this narrative overthrows timelessness.

IV

Like Dewart, Schubert Ogden also begins with an apprehension that man's contemporary experience of himself and his world is incompatible with faith in the God described by classical Christian theism. Our experience of life is "secular," it is an "affirmation of life here and now in the world, in all its aspects and in its proper autonomy. . . ."[32] In respect of knowledge, the paradigm of scientific work demands that our judgments be autonomous over against religious considerations or authority.[33] In respect of morality, we understand an action as moral, and its maxim as moral, exactly when it is the free choice of autonomous human will.[34]

But God as defined by classical theism empties our affirmation of life here and now.[35] God's nature is defined by attributes which mean that he can have no real active relation to anything but himself: immortality, impassivity, immateriality, etc.[36] Especially his eternity is understood as the "exclusion of the distinctions that . . . temporality entails."[37] To such a God, nothing that we do or that happens in time can make any difference. If such a being is the source and arbiter of meaning, then none of our temporal, "secular," doings and sufferings can be finally meaningful. Therefore secularity and classical theism are mutually exclusive: "Simply by deciding to be secular, one implicitly repudiates the conception of God whereby that decision is finally robbed of any force."[38] To be sure, the attributes which deny God's relation to temporal realities are not all that classical theism has to say of God. He is called Father, Creator, Reconciler and the like. But the *definition* of God is provided by the "metaphysical" attributes; these therefore interpret those predicates which speak of God's relatedness to the world. Such an interpretation inevitably ends by giving words like "know" or "love" "meanings exactly opposite to those we ordinarily understand."[39] God, for example, will be said to "know" us—but it will also be said this does not mean what it would mean in every other case, that his subjectivity is determined by what we are. In general, classical theism warns us not to take literally what the Scriptures tell of God's active relations with his creation. But what is a "nonliteral" relation?[40]

The thing is done by the doctrine of analogy. "Recognizing that the God of Holy Scripture is undeniably a God who is related to his creatures, theologians have generally allowed that relational concepts may be predicated of deity, provided they are understood analogically instead of literally. The difficulty, however, is that, on conventional metaphysical premises, to say that God is not literally related to the world could only mean that he is literally not related to it. . . ."[41] The traditional doctrine of analogy ends its explications of anything said about God that seems to involve his relatedness or temporality by flatly contradicting the meaning such assertions would ordinarily be supposed to have.[42]

It is a sign of the necessities of our theological situation, that we find here exactly the same critique of the method of analogy as in Dewart. Oddly, there is also the same failure to appreciate the place of the doctrine even in a purely metaphysical doctrine of God. This oversight allowed for, the critique is one we can make our own. And indeed, there is an obvious congruence between Ogden's entire critique of "classical theism" and Barth's concerns and those of this book.

V

But Ogden's method in reaching for a doctrine of God which will affirm secularity is very different from Barth's. He returns to the method which was the original target of Barth's whole attack: analysis of the phenomena of human life to show the inescapability of religion.[43] It is worth our time to work out why Ogden must make this move. We can thereby learn a great deal about the possible options in the present theological situation.

Ogden's starting point in theology was the original dialectical theology. The dialectical positions are represented for him by Bultmann, but the representative could just as well have been the Barth of the *Commentary on Romans*. He accepts without reservation dialectical theology's doctrine of the eternal moment of crisis, its doctrine that "the reality of God as Judge and Redeemer is not a particular event of the future, but the ever-present final consequence of each passing moment in the stream of time."[44] He accepts it because it is a consequence of the sort of existential interpretation which interprets all talk of God as the evocation or explication of possibilities of my present self-understanding. Ogden takes this method of interpretation from Bultmann, but could as well have found it in the *Commentary on Romans*.

But if this is so, no particular moment of time can be decisive for our eternity, for all moments of time are equally related to eternity. The most that can be said of any particular temporal event is that it is the final *revelation* of the possibility of faith in God, which is a real possibility of every moment and situation. As Ogden puts it, authentic existence is "man's universal possibility."[45] Ogden's charge against Bultmann is that Bultmann is half-hearted in facing up to this, and falls back into mythology by claiming that "Jesus not only decisively reveals God's love . . . , but actually constitutes it as an event, so that apart from him (or in witness of the church that proclaims him) man cannot actually realize his authentic life." Against such mythology we must say that God "in fact redeems every history." Our claim for Christ must not go past the claim that he is the decisive representation of God's redemptive action.[46]

But if the event of Christ is not constitutive for the event of God's reality for us, then we cannot get past the emptiness of dialectical theology's talk of God by a move like Barth's christological reversal. The only alternative is to develop the doctrine of God as explicitly natural theology. Ogden recognizes the theological vacuity of Bultmann's "one-sidedly existentialist" solution[47] and calls in the philosophical theology of Charles Hartshorne to make this up,[48] to give content to talk of God. A program like Ogden's is the antagonistic test of Barth's.

All religions are, according to Ogden, expressions of "an original confidence in the meaning and worth of life. . . ."[49] This confidence is the necessary condition of our moral life, and we do not and cannot ever actually lack this confidence. To act as a human being *is* to act on an existential faith in the worth of life, whether admitted or not. Moreover, to have this confidence is the same as to believe in God. For to be confident of the worth of life and to believe that the whole reality of which we are a part is such as to justify this confidence, come to the same thing—and the word "God" just means whatever it is about reality "that calls forth and justifies our original inescapable trust. . . ."[50] Thus atheism is possible only as more or less profound self-delusion. Faith in God is unavoidable, for God is "the ground of confidence in life's ultimate meaning" and therefore "the necessary condition of our existence as selves."[51]

It would be possible to raise objections to this argument,[52] to many of which Ogden's replies would also be available. But for our present purpose we need neither attack nor defend the argument. Our question is whether the argument, even granting its validity, suffices to provide a viable anti-religious, or in Ogden's language, "secular" doctrine of God.

Ogden's move is a simple one: an adequate conception of God will be one which describes him as an adequate reason for believing in the worth of our life, our "secular" life. This imposes two requirements on an adequate doctrine of God. First, "God must enjoy real internal relations to all our actions and so be affected by them in his own actual being." Otherwise he cannot be the ground of the significance of what we do, any more than I can be the ground of the significance of events which make no difference to me. Second, God's existence as the one whose actuality is thus relative to his creatures must itself be relative to nothing. Otherwise he could not be the object of inevitable confidence.[53] The natural theology of Hartshorne provides, thinks Ogden, just such a conception.

Classical metaphysics takes perceived things as the paradigm cases of reality, and so has as its primary category "substance," that which of itself and permanently has certain attributes. But if we base our thinking on our experience as selves, we will abandon this metaphysics. For the being of the self is both social and temporal. As a self, I am what I am in and by my relatedness to a world and other selves: and occasions in which the remembered past and anticipated future are integrated into a present whole of significance are my very reality. Our fundamental category must therefore be the "process" of "creative becoming."[54]

If we construe God's being in this category, in "strict analogy" to ourselves, we will conceive of him as the perfect instance of creative becoming, as eminently related and eminently temporal. God has real internal relations to the whole of reality, in a way of which our relation to our bodies is an imperfect reflection. And he is continually in process of self-creation, synthesizing in each new moment of his experience the whole of achieved actuality with the plenitude of possibility as yet unrealized.[55]

God is pure and limitless love. That is, he is the self whose response is *universal and direct*. In "each new present, he constitutes himself as God by participating fully and completely in the world of his creatures, thereby laying the ground for the next stage of the creative process."[56] He interacts with *all* events in a way analogous to the way in which we interact with events in our own bodies. "The whole world, as it were, is his sense organ. . . ." He has no external environment; all events are internal to him.[57]

We are surely representing Ogden's intentions if we say that God is the occurrence of mutual meaningfulness in which the universe coheres.[58] As such, he is eminently temporal, being in himself the occurrence of the world's creative act which in every present unites past actualization and future possibility. God is the "experiencing self" of all reality. He, like us but universally, "anticipates the future, and remembers the past," in creative present moments which therefore are "temporal occurrences."[59]

Yet God's relatedness and temporality are themselves absolute and eternal. God has relatedness and absoluteness as two poles of his being; he is "dipolar." The difference between this theology and classical theism is that here it is exactly God's *relatedness* which is absolute, whereas in classical theism relatedness and absoluteness are in contradiction with each other. Since God is internally related to all events, the fact of his existence as the supremely related one is itself relative to nothing. So also the fact that God is "ever-changing is itself the product . . . of no change whatever, but is . . . the ground of change as such. . . ."[60]

VI

It will be seen that this conception of God is very much that of Barth and this book—with one great exception: it is not trinitarian. Or rather, it is covertly trinitarian, *with the world where the Son would be*. Everything that Ogden says of God's relatedness is exactly what we want to say of the Father and the Son in the Spirit. God's temporality is in both doctrines his oneness with his own past and future, but whereas in the trinitarian doctrine the three hypostases in God are this past, present and future, here the actualities of the past history of this world are God's past and this world's future possibilities provide his future.

It would be possible to turn this observation directly into a critique. The identification or near identification of the Son with the world has been a recurrent phenomenon in the history of theology, and has always been rejected. It puts us where the Son would be, and since the general pattern of the trinitarian doctrine is preserved, amounts to our self-deification. But against Ogden this would not be a fair critique. The question must be whether a doctrine like Ogden's works; if it does, then the trinitarian doctrine is unveiled as a myth of which dipolar theism is the appropriate existential interpretation.

The key point is Ogden's doctrine of analogy, upon which everything depends. For it is by it that he proposes to move directly from analysis of our selfhood to the doctrine of God, without detouring over what happens with Christ. God is the *eminent* self, the *absolutely* related one, the *eminently* temporal one.[61] Ogden derives everything he says of God by analogy with what he says of man, and it is very clear that this is what he is doing.[62] In view of his critique of the classical doctrine of analogy, this is legitimate only if this method of analogy does not involve contradicting the meaning that words like "time" and "relation" have when used otherwise. Ogden is aware of this,[63] and this will be our test.

Ogden takes his analysis of man's temporality from Heidegger. Man is the one who projects himself into the future in terms of possibilities given by the past, who is temporally "ecstatic." But, says Ogden, whereas man is finitely temporal, God is infinitely temporal. Man is "thrown" into existence, he has a beginning and consequent range of possibilities which he himself did not choose. And he will die; there will be a time when he will not be. God is not so limited; he has neither beginning nor end. His temporality is therefore eminent temporality.[64]

The question is whether this eminent "temporality" of God contradicts the positive meaning of "temporality" predicated of man. It seems to me that it does, so that Ogden's program of analogy is open to his own critique of the classical program. According to Heidegger, our temporality is *constituted* by our mortality. It is exactly because we will someday not be, and know that this is so, that we are temporal. Moreover, our temporality *is* our relation to our arbitrary, "thrown," beginning.[65] Temporality was for Heidegger simply the chief category of a projected ontology of finite being. And *if* we leave out the new possibility opened by Christ's resurrection, surely Heidegger is right. But then to say that God is temporal without having beginning or end, is at least as incoherent as anything said by the classical analogies.

Temporality can be attributed to God without broken-backed analogies, only if temporality is itself understood not only from our being-unto-death, but also from Christ's being-unto-death-and-resurrection. Even then, we must be willing to say that God does in fact have a beginning and an end, which only the doctrine of the Trinity allows us to do. Unless we are willing to let the event of Christ be *constitutive* for the event of God, the attempt to speak of God's temporality will necessarily involve smuggling in determinants from the christological tradition without methodical warrants for so doing.[66]

The same sort of argument applies to what Ogden says about God's relatedness. Here we can put it as a question: in the sentence

"God is internally related to *everything*," can "related" mean anything at all? A doctrine of the Trinity, where *everything* is the second hypostasis, is really a doctrine of the significance of this world in itself, and needs no talk of a "relation" to God. Again Ogden's analogy empties his statements about God just as badly as the classical analogy. Only if we conceive God as the quite unanalogically understood relation between a particular being, Jesus, and transcendence, can we meaningfully speak of God's relatedness.

"Dipolar" theism is indeed what both the gospel and our secularity demand. That God is both related and absolute, and that it is exactly his relatedness which is absolute, is exactly what we must learn to understand. But dipolar theism will not work *as* natural theology. That God is both related and absolute is, as a mere pair of metaphysical assertions, just metaphysical paradox-mongering. But if God's relatedness is first his innertrinitarian relatedness, then it makes sense to say that *this* relatedness is his absoluteness over against all other being. If the creature that is "rather like a body" to God is not the creature-in-general, but *a* creature, the man Jesus, everything Ogden says can be said without need of analogy and without incoherence.

VII

But what then of Barth's use of analogy? It is a christological analogy to be sure, but does it carry no ambiguity into Barth's language about God's temporality and relatedness?

Sometimes Barth's theology reads as the first true theology of God-with-us: God occurs as what historically happens with Jesus Christ to give our secular lives concrete temporal structure. But then one turns one's head slightly—and the whole grandiose story of God and man seems to float away into the heavens, leaving us gazing up as spectators of our own drama. What is the true reading of Barth's thought? Both and neither—which is, of course, a very Barthian thing to have to say.

The meaning of Barth's theology could be that the eternal God of traditional theology came down to occur among us as Jesus' temporal relatedness. But it could also mean that both Jesus and our involvement with him occur in the abstract dwelling of the eternal God. What does it mean to say that the man Jesus preexists in God's eternity? That this "eternity" is Jesus' time? Or that Jesus' time is really not our time at all? Is what happens with Jesus what we mean by "eternity"? Or is Jesus "in" the *otherwise* eternal God? There is no doubt of Barth's intention. But this does not banish the ambiguity any more than in the case of Dewart.

We do not justify the critics who have spoken of Barth's isolation of God from the ordinary concerns of life. This vision of Barth's theology as a drama played on the stage of infinity opens only after one has penetrated deeply into it—and then it is precisely our own actual concerns and possibilities which seem to float away from us with Christ, so that it is as pure abstract spectator-ghosts that we are left behind to watch.

Just as the *Commentary on Romans* can be read as the perfected theology of a religion of timeless eternity, so the *Church Dogmatics* can be read as the most perfect eternalizing yet achieved of the gospel's themes and story. It is clear that this is the opposite of what Barth intends, and that when we read his theology so we are reading it wrongly—but there is something that compels us to read it wrongly in this way.[67]

What, we ask, *is* this time which God takes for us to be the form of his eternity? What is this reality of God in our time? What sort of time is Jesus' time which is God's eternity? It turns out, after all, not quite to be *our* time that God has as his time for us: "We would not understand God's revelation as revelation if we said without reserve that it occurred in 'our' time. . . ."[68] Revelation has its *own* time and is, "in distinction from our coming and going time, eternal time. . . ."[69]

We are reassured when we read that Jesus' time is "eternal" because it is "authentic, fulfilled time,"[70] that is, it is time with a genuine past and future, genuine because his past is not lost or his future merely dreamed of, and therefore also time with a genuine present.[71] His time heals our time by *bounding* and so determining it.[72] Our time is not yet this time, and just so our time is no longer endless, but is bounded by Jesus' time. Therefore our time has an end and goal —and just so is healed to be itself authentic time.[73] We remember Jesus—but to remember a time which was fulfilled time and therefore cannot slip back into the past is equally to *await* it.[74] Just so we have past and future that do not conflict, and our temporality is healed.

But when we ask *how* Jesus' time thus bounds our own, the ambiguity reappears. Jesus' time bounds ours because all our times are equally its immediate neighbor, because separations in time mean nothing to it.[75] Jesus' time is the "prototype" of our time;[76] our time is determined by it as the image by its model. This sort of language is rather too close for comfort to Plato's talk of time as the moving image of timeless eternity.

The discomfort is increased by Barth's final identification of the fulfilled time of Jesus, of the time which God takes for us. If, he says, we push the question, which is the fulfilled time, further than we perhaps should, the answer must be: the forty days of the resurrection appearances. The resurrection is *"the* event which is the real object of the rest of the narratives and doctrines of the New Testament." And the Easter-narratives speak, says Barth, "of a present without future, of an eternal presentness of God in time." Here is a time "which just as it is can never become past and needs no future —a time of pure presentness...."[77] *This* is why Jesus' time is both past and present to our time, because "it cannot become the past and has no future at all before it...."[78] The revelation "falls into time from above...."[79]

Now all this *can* be interpreted in terms of God's radical temporality. But it can also be read as itself an interpretation of what makes God's temporality radical, and in terms reminiscent of timelessness. It all depends on which way you look at it. Barth may have banished the Cheshire cat of timeless eternity from his theology, but the grin decidedly lingers on.

VIII

The difficulty is in the way Barth reckons with God's transcendence. He wants to say that God is in fact what happens with Christ, that we are in fact actors in his story, that God's Trinity is in fact his being Creator, Reconciler and Redeemer. But he also wants to proclaim the freedom and transcendence of God over against what he is for and with us. He thinks that to do this he must postulate a reality of God in himself distinct from God-for-us. But lest this God-in-himself become a different God *behind* God-for-us, and we be back in the situation of religion, God-in-himself is identified only as the prototype of God-in-his-revelation. All we are to say of God in himself is that the revelation is his image. Time is the image of eternity— which means that eternity is simply whatever it must be if time is to be its image.

But what can possibly be the content of saying that God in eternity is whatever is the prototype of his life in time? Either this sentence is perfectly empty; or the very form of the statement makes some sort of comparison between God's own characteristics and his temporal characteristics. Such a comparison can only be between timelessness and time. Either the introduction of analogy adds nothing at all to the fundamental claim that God could have been God otherwise than as God in and for *our* time, or what it indicates as the condition of this freedom must be a mode of being other than temporality, radical or otherwise.

The case seems to be that Barth has not discovered any new way of conceptualizing God's freedom over against his being for us—any way appropriate to the triune God, to the God who occurs. He has thus made do with the form of the old prototype-image way of comprehending the relation of eternity and time, while attempting to evade the substance. But if the whole of God's temporal story is to be analogous to something else, what can this something else be —if not a timeless deepest reality of God? The notion of the analogy of the whole of time to something else is itself the grin of the timeless cat.

Barth needs a way to say at once both that God is and is not in Jesus, both that the world is redeemed and lost, both that we already are what we are in Jesus' story and are not yet. The dialectic is indeed unavoidable to any Christian theology. Barth has found no way to sustain the dialectic to the end as a *temporal* dialectic.

When we are suddenly inclined to see Barth's whole tale as a tale about eternal beings who we are not, we are following the suggestion inherent in the very notion of the analogy of time to eternity. Indeed, this suggestion is the sole content of the notion. Failing a new way of positively describing God's transcendence to what we have of him, Barth relies on the shadow of the old way. This is what makes all Barth's assertions so shifting. Where the notion of analogy functions apart from its old metaphysical moorings, all assertions become uncontrollable. Always one ends by saying that what they mean depends on from which end you look at the matter.

Indeed, "analogously" is by itself but another way of saying "ambiguously"—and this is exactly the function of the notion of analogy in Barth's system. He wants to say that God *is* what happens with Jesus. But he does not want to do this in the way so much newer "radical" theology does, where talk of "God" really is superfluous. Therefore he wants also to say that God is free over against what happens with Jesus. He does not in fact have a way of doing both of these at once. The problem is systematically solved by making the great christological identifications—God *is* what happens with Christ; we *are* what we are for him; creation *is* the carrying out of his life—*ambiguous,* and so leaving a loophole for God's transcendence. But the ambiguity is precisely the shimmering possibility of reading all these statements in terms of timeless eternity.

IX

Barth's analogy is not intended to be the platonic analogy of moving time to unmoving eternity. And everything is indeed there for the creation of a *new* understanding of theological meaning, of a doctrine of "analogy" radically different from the old one.[80]

The "analogy" of which Barth wishes to speak is an analogy between relations, rather than between substances with partly similar and partly dissimilar attributes. It is the innertrinitarian *relation* between the Father and the Son that is "imitated" by that between the Father and Jesus. And this relating, which *is* Jesus' deity, is "imitated" by his humanity, i.e., by his relation to his fellows. Our relation to each other is again the image of our relation to him.[81]

Moreover, we should remember that these "relations" are all active relations. The love of the Father and the Son is an event, just as is Jesus' love for us and ours for each other. Thus these "analogies" are *correspondences* of one event to another. Barth can therefore use, parallel to "imitate," the word "repeat"; the innertrinitarian relations "are repeated and imitated in God's eternal covenant with man. . . ."[82] The analogy is that of *the same act repeated in new circumstances.*[83]

How we might understand this correspondence of acts is also suggested, at various points in the *Church Dogmatics,* in terms of language.[84] Thus Barth understands the creation as God's "Yes" to the creature, a "Yes" with which God interprets the "Yes" he speaks to himself in his choice to be what he is.[85] And our self-understanding as creatures is the "echo"—here truly a new notion of analogy —we bring to this promise of God.[86]

These are promising beginnings. Carrying them out would, however, lead to overcoming the whole notion of resemblance, of imitation and reflection. It would finally destroy the whole scheme of "analogy" as the scheme in which to cast our understanding of God's eternity. Barth does not achieve this.

X

If we drop the notion of analogy, we must try to understand God's transcendence within the terms of time itself. We will have to understand the radicalness of God's temporality as a certain pattern of that temporality itself.

It is clear how this is to be done. We will understand God's freedom over against what he is for and with us as his *futurity* to what he already is with and for us. And since Barth is indeed right in seeing God's freedom as one side of his deity, we will define God's deity as his futurity to himself and so to us.

We will have to find a new way to understand the continuities of God's reality and work in time: the oneness of the three modes of God, the coherence of what God is apart from Christ with what he is in Christ, of what we have been with what we will be. We will no longer be able to suppose these temporal separations bridged in timeless eternity. Again, it is fairly clear what categories offer themselves:

communication, utterance, language. We will learn to understand God as an *hermeneutic event,* as a Word.

I will be trying in these last two chapters to carry an understanding of God's trinity and temporality to some sort of completion. To do this, we will have to end our reliance on Barth, though were it not for Barth's work, we would not have a truly anti-religious conception of God to be trying to complete—or I, anyway, would not.

There is, moreover, much in Barth that can help us also here, and we will use it. But Barth's own backing we will not have.

Chapter Ten

The Futurity of God

I

Barth is right that the *resurrection* is the temporal event of God, that the post-crucifixion appearances of Jesus to his disciples are the center of God's self-revelation, their time the time taken from our time to be God's eternity. "He is risen" was—and is—the gospel.

But if we look at the tradition of Jesus' resurrection-appearances, we do not get the impression of a pure, perfectly fulfilled present without past or future. We may finally come to say that Jesus' risen presence is the present of God, at the union of his future and his past. But the appearances themselves—and so also God's present!—do not have the temporal structure of a moment possessing its future in itself.

On the contrary, the impression given by the tradition is rather that of events wholly elusive in their present, occurring only as pointers to their own future. The risen reality of Jesus is attested and described exactly as a series of *appearances,* not as a series of experiences of a reality generally available in the present. Had someone asked, "What do you mean, risen?" those to whom he had appeared were not in a position to reply: "You see that man over there? Go and talk to him, and you will be convinced he is the same Jesus who was crucified." Nor do the accounts attempt to pretend that the witnesses were in this position. The presence of the risen Jesus was not available beyond the witnesses' experiences of it; there was no currently available method of verifying the claim that he was risen.

That is to say, there was no way for them to *assure themselves* of this reality, no way to control their relation to it—which is a mere corollary of his appearances being the revelation of *God*.

This is not to say there is no verification of the claim that he is risen. "And the third day he rose again from the dead . . . ," and ". . . he shall come to judge both the quick and the dead" are but two ways of making the same claim—and if he does indeed come to judge all men, this will be the most decisive possible intersubjective verification of the claim of the resurrection. But this verification is not one we can perform; it is not one of the possibilities given in our present.

Many of the mythic elements of the resurrection accounts seem to express this elusiveness of the risen Jesus' present.[1] And the accounts make quite clear that the risen Jesus is transcendent to his present givenness because he is *not yet* what he is as the risen one: "Do not touch me, for I have not yet risen to the Father."[2] The risen Jesus is elusive because he is not present but future: his appearances are appearances of what is not yet.

The resurrection accounts depict the risen Jesus as a proclaimer of the Kingdom of God as before; but now he proclaims himself in that he proclaims the Kingdom. In the most characteristic of the resurrection utterances, he claims that the divine rule has in its totality been given to him.[3] The disciples confess that they had "hoped" that Jesus "would be the one who would redeem Israel," and the risen Jesus confirms their hope.

Yet the Kingdom does not thereby loose its futurity; there is no suggestion that *now* is the Kingdom. Rather Jesus himself, now personally identified with the Kingdom, has become future. Jesus confirms exactly their *hope* in him. The proclamation of the risen Jesus is wholly a matter of imperatives and promises for what is to be. The appearances of the risen Jesus were for those who experienced them commissions, *sendings*.[4] And they were promises of the final fulfillment, a fulfillment now characterized as fulfillment precisely of the resurrection: "And see, I am with you through the days left before the end of the age."[5]

Jesus' resurrection appearances, far from being pure fulfillment, were *pure promise*. The central accounts in Matthew and Luke are, despite wide differences of scenery, closely parallel in function and structure.[6] Both are accounts of appearances to the main body of disciples, following appearances to individuals. The heart of both is the missionary commission. And both end with a word of gospel for the disciples. These two final sayings are parallel even verbally: "And, see, I will. . . ." The saying in Matthew is a promise of Jesus' own presence with the disciples. The saying in Luke puts at this exact place the promise that *"the promise of the Father"* will come upon them. We are not over-interpreting if we recognize that the presence of the risen Lord and the *promise* of the Father play the same role in the two parallel sayings, that the risen Jesus' presence *is* a promise. We may put it so: promise is the ontological category for the reality of the risen Lord. Jesus appeared to the witnesses of the Resurrection as what he was not yet, but would be: the Lord of the End.

II

Thus, Jesus' appearances as risen were the occurrence of the transcendence of the God who justifies the ungodly, whose transcendence is his radical freedom from and to all that has come to be and so is. Jesus' appearances as risen were the revelation of the God whose transcendence is his futurity to what already is. They were therefore the revelation of victory over the God whose transcendence was his timelessness, his immunity in his present reality to the danger of an open future.[7]

It is, of course, not only the God of Jesus' resurrection who occurs in the appearance of the future. Also the God of religion enters our experience with the challenge which the future in general makes to each present. Human being is being in a not-yet: all that we do and suffer is our *doing* and *suffering* only in what comes of it. And what is to come of my deed stands then against my deed to qualify it as *not yet* what I must and shall become. It is in answer to this judgment of my future upon my past that I fall down to worship, and speak of God. If I bow down to wood and stone it is because I suppose that they have the power to free my tomorrow from today's sickness or poverty. If I prostrate myself before an eternal Judge, it is because I am torn in the contradiction between what I will to be and what I see I already am.

Indeed, only against what I am not yet, whether this be an ideal, a deity, an image of perfection, or the command of a personal God, *am* I now anything at all. The uninterpreted facts about me have no more interest for me than any other set of facts; they are not my life. Only interpreted by what is to come of them, only in relation to an ideal or command, do the facts about me have meaning for me. When I ask: "What am I?" the appropriate answer is not something like "brown-haired," but rather something like "ill-tempered" or "destined for heaven." I am by what I am not yet. The apprehension of God is the apprehension of this instrinsic determination by the future.

Yet the alienation of our lives from their truth is exactly that we apprehend our futurity only by attempting to evade it. The religious defense, in which we project a timeless Present which already is all that will be, has been the target of the polemic of this entire book.

But there is also a technological defense, where we neutralize the futurity of the future by planning for it in terms of present possibilities, where the future is allowed to be only what develops out of the present in ways we understand and can allow for. This the classic defense of the man who built his barns and filled them, in order to be able to reassure his soul about the morrow. The technological quest for security is the aggrandizement of the present at the expense of the future.

Whether the attempt to defend the given against the future is conducted by myth or science makes very little difference, and the way in which the utterances of believers in salvation by science reproduce the logical patterns of the most primitive religious mythology is a permanent irony of our age. The biblical technologist with his barns probably also called in a priest to bless them. Technology as a technique of defense against the future is but the secularization of religion. Both restrict the future to possibilities given in the present, and thereby neutralize its futurity.[8] This is not an attack on science or technology: science need not be cultivated as a way of salvation, nor technology as defense against an open future.

The pattern of alienated existence is, therefore, that the very present which the challenge of the future opens as a present, we live as the neutralization of the future. Religion and the God of its natural theology occur in the not-yet of life—as its neutralization. Scientism occurs in the same place in the same way.

Only if the challenge of the future has a particular content, and a content which is not among the possibilities of the present, can the challenge of the future overthrow our fortified present and the past which rules in it. Only if what is to come of our lives can be *narrated,* and only if that narration will not fit as a mere continuation of the narrative of what we have been, is our alienation healed. Such a future is proclaimed by the gospel proclamation that Jesus' story, the story of a past and therefore narratable event, is the story of what is to come of us all. For his story is the story of death and resurrection —and this is not among present possibilities. Not even death without resurrection is something I can *do*; it is never an event in my present.[9] We must discuss both of these points further: that there is a narratable final future (III-IV) and that what is narrated as our end is not our possibility (V-VIII).

III

All theology since the *Commentary on Romans* has agreed that Christianity is the discovery of *hope* as constituent of humanity. All agree that to be human is to hope, and that this assertion is central to Christian faith. But as the dialectical theology worked out this insight, a fateful twist occurred: the End was no longer understood as *what* is awaited in the whole of life, and became instead the ultimacy of each present moment. The awaited future became an "eternal" future, immediately related to every present. The content of the gospel is then no longer a narrative of what we may hopefully await, and is instead exhortation to hoping itself. The promised future is no longer a future, but futurity.

This conception could not remain unchallenged, and did not. For hope is evidently hope *for* something.[10] Yet as soon as one starts to think this through, one discovers an apparent antinomy. If the gospel's promise is of a particular, describable future, must this not mean that this future may one day become the present—so that hope will end? And if the hoped for authenticity of life will not itself be a life of hope, must this not mean that hope is not, after all, a necessary characteristic of human life? But then is not the whole theological project—and perhaps the gospel—emptied? If hope is to be fulfilled, hope is itself not essential; if hope is not to be fulfilled, it is ridiculous. Perhaps the very notion of hope as an ontological category is absurd.[11]

"So faith, hope, love abide, these three; but the greatest of these is love."[12] The antinomy seems confirmed. Hope will pass, obviated by the very End that is hoped for. Yet in fact the passage is Paul's solution to the antinomy, posed for him by the fanatics of Corinth. Love is said by Paul to be greater than faith or hope precisely because it is their eschatological reality; when neither faith nor hope is any more appropriate, love will be the fulfilled reality of both.

Love, in the entire New Testament, is the pattern of existence enacted in Jesus' being-unto-crucifixion: his giving over of all that he had earned, or that his fellows had forfeited, to the future he would be for them and they for him. Whether Jesus had more "loving" feelings for his fellows than others do, we have no idea. We do know he died for the future he proclaimed for them. The resurrection of Jesus promised his life itself as the future he died to give; that is, it promised love as what is to come of us. An existence of perfect mutuality is the final future promised by the resurrection.

Thus love transcends the antinomy of hope. On the one hand love is something we may hope *for*: we may hope for the overcoming of the barriers to our being-for one another, for a society in which we neither marry nor are given in marriage because what we now painfully realize with one will have been achieved with all. The resurrection was the success of Jesus' death for others; it is therefore the promise of the achieving of the love which is now the flickering value of our doings. The resurrection is the promise of an accomplished struggle toward each other.

Yet in love, hope's affirming openness to the future is preserved. For the very point of love is that I do not know what the one I love will do to me and with me, yet accept it fully in advance, expecting to *learn* what is good from his acts toward me. Thus the antinomy of hope is solved, for love is at once hope and something to be hoped for. Just so, love is the fulfillment of hope.

The End will not close the future—if the End is love. For to love is to be open to the other-than-me, to what I do not yet know or will. And yet love can be the End, for when love is achieved there is nothing left unaccomplished, no not-yet still to seek. The End is when the future is open as future, *without* an intervening time in which the future must be achieved or prepared for—so that life *is* an event of openness.

Love-in-general does not subsist, only particular loves. Defining love-in-general as God is the most insubstantial of all religious illusions. It is *Jesus'* love, his particular enactment of life in the pattern of being-unto-death, which is the open future. The gospel is the promise that the conclusion of our lives will be his utter affirmation of them, whatever they have been, as his chosen opportunities of acceptance, and our consequent ability to find each our particular love for the other. The gospel is the promise of the success of human society, a success achieved by Jesus' rule of man in entire self-abandonment.

The transcendence of the God who justifies the ungodly is thus the futurity of Jesus' love-unto-death. We said that God, though not a being, is the transcendence *of* the being Jesus. Now we can interpret this: God is the futurity *of* the past event Jesus. The mystery of Jesus' resurrection itself, of the event which must lie between his death and his coming in life, is the mystery of God. For faith, "God" equals, by definition, "Whoever raised Jesus." *That we have a narratable future,* that we live *for* this past and only therefore knowable person, *is itself an occurrence*. It is a temporal occurrence, for it came after Jesus' death and before his appearances. This event is the occurrence of God. And since the reality of the resurrection is the reality of a promise, we must say that God now is real as this promise.

It is the God who raised Jesus whose transcendence is the antireligious transcendence that limits us to the tasks of time, and just so frees us from and for them. For his transcendence *is* the fact of time, the "beyondness" of the future which gives us past and present and makes our lives temporal. But to speak of "the future" in general is empty. God's transcendence is the beyondness of a particular future; only because we live for a particular future do we have time.

Finally, this God is the God who is love. For God is achieved futurity, and this, we saw, is love. Or rather, God is *an* achieved futurity, and therefore is a particular act of love.

IV

Jesus' resurrection has promised him as the future. To live humanly is to await him. But what can it mean to await a man of the distant past, whose death is a matter of record?

First we must ask what it means to await any person at all. Suppose Jones leaves the room and a few minutes later someone enters. Under what circumstances will we say this person is Jones returning? Ordinarily we will go by appearance: if Jones is tall and the person who enters is short, we will not immediately be inclined to call the entering person Jones. But suppose a person enters who is shorter than Jones and of a different coloring, yet who in conversation gives all the answers we would have expected of Jones? Suppose this person remembers everything that Jones would be expected to remember and nothing else? And makes the choices we would expect Jones to make?

We do not, of course, expect such an occurrence. But this is only an empirical generalization, and open to correction; there is no *logical* impossibility to the case of Jones. By putting such unlikely cases to ourselves, we open the question of our final criterion of personal identity. Would we call this person Jones or not? What, at a minimum, are we expecting to happen if we are "waiting for Jones"? The issue would be a matter for choice: we would have to *decide* whether to extend our use of "same person" to a case where many of our former criteria for its use no longer applied. But the choice made would express our fundamental conviction about what it means to be human.

There seems little doubt what criterion of personal identity the gospel proposes. If our true self is what we are not yet but will be, then the unity of our lives must be like that of the plot of a drama, it must be a dramatic coherence: a life coheres in the way it leads up to its conclusion, its resolution and denouement. This means, of course, that only from the end can I know who I am—that only if there is a resurrection can my identity be something I myself experience. Yet even during the course of life we can meaningfully predict *that* life will cohere, just as during the course of a play we can, moved perhaps by confidence in the playwright, predict that it will "all work out" even though we are unable to predict what will happen to work it all out.

Moreover, from the course of the play so far we can predict *of what* sort the conclusion, and so the unity of the plot, will be: we can say that it would ruin the play if the author were so gauche as to reconcile the lovers in the last minute, or that the dramatic ironies require yet another flip-flop if they are to be profound. We can make, that is, predictions of *dramatic appropriateness* to what has already passed. We proceed just so also in life: we say that it would be "most unlike Jones" to marry in haste, or die in battle.

What—at a minimum—are we expecting when we await Jones? We are awaiting events *dramatically appropriate* to the story of Jones so far enacted. In looking for those events which will be the continuation of Jones' life, we are assured that whatever twists the plot of his life may take, after the event the plot will always be seen to cohere as a plot. And if someone we take on other grounds to be the continuation of Jones does marry in haste, we will either revise our narrative of his whole previous life, or, if the facts resist this new interpretation, conclude that Jones "is no longer himself."

We may therefore formulate the Christian hope so: we await events which will be dramatically appropriate as the conclusion of Jesus' life as already known, and dramatically appropriate as the conclusion of our lives as well. In any culture or cultural period, this hope will draw that culture's visions of love to itself, and build utopias and futurist mythologies, like those of biblical apocalypticism, Marxism, or liberalism. These utopias will come and go, born of and destroyed by the hope for the conclusion of Jesus' life-for-us.

But we have run over the main point: if we await Jesus—rather than Jones—we await one who has died. The resurrection appearances followed Jesus' death. The proclamation of the case where the awaited one's departure was the departure of death is the most violent possible challenge to our ordinary criteria of personal identity. Yet it could not be otherwise, for if the future is free, then only in resurrection is there any personal identity at all. And there is, after all, one plot of life which spans death and futurity: the plot of love. For love is the release of all that is past, for the sake of the loved one's future. Love is both death and hope for the future. To say that Jesus loved is the same as to say that he has died, and that we *await* this act of love—that he lives as the crucified one. Love is the dramatic coherence of Jesus' plot of death and future action.

Again we arrive at the proposition: God is love. For God is the possibility of death's *future*. He is the reconciliation of death and hope. Which is to say: he is the success of love.

V

With these last reflections we are well into the next problem. Why can we not hope simply for love? Why must we say that love will be realized under *Jesus'* love for us? Why can we not simply be utopians? Or perhaps posit the society of love as an unrealizable ideal, and hope and work for daily partial realizations? Why must we hope for the action of someone other than we? Must we not demythologize the hope for Christ's coming into a hope for the better success of *our* love for each other? Why must hope be hope in a transcendent reality?

The gospel's answer has two forms. The first is: the future which is promised is love, and love is something we do not succeed at. There is no reason why we cannot, but in fact we do not. Nor are there any grounds for supposing that we shall—unless in the promise that love will be realized among us by the one who has already succeeded at love. If there is to be love among men, it will be because someone other than we will love us.

The second form of the answer is: resurrection is not among our possibilities. Resurrection is a hope for life in its *totality,* a totality constituted by the limit of death. Resurrection is not one of the possibilities in this world; it is a possibility *for* this world. By "this world" we mean that entire present which we may aggrandize by religious or technological raids on the future, all that is and all that can be foreseen or made to be. At the end, this world will still be bounded by death. The future of the gospel is a future for this world. Just and only so it is a future unassailable in its futurity. But just so it is also beyond our possibilities. Indeed, it is only the proclamation of resurrection that makes our dying world a whole, so that there can be at all a future we cannot take over into any present.[13]

Every hope is a contradiction of the present, it is hope for what the world now is not. Yet our plans, techniques and religious illusions mediate these contradictions. Only Jesus' resurrection from the dead is so total a contradiction of the standing order that mediation is beyond us. The mediation of this contradiction could only be the beginning of a new world, an act of creation explicable by no evolutionary hypotheses.[14]

A true future is thus no mere possible rectification of one or another shortcoming of the present. If we hope, we do not see the present as the basis of life, needing only to be perfected. A true future is not merely the goal of a teleologically conceived world-process. Hope is directed rather to a not-yet which is an essential character of all that can become present, to a missing reality which is exactly the required possibility of life.[15]

If the future is ontologically prior to the present, it must subsist in its futurity of itself, and not of our will or the present possibilities our wills seize. Only if the future is someone else's future, *God's* future, is there a future at all. The not-yet which is opened by Jesus' resurrection appearances is not a mere lack in the given, discovered over against the relative fulfillment of the given; it is the not-yet opened by one who promises what he will do. It is *God's* not-yet.[16] Hope does not project the future from possibilities given in the present by the past; it projects the past—its interpretation of and relation to what is recollected—from the new future possibilities given by God.

God, therefore, is "the power of the future, of the future conceived from its futurity, from its coming. . . ."[17] *That* future which confronts us when the resurrection ends our religious and technological attempts to incorporate the future into the present, the future "conceived from its futurity," is the otherness which is the otherness of God. God is "present as the coming one";[18] faith "has Christ in that it hopes for him."[19]

VI

God is not only transcendent; that is, he is not only future. He is the "dipolar" God whose transcendence is the transcendence of his relatedness; that is, his futurity is the future of Jesus, a past event remembered in our present. If we may hope to meet God, it must be possible to describe his coming—otherwise we are not waiting for the particular event of God, but only for whatever may chance to come next. That the coming of God is describable means that the promise of his coming is specific, that is, has content. Since the only promises we can know are those which have in fact been made, knowledge of the content of the promise—and so of the coming God—is knowledge of a past event. But if to know God is to know a past event, then unless we are to seek God religiously beyond his revelation, God must be a past event. God is not only future, he is also past.[20]

This is not a new and independent theme over against God's futurity—though religion makes it be so. God is radically future because his occurrence is resurrection *from the dead*. Hope is hope for the crucifixion. Just so it is hope for this world, in its injustice and suffering and death.[21] It is hope for the present, just as the past has brought it forth.

Only, after all, in hope is it possible to accept the world just as it is. If I have no hope that things will be different, I have only the choice between hatred of the given world and my life in it, and the attempt to persuade myself that at some deeper level this world is not as it manifestly is. But the promise of resurrection both tells us we are dying, and makes it possible to affirm this creatively. It both compels us to face the radical not-yet of the world, and makes such honesty possible and fruitful. Only under the transcendence of the impossible future of resurrection must and can we own the present as the past has in fact led to it. Apart from this promise, we will always flee from the true present into some degree of religious or scientific self-delusion. We will talk much about sticking to reality and the present and not going after pie-in-the sky—but our reality will be a self-invented superworld of one sort or another, our present a timeless present abstracted from the history which in fact shapes our life.

The gospel-promise thus raises the question of how we will own our past. Our past is the past of our own actions; it is also the greater past which is mediated to us by the tradition, as this poses to us the possibilities of human life from which we must choose. We may own our past by leaving the choices of our lives to the tradition—manifestos of indifference to the past are no proof we are not doing this, for it does not matter how recent the tradition may be. We may claim justification by the past, by what we have done and by the superiority of the culture within which we do it. We may rebel, or despair. We may win sufficient freedom from the past to make free choices for the future among the possibilities it poses us. We may even be creative over against it.

The gospel-promise calls and enables us to own the past in *repentance*. When we own our past in repentance, we confess that between our past and any true future there is no continuity we can achieve. We confess that in what we and our fellows have made of ourselves and our world, there are no possibilities which could fulfill the not-yet of that world. Just so, we are set free to recollect and research the past objectively; we have no more reason to twist the past, to interpret it to fit a priori demands for our or our culture's justification—or for our condemnation. Yet this does not mean that we simply turn away from the past. On the contrary, this repentant concern with the past is our appropriate response to the promise of the fulfillment of our lives—in our repentant concern for the past we are concerned for our final destiny. In repentance we grasp the meaning of what we are as the past has made us, the meaning which God will give our acts in his final acceptance.[22]

Thus God occurs as the transcendence of the future, and just so as the transcendence of the past. In the past is the event of Jesus; and in the past is the self I possess and that possesses me, for the only self I have to deal with is my past history. The coming of God is the meaning of the one for the other. In every present I come from God precisely in that I go toward him.

VII

The pastness of God is most fully expressed by calling him "Creator." Here hope, as hope for the world that already is and as hope in an event that has occurred in that world, makes its promise to that world universal. The God of hope encounters the God of the past in his role of universal origin, and seizes the role for himself. Hope looks back at the story of what has been and so now is, and says that it all will have led up to the victory of Christ's love—in spite of all the evil that has been. The promise is the possibility of interpreting the past as a story of opportunities of love, waiting to be realized—an interpretation otherwise not possible.

In the history of theology, the doctrine of creation has been at once the sharpest expression of the specifically believing apprehension of God, and the place where, within the Christian synthesis, faith has repeatedly capitulated to religion. Repeatedly the Creator has been identified with the primary cause, or underlying principle, or creative force which religion seeks behind the world. But that God is Creator means exactly that he is none of these things. It means that the relation between the world and the transcendence which justifies it is neither causal nor logical nor organic. The relation is rather that between a will and what is willed. God *decides* that we are.

What a *decision* calls into being is history. What God "has" created is precisely history, precisely the reality of the future's transcendence of its concrete past. If there is a philosophical achievement which can be credited to Israel, it is that of the second chapter of the book of Daniel and the other "apocalyptic" thinkers: they overcame the religious way of conceiving the whole of reality. Ancient religion conceived reality as a whole by conceiving it as a fixed universal order springing from a common ground, which was potent in the beginning and is repeated in each seasonal or cultic return to the roots. When science, contrary to its own inner meaning, becomes a world-view, it has this same structure. Israel learned to see the world as a whole by seeing it rather as a story with a plot.[23]

History—as against a cosmos—is created by *promises*. The creating word of God is his call that what is not shall be, his commands and promises which contradict every status quo and upset every equilibrium. The creating word of God is: "Come, I will send you to Pharaoh that you may bring forth my people . . . out of Egypt."[24] The history which God creates is not world-history as an artifact which is only incidentally not yet finished. It is not a whole which will be total only when it shall be completed in the past. What God creates is the *fact* of history, the fact of transcendence in time as this involves both the transcending future and the transcended past. And he creates this fact in its quality as the openness of love—rather than as the openness of fear or blind obedience.

VIII

Thus God is both future and past. That our lives are so bracketed in time, that we may live *for* someone, *as* the concrete particular persons the past has made us, is itself an occurrence: the setting of the plot of life. This occurrence is God. Yet more must be said; we cannot simply take the bracketing future and past as separate and independent mysteries. The natural triplicity of time, as past, present and future, is never symmetrical. Either the future or the past will be materially the root of time. The present moment of decision and action will be either the anticipation of the future or the repetition of the past. Either the past will be a story of opportunities of future transformation, or the future will be the prolongation of the past. The range of possibilities which stand in question in every present choice will be discovered either by promises or research. Time is either *historical* time or *cosmic* time.

In both historical and cosmic time, a transcendence asserts itself: the transcendence of the future or the transcendence of the past. Neither is in itself false; we cannot live as if there were no future before us, or as if there were no past behind us. In both historical and cosmic time one transcendence asserts itself against the other; in this confrontation with the other, and only therein, it asserts itself as God. The transcendence of the past is the transcendence of the God of religion only in that the past arbitrates the future so that true reality becomes a timeless and therefore supernatural special reality. The Father of Jesus is a God at all only in that he overcomes and takes the place of this God of religion.

The God of religion is the arbiter of the future, whose transcendence as lord and arbiter is that of the past. The God of faith is the arbiter of the past, whose transcendence as lord and arbiter is that of the future. Only in that time is thus, in the one way or the other, asymmetrical, is it *time*. Thus God and time belong together: atheism would be unconsciousness of time.

God is a polemic reality. He occurs as the victory of the future over the past, or the past over the future. Therefore there are only two possible Gods. Which is the true God depends on whether the future or the past rules. Or rather, whether the future or the past rules, whether historical or cosmic time is real, depends on which god is true. The gospel is the promise of the rule of the future. It is in the polemic of future time against cosmic time that the true God occurs. It is in the future's attack on the god of religion, enacted as Jesus' crucifixion and resurrection, that God occurs.

Barth's christological reversal is the apprehension of historical time and its transcendence. But in its isolation, it is not yet the apprehension of *God*. God will be apprehended only when the transcendence of the future is alive in our thought *in* its polemic relation to the realities of religion and the self-contained world of technology. Cosmic time is either mythic or scientific. Attacking the first form of cosmic time, the transcendence of the future is apprehended in anti-religious theology. Against the second, a-religious theologies are formed. We need both the self-explication of our religious and scientific ways to transcendence and the christological reversal of those ways—*theology* occurs only as critique of the one by the other.

The hold of the future on the past is the identity of the risen Christ with the crucified. Within cosmic time, the unity of reality would not be problematic: the future would simply grow out of the past. But in historical time, the unity of the transcendence of the future with that of the past, where the future is free from and for the past, occurs as contradiction, suffering and overcoming. It occurs as the *cross*. It occurs as the death which the religion even of Israel inflicted on the one who spoke for and lived from the future, and as his acceptance of that death. As we live in historical time, the unity of our lives is not to be found in their own immanent development. It occurs as the unity of past and future which happened as Jesus' crucifixion.

We have the account of Jesus' crucifixion. We have also the accounts of the appearances which promise his coming. Between, there must have been "resurrection." But we have no account of this event.[25] The personal identity of the risen and crucified Jesus is not given us except in the contradiction of death and life. This identity in contradiction is God.

The account of Jesus' crucifixion talks of the abandonment by God of the one who radically trusted in him, of the end of hope for the proclaimer of hope at all costs. The account of his resurrection is the promise that this one will be our destiny. It is therefore the proclamation of hope after the end of all possible hope, of the future of every possible dead end, of God as the occurrence of the open future of the futureless. God *is* hope after our hope.[26]

In the denial of hope to the only consistent spokesman of hope in God, God was acted out—*as* damnation. The crucifixion was the enactment of God because it was the inevitable conclusion of Israel's history, of the history which had been lived for a goal. Here the goal occurred as death. God as death, or death as God, *occurred* in the crucifixion. But it is only from the resurrection that God can be seen in the crucifixion; only because of the resurrection can we call the crucifixion the goal of Israel's history. The crucifixion of Jesus was the enactment of God as death only in that he thereafter is promised as the living future—here is the paradigm case of the determination of an event by its future. Therefore only in and with the event of the overcoming of death is God enacted as death. In the crucifixion and resurrection, God occurs as death *and* promise, as the *overcoming* of death, as the triumph of the future.

If God is this, he is triune. Only a trinitarian concept of God can contain this dialectic within itself. Or rather, the trinitarian concept of God conceives God as the reality of this dialectic. Just so, it is the triumph of the polemic against religion.

IX

If God's transcendence is his futurity rather than his timelessness, many of the traditional assertions about God need reexamining. We have already discussed the question of God's *substantiality,* of the justification of speaking of God as "he" or even "it";[27] and we will discuss it again in the next chapter. The necessary minimum about God's *personality* has been said by Wolfhart Pannenberg, whose work we will report in the next section. Here we will say something about God's *eternity,* about the notion of his *nature,* and about the consequent revision of the notion of *"being."*

The religious idea of God's eternity is, at bottom, the belief that he is the one able always to persist in what he already is. But, purely formally, an exactly opposite notion of eternity is entirely possible, and is required if the future and not the past is the fount of time. This is that God is always open to what he will be. If we abstract from the existential significance of this language, it may seem that there is no difference between the two formulations. But the difference is real: it is whether we think of God as the great Reactionary or the great Revolutionary.

God's eternity is not that for him everything is really already past, but that in love everything is still open, including the past. His eternity is that he can never be surpassed, never caught up with. He anticipates the future in the sense that however we press forward in time, we always find that God has already been there and is now ahead calling us on. God is not a presence possessing his past and future in himself; he is a future possessing his past in himself and therefore always present.

God's nature, therefore, is not the set of attributes he may be permanently relied on to exemplify; it is the plot of his history. His nature is the coherence of his acts, such that after the fact we can always say: "Yes, that's just what the God of Abraham, Moses and

Isaiah *would* do—though I would never have been able to predict it." God occurs, and *what* occurs is this plot of a history. But, because this history is that which makes all reality temporal, we must also say: God occurs, and *what* occurs is that life has the plot of historical time rather than mythic time.

Finally, the futurity of God demands that we go to the end with a Christian revision of our ontological schema. In religious metaphysics, "being" is resistance to change, immunity to time. If God's transcendence is futurity, then "being" is historical temporality, it is exactly the call to change. In religious metaphysics, that I am is guaranteed by something about *me,* by a resistance to cessation which is a characteristic of the substance "I," rather like being mammalian or intelligent. In a truly theological ontology, "being" is the possibility of becoming other than I am, and is therefore necessarily not a characteristic of myself. The guarantee that I am is beyond me; it occurs as the call to change.

By itself, "being" is an empty word, whether it means resistance to change or the call to change. In either case, the word "being" gets its content from material assertions of the thinking which uses it. In the one case, these are the metaphysical assertions that "being" is convertible with "unity," "goodness" and "truth." In the other, they are eschatological narration: to be is to be underway toward a conclusion narrated by the story of Jesus. It is to be living a story which will be resolved by involvement in his.

Classically, the notion of being has pointed to the meeting between what already is and what is to be. An historical apprehension of reality needs a way to point to the same mystery; otherwise there would be no reason to retain the word. But whereas classically "being" has meant the way—however mysterious—in which everything that is to be already is, contemporary ontology is more likely to use the word to point to the *difference* between what is and what is to be, the difference in which freedom occurs.[28] Being is the possibility of this freedom. Being is not identical with freedom; being is the fact about any reality that it is not yet what it must be, insofar as this "not" upsets and moves the status quo away from itself. God, finally, is the miracle that this happens.

X

God is the occurrence of the temporal bracketing of our lives by origin and goal. Moreover, he is both origin and goal not as timeless transcendence above past and future, but as suffering and overcoming, as the unity of past and future in Jesus' crucifixion. Only the trinitarian concept of God can be the concept of a God who contains this temporal difference. Indeed, only such radical affirmation of the futurity of God makes finally clear why Christian faith must identify God as the triune one.

The temporality of the triune God is thoroughly worked out by Barth: "He is the Beginning, without whom there is no Middle and no End; the Middle, that can only come from the Beginning and without whom there would be no End; the End that comes altogether from the Beginning." We can simply adopt and carry forward almost all the formulations we discussed in Chapter Seven.

Yet in this very passage, the shadow of religious direction to the past, of the "analogous" notion of eternity, is dark and well-defined. The "Middle" and the "End" are rightly said to come from the "Beginning"—but nothing is said about the Beginning and Middle going toward the End. Without the Father there would be no Son or Spirit—but it is not said that without the Spirit the Father and the Son would not occur. In every nuance of his formulations, Barth displays the doctrine that the Father is "the fount of the Trinity." But that the Trinity also has a goal in the Spirit remains a mere occasional assertion. This gathering to the past, to the Beginning in which all has already been decided, pervades all Barth's thinking.[29]

The direction of the trinitarian formulations toward the past is something Barth shares with the tradition. The necessities of the historical circumstances of their origin dictated this. But if the true temporality of the triune God, and the true meaning of the doctrine of the Trinity, is at last to appear without ambiguity, this shadow must be banished. That is, the futurity of the triune God must be made plain.

The formal pattern of the doctrine must be reversed, to give the "Spirit" some of the formal role which the "Father" has had. It is noteworthy that also in the traditional formulation, only the third hypostasis, the hypostasis of God's futurity, has as its particular name a word which can also define God as such. Indeed, "God is Spirit" is the Bible's only approach to a definition of God's essence. Instead of defining all three hypostases by their relation to origin, they must be defined by their relation to goal. The Spirit is the goal of the Trinity, and this doctrine must be given the function which has belonged to the doctrine that the Father is the "fount of the Trinity."

The Spirit, says Barth, is the "historicity" of God—we might say the Spirit is God's existentiality. The Spirit is at once God and our experience of God, God and our possibility of faith in God.[30] But Barth does not seem to see clearly that the Spirit can be both because he is God-future, God as what we may live *for*. In general, Barth's discussions of the Spirit are not so convincing as his discussions of the Father and the Son.[31] It is hard to see what is said that had not been said before. In contrast to Barth's usual fullness and determination to be understood at all costs, we find here brief concatenations of hints and dicta. One is even tempted to think that the incompletion of the *Church Dogmatics,* with the eschatology and doctrine of the Spirit missing, is not merely a matter of chronology.

The Spirit is the hypostasis of God's futurity and so of God's relatedness. The Spirit is therefore the determination of the nature of the triune—that is, future and related—God. We therefore replace the formula that in the Trinity there is an Origin and two Originateds with the formula that in God there is a Goal and two Anticipations, an anticipated Anticipation and a pure Anticipation. God goes before, God follows and God is preceded—and *these* are the relations subsisting as modes of being in God.

The relations which are modes of being in God are active personal relations. We must now make explicit what theology has not made explicit before: active personal relations are relations to a future. The relation of the Father to the Son in the Spirit is the Father's relation to his future. And the relation of the Son to the Father in the Spirit is the Son's relation to his future. If then God *is* the mutuality of the trinitarian relations, then God is his openness to himself as a true future not fixed by any past—which is where we started: God is love.

This God, and only this God, contains within himself the difference of past and future, in the actual reality of that difference as the conflict of death and life, despair and hope, guilt and the justification of the guilty, the transcendence of wrath and the transcendence of promise. Or rather, only this God *is* this difference of past and future. God is the reconciliation of the transcendence of the past by the transcendence of the future, in the present of Jesus' crucifixion.

If the futurity of God is thus the structure of his trinitarian life with and for us, we do not need to safeguard God's freedom by the clumsy device of calling the "dispensational Trinity" the "image" of an "immanent Trinity." For futurity *is* the condition of freedom. God is free over against the realized actualities of his trinitarian life with us, because he is always ahead of them; he always can be otherwise triune than he has so far been. This freedom *is* his trinitarian life. It is a permanent, transcendent freedom, because it is love's complete but never-ended openness to the future. Just so, as love's openness, this unpredictability of God is gospel and not threat: we do not know what God will be, but we know that every new event of his eternal creativity will be seen, when it has occurred, as an inevitable step in the life of the good God we have known.

"Appropriations," therefore, are all those descriptions of God's triune life made possible by the past history of that life. There is nothing "analogous" about them. They are transcended not by some other description which would be literal if it were available, but rather by God's futurity, as the endless newness of seeing God "face to face," a newness from which also our descriptions learned on the way have sprung.

XI

Even the footnotes will have shown how closely related sections I-VII of this chapter are to the movement in theology led by Wolfhart Pannenberg and Jürgen Moltmann. Exactly how directly indebted my reflections are to these men, I am not sure. The indebtedness is doubtless considerable. Without implying that Pannenberg and Moltmann have the same theology, we will choose only one for explicit discussion: Pannenberg, who has claim to priority.

Unlike with some of the others now developing eschatological theologies, a passion for the future as such does not seem to be Pannenberg's original concern. Rather, his thinking starts with a concern for wholeness: ". . . the need for inclusive unity . . . is so deeply rooted in man . . . , that the question how far this or that religion is able to establish a universal unity of the experience of reality can very well [be] the criterion of its relevance, saving power—and perhaps also of its truth. . . ."[32]

The wholeness of reality which Pannenberg seeks is the wholeness of history. The biblical revelation has opened the vision of reality as history, and of God as the God of history:[33] "It is specific for Israel, that she did not experience the reality of her God in reflections of a mythic primal event, but rather, and ever more decisively, in historical change itself."[34] History is whole only from its end. Thus the God of history is his own truth only as the End of history—and so Pannenberg arrives at the futurity of God.

Pannenberg shares the general apprehension of the problematical character of the concept of God. For him, this too arises out of the concern for universality. He locates the decisive step in our loss of the traditional God in German idealism. This movement discovered the contradiction between the necessity that God, as the meaning of all reality, be infinite, and the idea, seemingly contained in the very notion of God, that he is a particular being. A "highest being" is a contradiction.[35] Yet a "God" who lacked universality, or who lacked individual personality, would not be God. Only if we can find a new way to think of God as at once universal and individually personal can the crisis of western religion be overcome.

We will present Pannenberg's argument in very compressed form. In man's search for the wholeness of his own existence, the "primacy of the future" immediately announces itself. Man's life is a whole only from the end. But the end of man's life is death, which does not complete life but rather breaks it off. Only in a conclusion beyond death could our lives be whole. But this means that every grasp of my life as a distinct reality, as a whole, is an anticipation of what is not and cannot yet be, of a transcendent future. We anticipate a goal of life, and only so do we have our life.[36]

Moreover, our lives are what they are only within the whole of history. Every attempt to probe the meaning of life is, therefore, an anticipation of the end of history, of the wholeness of "universal history";[37] only in the horizon of world history can any individual event be understood in its full consequences.[38] Therefore our attempt to understand our lives always involves some projection of the plot of universal history, i.e., some anticipation of the end. Yet such an anticipation of the future must not close us off from the contingency and unpredictability of the future—which is the very nature of the experience of reality as history.[39] Such anticipation of the End, *as open*, is possible only by the particular nature of the revelation in Christ, or what is the same thing, by the particular nature of the Christian apprehension of God.

The gospel proclaims Jesus Christ as the end of history, which has occurred ahead of time *in* history. Just and only so, he is the revelation of the God of history, of the meaning of history as a whole.[40] The earthly Jesus spoke and acted with the authority of the Kingdom of God, enacting the last judgment ahead of time.[41] This claim of Jesus could only be justified by the future; within Judaism's historical apprehension of reality, his resurrection was that justification.[42] If Jesus was risen, then the end was already begun, and begun with Jesus, thus confirming the claim made by his life.[43] Moreover, if the end is begun with Jesus, then he is the revelation of God; then the Lord of history's wholeness is on the scene in what happens with him.[44]

Yet Jesus' anticipation of the end of history, though it makes it possible for us to see history whole, does not diminish the openness and unpredictability of what is coming. For although he is risen, we are not—and therefore we do know what the metaphor "resurrection from the dead" means. We wait to rise as he did, but what happened to him we do not know.[45]

Rather, the universality and finality of Jesus' resurrection expresses itself exactly as the "commission to go to all peoples, and to integrate all areas of life into the . . . truth which has appeared in Jesus. . . ."[46] Thus the resurrection of Jesus inaugurates a new history, the history of the ever new and unpredictable interpretations of the finality and universality of what has happened with Jesus[47]—

of what "resurrection" can mean. "In the continuing tradition of God's revelation in Jesus of Nazareth the totality of history is . . . ever constituted anew. With his revelation, God, who constitutes the totality of history, has himself entered into the process of history."[48] Thus in the history of the gospel, we are given ever new apprehensions of the wholeness of history—and just so history remains open, for we must always expect new apprehensions.[49]

This revelation in Christ defines who and what God is.[50] The myths through which religion grasps reality whole we do not conceive themselves as preliminary, as due to be transcended by future interpretations. In fact they are in history so transcended: but they themselves are "turned toward primeval time, and closed against the future of their own transformation." Thus the gods of religion are fixed to their given forms—they are mountain-gods, sun-gods, etc.— and serve as protection against the dark power of the future.[51] The biblical revelation, on the contrary, is the "appearance of divine reality as infinite," and just so does "not distort, but rather opens the openness of the future, the uncloseableness of man's history—also in respect of his knowledge of God."[52] God is "the power of the future."[53]

Man *must,* says Pannenberg, ask after the possibility of the wholeness of his life, after the "ground of being." The question is whether it is any longer possible to speak of *God* as the object of man's necessary question.[54] The God of "theism," God as a person-type thing, is no longer thinkable—precisely because of our grasp of the historical character of reality, of the futurity of our lives.[55] But the primacy of the future is itself only secure if it is grounded in itself,[56] if the power of the future is a reality, i.e., if there is God.

God "is God only in carrying-out his lordship. . . . Therefore his deity will only be revealed with the coming of his kingdom." But God's deity and the revelation of his deity cannot be separated. "Does this not mean: God is not yet, but will be? In any case, he is now only in the way that the future has power over the present. . . ." It is because he is not but will be that God is transcendent. Yet he is real, for the power of the future *is* Being.[57]

God as the power of the future does not take away our freedom, he frees us for our future. He is "the power of contradiction" to the status quo, and just therefore can save and preserve. He is the only possible object of hope and trust.[58]

Yet we have still not established that we can speak of the power of the future as "he," as God, at all. At this most sensitive point of his project, Pannenberg's move is direct. "Personality" *means,* he asserts, freedom and futurity. The power of the future, which is free from every present and challenges it with the possibility of its transformation, is just so a personal power.⁵⁹ The mark of a person is that he is not wholly "disposable." Whether we speak of "God" depends therefore "on whether that whole which expresses itself in the individual events of history is in principle . . . disposable or not disposable. The latter is the case, *if* we understand the whole of reality as the history of ever new occurrence."⁶⁰

This God, and only this God, can give us *history* as a *whole*—and so the meaning we seek for life. History is contingency, which a knowledge of history as a whole would seem to cancel. Therefore, the wholeness of history "can perhaps only so be thought, that the contingency of events and their connection" somehow "have a common root." The Power of the Future is this root: he is at once by his futurity the "origin of the contingency of events" and by his personal oneness the "origin of their connection. . . ." That contingent events fit together to make a whole is the expression of the "faithfulness" of God.⁶¹

XII

Obviously, the whole of what is here outlined of Pannenberg's position is affirmed by the viewpoint of this book. We can simply accept each of his propositions as a confirmation of or addition to what we have ourselves been led to say. Indeed, Pannenberg must be regarded as a pioneer of the sort of thinking active in the earlier sections of this chapter.

Yet we must ask if Pannenberg's fundamental and overriding concern for wholeness and universality does not pull him in a direction opposed to the direction we have been going. His thinking is guided by the postulate of a totality of history. This totality seems to be the sort of totality on which one would look back when history had stopped. It is not clear whether Pannenberg expects such a stop of history, or whether the process of new interpretations of the wholeness of history is itself expected to go on indefinitely. In either case, the ideal itself is of the totality of *completed* history. But if God is God in that history stops and becomes a completed entity, this God is the God of *past* history after all; and what we are bidden to await is the transformation of the God who is the power of the future into the God who *was* the power of the future.⁶²

There is nothing in what Pannenberg says that absolutely necessitates such a conclusion. But to avoid it, we must reflect not only on how the end as *anticipated* does not close the openness of reality, but also on how the end simply as the end will not close the openness of reality. Pannenberg has taken up the first task, and more fully and subtly than we could report here. But he has not yet taken up the second. He has not dealt with what we called "the antinomy of hope." Moreover, that he has not seems consistent with his basic motif of wholeness—which does not naturally lead to the notion of an essentially and eternally unclosed reality.

It fits with this tendency that the contradiction of death and life, which *is* for us the unity of reality, is not given any such ontological role by Pannenberg. Indeed, the crucifixion does not in general have the theological place that we might expect. Pannenberg makes wholeness his *starting* point, and must therefore iron out all dualisms as far as possible. In contrast, we have identified the suffering unity of the crucified and future one as the very being of God.

These motifs in Pannenberg's thought give the whole structure a surprising resemblance to the *Church Dogmatics,* and in just that aspect from which we have tried to break away. One is tempted to say that Pannenberg is Barth inside out: Barth with past and future reversed, and therefore with history as a whole replacing analogous eternity. This, of course, would be too neat, and not quite fair. But both Barth and Pannenberg have the same passion to avoid theological "ands," and both are nevertheless determined to encompass all of reality, all of culture and learning, as the object of theological reflection. It was the need to satisfy these two concerns at once that drove Barth to his fatal use of "analogy," and to the strange unreality which his depiction of our life in God sometimes acquires. Pannenberg's work sometimes gives a similar impression of construing the reality of God and man from a distance.

If our own reflection on God's futurity is to avoid abstraction, we have one big step left to take. We must hear the reality of God as *Word*.

Chapter Eleven
God as Word

I

The long worry of philosophy about "being" is at its heart the history of the question: who *am* I? This question can easily be a muddle, perhaps a muddle deliberately chosen to hide behind. For we all know, in one way, quite well enough what we are, and the attempt to pretend we do not, so as to create scope for profundity, may merely be mystery-mongering. Yet it is hardly plausible to dismiss as *merely* logical confusion the fascination which this question—or pseudo-question—has had from Socrates on.

In the case of Socrates, it is easy to see the source of the fascination. What he was concerned with all his life was what he *ought* to be, what he should *become*. And this is of course a question we cannot avoid, once asking it has become a possibility, for by every decision, by every word and act, we pose and answer it. But why then did he claim to be puzzled by what he *was*? Because he believed that only in what he ought to be could he find his self, the very same self which —since here he indubitably was, with his talk and questions—he already *was*. So Plato and Aristotle were convinced that what we ought to become is the reason of what we already have become, that the future is present in what we now are as its rule and direction. They may have been wrong, or even muddled; but the relation between what we are and what we shall or ought to be is clearly the basic human problem they have left us.

When I ask, "What is to become of me?" the "me" about whom I can inquire, as about an object of some sort, is my past history. The self I can examine is a set of past events, which I collect as "my" life and could put in an autobiography if I thought it worth doing. But when I ask this question, I also project a future self which I cannot examine, which I hope for, or believe in, or perhaps just plan for. Thus when I seek to understand myself, to "get hold of" myself, the act I perform is indivisibly both the examination of an object and the positing of a value, the description of a past and the choice of a future. That such an act occurs shows that between what I am and what I ought to be there is some relation other than that between successive observable states of an object; it shows that Socrates' question is not without point. Indeed, we have a whole language in which we thus seek *self-understanding*.

The qualitative difference between knowing the past and choosing the future, and their coincidence in the act of self-understanding, are equally essential to this act. It is here that the classical talk of metaphysics about "being" has its home. What has been meant by "being" has been what comes between given past and fulfilling future, between facts and hopes; whether to unite or separate them is what has been in dispute.

We have passed over a point, which leads us to the same result. How do I know which past events belong together as the sequence of my life? Clearly, all and only those are candidates which have in one way or another happened to a certain particular thing, my body.[1] Yet what I can on any occasion mean by "my" life is a *selection* from the vast class of events which I might discover to have happened to my body. As soon as we reflect we see that the principle of selection is one we have already encountered: by *my* life I mean a selection of past events which in their sequence make a story, which belong together by dramatic coherence.[2] But the dramatic coherence of a story is given by its *conclusion*. Only by virtue of my hopes or fears do I have a self at all. Socrates' question is by no means pointless.

One possible answer to the question of our being is that we already are what we are to be, so that the present choice and decision is not a break, but the immanent development of a changeless essential nature. This whole book has been a polemic against the religious version of this: that in the mind of the changeless God all newness and all conflict are always already reconciled. A scientific version merely substitutes evolution for God.[3] In both religion and scientism, my being is an "essence," a changeless and certain "human nature" within which, in all strivings and sufferings, I am secure of fulfillment.

Evidently, the opposite view must be that what I am to be must always be *won from* what I am, that the choice of purpose is a true choice only if it is defiance of what the past would dictate, even if I finally choose just that. My being is my winning of freedom from the past. If my choice is authentic, what is "between" what I am and what I choose to be is exactly their "difference."[4] What stands between is negation; and if we continue to use traditional language we will get nihilist or existentialist formulations: being and nothingness are the same.[5]

Believing positions result from critique of the religious option, and it has been convincingly argued that the nihilist option has also resulted from this same critique. The gospel says of us that our given reality is a denial of what God wills us to be. And its promise is that God will indeed make of us what he wills us to be. We are not bound to a predetermined human nature; we are freed from the law which would predetermine our choice of fulfillment.

Yet faith's criticism of the nihilist options is equally urgent, for these all amount to the assertion that man is his own God, creating his meaning out of nothing but his miraculous choice. Consistent nihilism only adds the recognition that if I am God, then God is the devil. Faith insists that if we are creatures, then there already *is* a reason for our living; we do not need to invent one. Faith's understanding of our being insists both that our being is freedom, and that we do not create our purposes by choosing them. But how can both be so?

At just this point, Christian thought has persistently talked of the *word*—in however crippled or ambiguous a fashion. I am called to what I am to be: I am *called,* and just so given the possibility of choice, yet given this choice not by myself but by the one who calls me. The possibility of freedom which is not self-deification is that we live in *communication.* It is because we are born into communication that our existence may be both freedom and obedience, openness for the future and responsibility for the past. It is because we are born into communication that our free choice of what we will to be need not be the fantastic effort to create new selves out of nothing, and can instead be creative acceptance of what we are.

I can live for what I am not yet only in that I am confronted by one who is what I am not, who offers possibilities strange to those I have already accepted or rejected. This occurs in address, in the event of communication. Any address whatever does this. It you say to me, "Nice weather," you break open my enclosure and make me hearken to you, to an other-than-me. We take up a new task together, the task of coming to an understanding with each other, and with the new and strange that each of us brings to the other, at however trivial a level. Yet with your entrance into my life the past also enters. "Nice weather" is a communication only because it is a sentence in a language, only because of a multitude of already arrived-at understandings which you and I share with all whom we could understand. These are inherited from the past. Yet what you say opens a future. Here past and future cohere—and we are at "being."

We are at being, but we have not achieved it. For when we ask what we are, we ask after *the* future, after the particular event which will be the conclusion of all. It is thus a *particular* word which believers speak as the address which unites all the past with the last future. We have already repeatedly insisted: the gospel is the story of the past history of Jesus, told as the story from which those addressed may learn their destiny. It is the story of a past event as the future, so that if I play my life as a role in this story, my past and future are one, yet not in what I do, but in the whole plot in which I have my role.

This word is the story of the one who proclaimed the radical freedom of the future—and was crucified for it. Here is a judgment on the other words of which our lives are made. Each of them calls to a future. "Nice weather" opens the possibility of a new friend, or of a new start on the day. A scientific hypothesis opens a task of investigation. The judgment of the gospel is that our invariable response to these calls—beneath however many layers of irony or evasion—is a refusal to step out of ourselves, a refusal to let go to the future. The judgment of the gospel is that in the conversation of our lives we use language to shield ourselves from the future which is in each other: so we use ideology, lies, mere prattle, sincerity and a great many other sorts of noncommunication. In all the comunication which is our lives each of us says to the other, "Keep off." Just so he also speaks judgment to the other: that he too has refused the call of the future and therefore has none.

Just so, Jesus' story is about our pasts. For it is the story of his love exactly for those who refuse the call to the future. When we hear his story as a call to our last and preliminary futures, and respond, as usual and in continuation of the pattern of all our past conversation, by retreating to what we already are, this *confirms* us as exactly those to whom he promises his love as future.

Jesus' story is the word by which we are what we have always been—and just so are free from all that we have been, free in every new choice to choose fulfillment. It is the word by which we may "be."

II

"By 'being' I mean . . . the possibility of letting oneself be called into question."[6] Ernst Fuchs' definition is, at least apparently, a good summary of all we have said on this line, especially if we attend to the words "called" and "question."

This ontological intuition is another widespread motif in contemporary theology and philosophy. We will use Fuchs to lead us further into it, though there are many other thinkers who might serve as well.[7] Fuchs' path of hermeneutical ontology will prove to be the very one we wish to travel, but in the other direction. This result will be the beginning of our own reflections. We will begin by seeing what Fuchs makes of the apprehension that to be is to be called; then we will ask what we want to make of it.

Fuchs' final ontological intuition can be set at the very beginning: if being is the possibility of being called into question, *time* is being. Time is the "ground" of our questioned and questioning existence. The gospel saves because it *promises* us time, thus ending our attempt to *have* time, and so freeing us to be ourselves in time. "The self-abandonment demanded by Jesus was not a matter of morality. It meant giving up the attempt to dispose of time as the ground of our existence—as did the prodigal Son who would not await his time"—and letting time be the ground of our life.[8] That *time* is "being" is the interpretation of existence which is both the creation and the undiscussed presupposition of the New Testament message, which we come to as the summary expression of existential interpretation of its texts.[9]

The gospel speaks to and raises the question of how we will understand our lives, of what "ground" we find for them, and just so involves us with and in *history*. The question put to us by our own existence is "how we address reality in pain and joy, anxiety and calm . . ."[10]—and just this address to reality is history.

Being, so understood, occurs only in "call" and "address," in the event of *speech*.[11] We may perhaps summarize Fuchs' dialectic so, departing from Fuchs' own terminology: language as we receive it, as it precedes us as tradition, is the reality for us of our past, and of the determination of our self-understanding by the past. Yet the *event* of language, speech in our received language, is precisely the possibility of decision and, therefore, our openness to the future. Thus language is the meeting of past and future, it is the challenge to the future, given by the past: this is "being." We must go through this argument more in detail, and stay more closely with Fuchs' own formulations.

To understand myself is to *answer* for myself, to someone who challenges me.[12] Thus we achieve self-understanding in that we seek understanding with each other. And the understanding we have already come to with each other sets the limits for how each of us can come to understand himself.[13]

Moreover, when we seek and enact our understanding of what we are for, we always already have language. This language is itself the creation of all the ways in which we have come to understanding with each other in the past. It is an inherited *interpretation* of the realities which impinge on us, in terms of our understanding with each other. It is reality so interpreted in inherited language that we mean by "the world."[14]

It is *this* reality over against which each of us has to understand himself, a reality interpreted by the common past understandings in which we *have* understood ourselves. Over against an uninterpreted reality, there would be no decisions to make.[15] Thus our whole history "is taken over 'of itself' in the concrete decision of the individual."[16] In "our" language we begin with an established understanding inherited from earlier agreement, with common understanding that is "self-understood." It is only over against this that "the individual's 'self-understanding' becomes a task and a problem." Indeed, the question of our self-understanding, of our way of dwelling "in a meaningful world," is precisely the question of "whether and how we take over, preserve or dispute the 'self-understood' common understanding given us by tradition."[17]

What usually happens is that my self-understanding is *hidden* under the self-understood. "If it becomes acute, it is because the self-understood has become problematical."[18] And again, it is precisely language which is the possibility of the call that challenges everything that is self-understood, which by opening an interpreted, meaningful world, gives the possibility of decision.[19] Language is always ahead of us in our history, awaiting us where our reality will be fulfilled. In language and only in our language we are future to ourselves, called by what we are not yet. "The true love-poem, for example, does not set limits to love, but projects it before us, without ulterior motives, thus setting it free as a true possibility, in which we are awaited and will perhaps find ourselves."[20] *The word is the call to being.* It calls in time to time.[21]

When the self-understood is thus made problematic, our common understanding in our world is shaken. The achievement of self-understanding occurs, therefore, as the achievement of the *new* language of a *new* common understanding. The question of my existence is whether I question the self-understood interpretation we inherit together—which is to seek new common interpretations, to create new language. The language in which I can understand myself is, therefore, always new language, the language which is my "unique possibility." Just *this* language is what is really bespoken to me by the past as it gives itself to me in the tradition of language.[22]

Thus the alienated man does not properly have a "self-understanding." For he seeks to master time, and so does not wish new language.[23] Only the "believer," who understands exactly that the meaning of the past is the possibility of true self-understanding, of a language *new* over against the past and its self-understood interpretations, understands him*self*.[24]

Truth is what is said in the always new language of self-understanding; it is the utterance in which we challenge each other to self-understanding, yet do this in *language,* in words that can be understood because with them we can talk about our shared world. The truth is what is said when what comes "of itself" to us from the past—the "self-understood"—is exactly the new language of openness to the future.[25] "Faith . . . follows the inner tendency of language itself to grasp the truth in that new word which puts it up to . . . man . . . to become himself. . . . What thus seeks to build itself is the language of self-understanding."[26]

So we arrive at the concept of being. "Being is the possibility—which addresses itself to us in the truth—of what 'of itself' makes what we call 'existence' possible for us."[27] Being is the possibility of what is both just there, inherited without question from the past, and yet opens a life lived into the future in question and decision.[28] "Being is . . . the place of our original unity, where each thing appears as itself of itself."[29]

This something that can without our decision free us for decision is "speech 'about' something 'to' someone."[30] It is speech which can be "about" our world because we share a common unquestioned inherited language, yet is speech of mutual challenge. Being is the possibility of such language. We are clearly following Fuchs' intention if we say: "I am" means "I have the possibility of so speaking and being bespoken."

Time is this possibility. There is no logically necessary connection between the concepts of time and being; had we been timeless beings our existence would be otherwise grounded. But the contingent truth about being is: "There is time. There was time. There will be time." The "there" in these three sentences is the pointer to being. Therefore *true* being occurs as "Decision, Remembrance and Expectation."[31] To "be in the truth" is to be able to decide, remember and expect.

Therefore also the question of what I am, or what is the same, of what I now understand that I am to be, is the question of what I have to say for myself. The question is what word I have, when my life is at stake; better, the question is whether I have *any* word equal to this situation. To understand myself is to know when I am to speak.[32]

If we could sustain this "harmony" of our given selves and our true selves, if we could sustain the question after ourselves as an utterance in new language, we would not need to have the truth *communicated* to us. But we do not.[33] We do not hold onto the ever-new word of faith.[34] We can speak the language of self-understanding only if it is spoken independently of us and is communicated to us. We can speak new language if it has been spoken in history so as to be always there as one of the items in the tradition, ready always to be communicated to us afresh.[35]

We should note what has happened in this last reflection. The new language of self-understanding must, it is said, be given not only *by* history but *in* history. For alienated man, the call of given language to speak new language can succeed only if the new language itself *is* a given language. Here is a sort of redoubling of the union of past and future in language. We need a language which is, as it were, *about* what all language *is*.

Moreover, it is apparent what language Fuchs has in mind. "The" language is "christological."[36] The language of self-understanding, in which the "inner tendency of language itself" is fulfilled, is that taught us by the texts about Jesus.[37] "The New Testament makes the 'world' and . . . the self-understood questionable, in that it historically hands on to us that new language, which can unite us in truth": the language of Jesus Christ.[38]

The essential language is the language of love, which provides the *needed* word as we come together in speech. If I have the language of love, I know when to speak and when to keep silent: I understand myself.[39] Love *is* achieved communication.[40] The New Testament instructs us "in the language of Jesus' Cross. This language is indeed the language of *decision,* of self-surrender. . . ." What is given up by those who come to use this language is "the will to found our own existence . . . in the time we ourselves dispose of. Instead, time becomes God's gift."[41] In this language we have freedom from the past, and that is, freedom to say what must be said.[42]

We come to speak the language of love and self-understanding as we build new language in seeking to achieve common understanding with Jesus.[43] What happened with Jesus was that love came to be spoken, and spoken so as to seek to instruct us in this speech.[44] We live *between* our old failed self-understanding and the communication to us of the language which was spoken by and about Jesus. Just this is our salvation.[45] The *historicity* of Jesus means that his language is always there, always ready to be communicated—that we cannot neutralize it into our own given self-understanding.[46] In Jesus' proclamation "the word has created for itself the dynamic of being which is in man's language, and done so even as the historical creation of an historical fact. . . ."[47]

III

Fuchs is altogether right and altogether wrong. We can simply incorporate his analysis. Yet through it all the future to which we are called to live is the eternal future of all the dialectical theologians. We end in the past after all: "History wants to call us *back* . . . to the essential language. . . ." (My emphasis.)[48]

If we want to say instead that history calls us *forward* to the essential language, what alterations must we make to Fuchs' analysis? Only one is needed, but it is central. Instead of saying that time is the possibility of the true word, we must say that the word is the possibility of true time.

The clock time by which we measure space inside our aggrandized present subsists, of course, with or without words. So does that future which is merely that part of this present which lies beyond whatever line we, on a particular occasion and for its purposes, choose to regard as the boundary of "now." The past, present and future of cosmic time are all there for us prior to the word. But if time is historical time, it depends on the word. For the future which is a specific new possibility that challenges and just so grounds the past, and is not merely an unfilled continuation of the past, is there only in a word, in a *promise*. If the future is the fount of time, if anticipation is the ground of remembrance and decision, then the future must have a content other than and independent of the content our present decision gives it as the extension of the remembered past. We must have something to hope for which we would and could hope for no matter what the past or present might be. Such an object of hope must be one that does not itself restore the rule of the past, which can be achieved while remaining future. We have seen that love is such an object. The present point is that only the word can present a future to us as an independent possibility of hope. Thus, also, love *is* communication.

The prior reality of the future is a self-contradiction under all conditions but one: that love is promised. On the one hand, it seems that hope must not be hope for anything specific. For the futurity of the future is exactly its openness, and if we may know what is coming at the last, it seems that all time is put within our present grasp, and just thereby loses is futurity. On the other hand, if hope is not for something specific, the future becomes a mere blank to be filled in as it becomes past, a mere logical possibility for the aggrandizement of a present. The word which promises love overcomes this contradiction. This word is the presence of the future which yet does not bind the future to its present.

Fuchs has worked out how every event of communication is, merely as such, an opening to future new language, given by the tradition of past language. He has also described a particular language which redoubles this relation: the language spoken in the texts about Jesus is new language available as a particular item in history. For alienated man, this redoubling is essential. But Fuchs omits another prior redoubling. The hope of alienated man indeed lives from this double formal and material anchor in the past. But hope, alienated or not, requires a prior anchor in the future, which is also both formal and material. We need not only a language for hoping, but a word *about* the specific object of hope.

All utterance is opening to the future. But only promise *gives* that future. If there is no promise, the way in which the formal structure of the event of communication turns us to the future is but the way in which we confront nothingness.[49] The essential language is the language of Jesus, not just in its formality, but materially as the language which *narrates* the last future. The essential language is the promise of Jesus' love. The gospel is the communication of the story of Jesus, with the claim that this story is about us. As we seek to tell it about ourselves, we come—or do not come—to a way of speaking in which this narrative *can* be about us. Thus the work of the gospel-word is at once its narration and its language-creating challenge, and must be both to be either. If we come to speak in answer to the gospel, we acquire both a narrative of the last future and the language which so interprets reality that we can understand ourselves as having that last future. The essential utterance gives the future both in what it says and the way it says it: it is *promise*.

A promise, we have already said, has to have been made. The material—as well as formal—past historicity of the language of love is thus not merely grace for alienated man. Also Adam before the fall would have been able to live in time only because of a specific promise remembered in his past. The mark of our alienation is the contingent fact that the utterance of the promise was a *crucifixion*, and the promise a promise of sharing the cross. The promise creates the future, not the future the promise. The future is simply "that reality in which the promise fulfills itself and comes to rest. . . ."[50] Therefore the word is prior to time, if indeed time is historical time. Our existence is temporal self-transcendence because we are addressed, because we live in communication, not the other way around. To live in time is to hope, and the call to the future is the ground of hope.[51]

IV

Therefore communication is being. To be is to be addressed. I am in that I am addressed and respond. And to the question "What am I?" the answer must be a description of my conversation: the answer will be repetition of the word to which I hearken and analysis of the temporality it evokes.

But we are concerned with God, not with being. Nor do we now intend to derive a doctrine of God, by analogy, from an independent analysis of being-in-general. Rather, if the doctrine of being we have developed is true, it is a consequence of the gospel's use of the word "God."

God is an utterance. He occurs as the utterance of one man to another—in English or Swahili or Greek—which in what it says and how it says it creates communication, creates the possibility of temporality: God is the utterance that creates being. He is therefore neither above nor within us; he occurs *between us*. We seek our being in the communication between us—and we have our being to seek from God.

God is the communication that creates our communication—as the possibility of history. God is the word to which all other words respond. God's transcendence, we said, is his insurpassable futurity. That is to say, God is the word whose future-opening utterance does not depend on a prior word, on a language which would subsist even were this word not spoken. The word which God is does not depend on some other word already having been spoken to create the language now used. The language in which God is uttered and which he presupposes is always and only the new language which that utterance seeks as its future. We may put it so: the futurity of God is that the distinction of language and utterance does not apply to him. An utterance which utters its own language is a word whose futurity cannot be overtaken.

The utterance that God is, is the gospel, the story of Jesus addressed by one man to another as their mutual personal address, as their mutual possibility of true temporality. But not only believers live between future and past. Whenever one man calls another out of what he is toward what he is not yet—i.e., whenever one man makes another hearken, God is speaking.

Every utterance is a demand upon the one to whom it is addressed. The demands which life makes upon us are thus endlessly varied, contradictory, and above all never-ending. Thus, in the end, one demand is made in all the utterances of life: that we open to the future—the anonymous future. The God who bespeaks himself to us in all the communication of life, merely by the temporal structure of utterance, is the hidden God whose existence for us is naked empty demand.

The judgment of the gospel is that our response to the address of life is prayer and praise—or perhaps defiance—to the God of religion. The God of religion lives exactly as this conversation between the hidden God and hiding man. Over against this response, and the idols created in it, the communication of life becomes judgment and condemnation: the word that tells us we have no future, or rather that we have the endless past of death as our future. The gospel makes this word its own, and so claims the hidden God as its own speaker. But although the gospel makes this condemnation its own, it is itself the justification of those it thus agrees are ungodly.

Thus God occurs as the polemic of the word of the future against our prayer and praise to the God we create to defend us against the future's hiddenness. Following Barth, we can say that God could utter himself otherwise, but that the surprising fact of grace is that he utters himself so. God might have spoken himself without, or past, or against us. But in fact he speaks himself against our self-condemnation: he occurs as the word of forgiveness.

V

As is obvious, this conception of God is trinitarian. Indeed, it is perhaps but a drastic statement of the sense of Barth's doctrine. For if indeed "the point of all that happens in revelation . . . is that God speaks as an 'I' and is heard by the 'you' he addresses . . . ,"[52] and if what the doctrine of the Trinity has to say is that God in himself is the formal pattern of his revealing action, must this not mean that God is the address of an "I" to a "you"? If the event of Jesus is God's interpretation of himself both to us and to himself, and if in fact the Son *is* Jesus, then the innertrinitarian active relations which are the being of God must be precisely this event of *interpretation*—must be a "word-event."[53]

As Father, Son and Spirit, God is "I" and "You" in himself. He is that reality of a person in his communication who needs no *other* person to occur. God is for himself Speaker and Hearer, Address and Response. He is, if one likes, a *Conversation*—the conversation which is complete in itself and of which all other being is side-conversation. God is in fact the conversation in which the promise of love is made to us, and in which we respond by asserting our lovelessness. But this Conversation does not need us to occur: God as triune is free. In the conversation which in fact takes place, this freedom is spoken by the way in which the word of love is "nevertheless" to our rejection of it. As the triune word, God is the word of the justification of the ungodly.

Let us try now to put the trinitarian doctrine itself in the terms suggested by our final discussions—acknowledging the speculative character of the attempt, and the dangers of speculation. God is in himself Spirit, Father and Son: Future, Past and Present. That is, he is in himself Self-understanding, Language and Utterance—remembering that self-understanding is also a communication-event, and using "language" is the sense of presupposed past utterance. He is insurpassably future because the givenness of the possibility of his utterance is no other God than the new language toward which he utters himself, because the Father and the Spirit are the one God.

Though it might have been otherwise, the presupposed utterance (the Father) is the hidden God's judgment of our clinging to the past. Though it might have been otherwise, God's utterance itself (the Son) is the event of Jesus *as* his story is told again and again in antiphony with the ever-new apprehension of judgment. The reality of this antiphony is God's opening, for us and for himself, to the future identity of judgment and acceptance, wrath and favor (the Spirit), which we call "love" and in which God will be God and we will live thereby. God's Trinity is the plot of the conversation which embraces in its living exchange all the suffering conflicts of past and future. Only the triune Word is the God of what is and what is to be.

This is why, finally, God is both deed and doer, word and speaker, why we call him an "utterance" yet speak of him as "he." As triune, he *is* the achievement of the unity of the conflicting words which drive apart our past and future, and make us dream of timeless and immune "selves" to save our identity. Thus *God* needs no *such* "self"; he needs no other substantiality than the sure hope that he will as the End be no other communication than he has been as the Beginning. What he has begun is, contingently, a conversation that includes us. The hope that God is for himself is, therefore, the achievement of the justifying word to the ungodly. The resurrection, between crucifixion and coming, is the enactment of that hope, its telling the word of God.

The resurrection has been proclaimed also to us. Therefore, we too are called to hope that we will hear at the End the same word that was spoken in Jesus, hear it as the final reply that will incorporate all our answers, good and bad, into the language of self-understanding in love. This hope is our knowledge of the substantiality of God.

VI

God is the first and last word, the call we have always already heard and will hear as the conclusion. He is the event of the address whose gift and attaining of self-understanding is perfectly free from and for its own past. Therefore he is achieved temporal self-transcendence. Therefore he is the call *between* whose past and future we may and do live.

God is the first word, the Creator. He is the Utterance that begins the conversation in which all things come to be, that begins the splendidly and intricately ramified communication that is our being and the being of our world. All our communication presupposes language, and language presupposes past communication. The givenness of language is the mystery and presupposition of all that we will be and are, and of the fact that we are anything at all. God is this mystery and presupposition, as the Call that calls forth all things, as the Utterance who presupposes no other utterance than himself. This is not an attempt at a "proof" of God's reality, for that "communication" in the sense used here occurs at all is but a corollary of the self-interpretation enforced on us by the gospel.

We "appropriate" creation to the Father. For the *givenness* of language, of cultural tradition as such, in which communication is always newly possible, is the locus of the teaching of creation. God is the enabling word, of his own futurity and—as he has in fact bespoken himself—of ours.

God is the last word, the Fulfiller. He is the Utterance in which all our conversation will come to its meaning. We must now amend an earlier statement. In hearing and repeating the story of Christ, we do not simply acquire the language in which we may tell this story of love as a story about ourselves. Rather, we come to *hope for* such language. What we await is that we will become able to be told and tell to each other the manifold story of our life in this world as one story with the narrative of Jesus' self-giving unto death—and so exist with and for each other as a communication of ourselves as love. We wait to hear "Come unto me," as the word with endless future but no not-yet. God will be that Word.

Therefore God is the present word. We live, "move and have our being" *in* his utterance; he is the future and past call which gives us time, and so gives us the present moment. That is, he goes with us as the word of Jesus Christ, as the present reality of the speaking from one to another of the concrete tale of hope.

VII

God is the occurrence of the word in which Jesus' crucifixion and resurrection is our last future, i.e., he is triune. Whether this identification and concept of God is that to which we are called after the *Commentary on Romans,* after the self-destruction of the God of past history, someone else must judge. And what about Karl Barth? In saying this have I merely repeated what he had already gone on to say? Have I perverted it? Or have we made a step toward the future transformation in which his theology—as that of every theologian—will be fulfilled by being redone? Even this someone else must judge.

NOTES—Chapter One

1. *Commentary on Romans*, p. 13.
2. Ibid., p. 12.
3. Ibid., p. 16.
4. Ibid., pp. 95-6.
5. Ibid., p. 7.
6. Ibid., p. 72.
7. Ibid., p. 132.
8. Ibid., p. 14.
9. Ibid., p. 84.
10. Ibid., p. 129.
11. Ibid., p. 388.
12. For all points of information about Barth there is a sort of Barth-encyclopedia: Henri Bouillard, *Karl Barth*.
13. E.g., Nels Ferre in the *Christian Century* for December 26, 1962: Barth "isolated transcendence, removing it from man's general knowledge and concerns. . . ." Or again, Schubert Ogden, *The Reality of God*, p. 5: "Especially through the influence of Barth's later work in *Die Kirkliche Dogmatik*, the theological task came to be received as entailing a radical separation of Christian faith and modern culture." The first step toward understanding Barth is to grasp that this is the precise and compendious opposite of the case.
14. See below, 24ff.
15. For a thorough if sometimes labored analysis of the *Commentary on Romans* and the rest of Barth's early theology, exactly from the viewpoint of the relation of time and eternity, see Tjarko Stadtland, *Eschatologie und Geschichte in der Theologie des jungen Karl Barth*.
16. Ibid., XIII.
17. Ibid., p. 95.
18. Ibid., p. 66.
19. E.g., ibid., p. 143.
20. Ibid., p. 6.
21. Ibid., p. 5.
22. Ibid., p. 12.
23. Ibid., p. 32.
24. Ibid., p. 32.
25. Ibid., p. 350.
26. Ibid., p. 207.
27. Ibid., p. 162.
28. Ibid., p. 85.
29. Ibid., p. 316.
30. Ibid., p. 220.
31. Ibid., p. 259.
32. Ibid., p. 137.
33. Ibid., p. 222.
34. Ibid., p. 112.
35. Ibid., p. 112.
36. Ibid., p. 226.
37. Ibid., p. 20.
38. Ibid., p. 228.
39. Ibid., p. 390.
40. Ibid., p. 235.
41. Ibid., p. 218.
42. Ibid., p. 20.
43. Ibid., pp. 163ff.
44. Ibid., p. 170.
45. Ibid., p. 218.
46. Ibid., p. 228.
47. Ibid., p. 112.

48. Ibid., pp. 215f.
49. Ibid., p. 165.
50. Ibid., p. 352.
51. Parmenides, Fragment 1.
52. Fragment 2.
53. Fragment 3.
54. Fragment 8.
55. Fragment 8, lines 50ff.
56. This whole side of Plato is best discussed by Paul Friedlander, *Plato*.
57. Bekker ed., vol. V, p. 74.
58. V, p. 88.
59. See esp. Werner Marx, *The Meaning of Aristotle's Ontology*, pp. 9ff., 63f.
60. τὸ τί ἦν εἶναι, *Metaphysics*, 1029b.
61. *Metaphysics*, 1051b, 29f.
62. *Metaphysics*, 10726. For sudden understanding of the point of Aristotle's theology, I am indebted to H. G. Gadamer's lectures at Heidelberg in the spring of 1965.
63. Ibid., p. 71.
64. Ibid., p. 22.
65. Ibid., p. 83.
66. Ibid., p. 51.
67. Ibid., p. 91.
68. Ibid., p. 51.
69. Ibid., p. 82.
70. Ibid., p. 70.
71. Ibid., p. 81.
72. Ibid., p. 70.
73. Ibid., p. 70.
74. Ibid., p. 183.
75. Ibid., p. 137.
76. Ibid., p. 82.
77. Ibid., p. 220.
78. Ibid., p. 221.
79. Ibid., p. 276.
80. Ibid., p. 286.
81. Ibid., p. 286.
82. Ibid., p. 212.
83. Ibid., p. 26.
84. Ibid., p. 25.
85. Ibid., p. 286.
86. Ibid., p. 16.
87. Ibid., p. 213.
88. Ibid., p. 315.
89. Ibid., p. 26.
90. Ibid., p. 286.
91. Ibid., p. 23.
92. Ibid., p. 32.
93. Ibid., p. 177.
94. Ibid., p. 17.
95. *Romans* 5.
96. *Isaiah* 44: 18-19.
97. *Jeremiah* 31: 31-2.
98. See Gerhard von Rad, *Theologie des Alten Testaments*, vol. II., pp. 271ff., and passim.
99. To all this see the standard "Jesus-books" by Dibelius, Bultmann and Bornkamm.
100. Kirchliche Dogmatik (hereafter cited as) KD, III/2, pp. 189.
101. To the whole following discussion of Origen, see: Robert Jenson, *The Knowledge of Things Hoped For*, passim. There also bibliography.
102. *Fragments to John*, XIII.
103. *Commentary on John*, XXII, 29.

104. Ibid., I, 7.
105. *First Principles,* IV, 2, 6.
106. *Commentary on John,* V, 4.
107. *Confessions,* I, I.
108. Ibid., XIII, I.
109. Ibid., VII, IX.

NOTES—Chapter Two

1. *Commentary on Romans,* p. 229.
2. Ibid., pp. 229f.
3. Ibid., p. 145.
4. Ibid., p. 230.
5. Ibid., p. 40.
6. Ibid., p. 105.
7. Ibid., p. 236.
8. Ibid., pp. 224-6.
9. Ibid., p. 225.
10. Ibid., p. 235.
11. Ibid., p. 238.
12. Ibid., p. 250.
13. Ibid., p. 52.
14. Ibid., p. 147.
15. Ibid., p. 88.
16. Ibid., p. 263.
17. Ibid., p. 156.
18. Ibid., p. 203.
19. Ibid., p. 88.
20. Ibid., p. 280.
21. Ibid., p. 129.
22. Ibid., p. 271.
23. Ibid., p. 271.
24. Ibid., p. 216.
25. Ibid., p. 51.
26. Ibid., p. 65.
27. Ibid., p. 143.
28. Ibid., p. 143.
29. Ibid., p. 280.
30. Ibid., p. 305.
31. Ibid., p. 105.
32. Ibid., p. 105.
33. Ibid., p. 5.
34. Ibid., p. 58.
35. Ibid., p. 248.
36. Ibid., p. 363.
37. Ibid., p. 115.
38. Ibid., p. 118.
39. Ibid., p. 39.
40. Ibid., p. 114.
41. Ibid., pp. 159f.
42. Ibid., p. 407.
43. Ibid., pp. 334-7.
44. Ibid., p. 307.
45. Ibid., p. 267.
46. Ibid., p. 149.
47. Ibid., p. 342.
48. Ibid., p. 333.
49. Ibid., p. 332.
50. Ibid., pp. 267f.
51. Ibid., p. 343.

52. Ibid., p. 154.
53. Ibid., p. 305.
54. Ibid., p. 50.
55. Ibid., p. 170.
56. Ibid., p. 105.
57. Ibid., p. 163.
58. Ibid., p. 71.
59. Ibid., p. 281.
60. Ibid., p. 3.
61. Ibid., p. 258.
62. Ibid., p. 96.
63. Ibid., p. 278.
64. Cf. Stadtland, pp. 98, 116.
65. *Commentary on Romans*, p. 294.
66. Ibid., p. 322.
67. Ibid., p. 175.
68. Ibid., p. 311.
69. Ibid., pp. 200-6.
70. Ibid., p. 369.
71. Cf. Stadtland, pp. 98, 116.
72. My list of suggested accounts in the current sociological style is the same as anyone's: Peter Berger, *The Noise of Solemn Assemblies;* Gibson Winter, *The Suburban Captivity of the Church;* Thomas Luckmann, *The Invisible Religion.*
73. Luckmann, p. 108.
74. Cf. Luckmann, pp. 50-106.
75. *Encyclopädie der philosophischen Wissenchaften,* here cited from Berlin edition of 1840, vol. VI, pp. 310f.
76. Ibid., pp. 19f.
77. *Phänomenologie des Geistes,* here cited from edition of 1948, pp. 414ff., 420ff.
78. *Encyclopädie,* VI, pp. 59ff.
79. Ibid., VI, pp. 151ff.
80. Ibid., VI, p. 14.
81. Ibid., VI, pp. 44, 49, 63.
82. Ibid., VI, p. 413.
83. E.g., ibid., VI, pp. 47, 408
84. Ibid., VI, p. 63.
85. Ibid., VI, p. 49.
86. Even the motive for *dialectical* thinking is much the same in both. Cf. Stadtland, pp. 60-4.
87. *After Auschwitz,* p. 153.
88. Ibid., pp. 52, 58, 204, 227.
89. And even more remarkable that Rubenstein does not seem to have noticed this. Cf. Gerhard von Rad, *Theologie des alten Testaments,* I, pp. 451ff.
90. Ibid., p. 135.
91. Ibid., p. 20.
92. Ibid., p. 154.
93. Ibid., p. 141.
94. Ibid., p. 67.
95. Ibid., p. 154.
96. *Commentary on Romans,* pp. 97, 102, 136, 148, 186f., 370.
97. *After Auschwitz,* p. 198.
98. Ibid., p. 220. More on Rubenstein, pp. 51-57.

NOTES—Chapter Three

1. *Commentary on Romans,* p. 283.
2. William Hamilton seems, a few years ago, not to have stopped to think through the way in which a polemical concept works. Surely, if he had, he

would not have permitted himself to say: "Barth defines religion, in his attack on it, as something like man's arrogant and grasping attempt to become God, so it is hard to see what all the posturing is about. If by definition religion equals sin, and you then say revelation ought to be against religion . . . , you have not forwarded theological clarity very much." *Radical Theology and the Death of God*, with Thomas Altizer, p. 39. What Barth's concept of religion does is to enable us to see that *in fact* what we have always called "religion" *is* an attempt to be more like God. Moreover, it would be quite in order to object to a polemic use of "religion," or to object to Barth's particular use and propose another. But to do the latter, one must propose a different polemic use of "religion" and not simply reproduce Barth's, which is in fact what Hamilton does.
3. The best starting point on Bonhoeffer is now Heinrich Ott, *Wirklichkeit und Glaube*, vol. I, despite a slightly tendentious interpretation.
4. *Widerstand und Ergebung*, p. 137.
5. Ibid., p. 136.
6. Ibid., pp. 134f.
7. Ibid., p. 178.
8. Ibid., p. 93
9. Ibid., p. 135.
10. Ibid., pp. 136f.
11. Ibid., p. 136.
12. Ibid., p. 133.
13. Remarks like the following are unduly self-congratulatory: "An ironic dilemma of contemporary theology derives from its increasing insistence that Christianity both transcends and negates religion even while theology refuses to open itself to an understanding of the actual nature or the historical phenomenon of religion. The persistent calls for a 'religionless Christianity' can have little meaning so long as religion is conceived of as merely a fake righteousness or a shallow pity." *The Gospel of Christian Atheism*, p. 31.
14. Eliade has been important for the background also of the present work. See especially *Cosmos and History*.
15. *The Gospel of Christian Atheism*, p. 34.
16. Ibid., p. 35.
17. Ibid., pp. 35ff.
18. *The Secular City*, p. 1113.
19. This extremely compressed version of Cox's analysis is put together out of pp. 1-13, 38-84 of *The Secular City*.
20. "Welchen Sinn hat es, von Gott zu sprechen?"
21. Robert Jenson, *The Knowledge of Things Hoped For*, pp. 158-201.
22. Cf. Ogden, *The Reality of God*, p. 1: ". . . the reality of God has now become the central theological problem." But it is a mystery how Ogden can go on to say: "The fact remains that for much of the theology of the first half of our century the reality of God was not the one great theme."
23. Cf. the perfectly splendid account of the incompleteness of the Fathers' transformation of the philosophical concept of God by Wolfhart Pannenberg.
24. I have handled this question at length—though not in connection with Barth—in a study devoted to it alone: *Five Words with the Mind*.

NOTES—Chapter Four

1. *After Auschwitz*, p. 153.
2. *Commentary on Romans*, p. 280.
3. A good standard is still Martin Marty, *The New Shape of American Religion*. For a bibliography of evidence, see the notes in Luckmann.
4. *After Auschwitz*, p. 119.
5. Ibid., p. 205.
6. Ibid., p. 76.

7. Ibid., p. 79.
8. Ibid., p. 116.
9. Ibid., p. 78.
10. Ibid., p. 79.
11. Ibid., p. 222.
12. Ibid., pp. 133-5.
13. Ibid., p. 264.
14. Ibid., pp. 259, 264.
15. Ibid., p. 68.
16. The move is exactly that from Hinayana to Mahayana Buddhism.
17. *After Auschwitz*, p. 125.
18. Ibid., p. 139.
19. Ibid., p. 70.
20. Ibid., p. 140.
21. Ibid., pp. 102, 153.
22. Ibid., pp. 1-44.
23. *Radical Theology and the Death of God*, p. 92.
24. Ibid., p. 40.
25. Ibid., pp. 46-8.
26. Ibid., pp. 157-169.
27. Ibid., pp. 48-50.
28. E.g., the recent conversion of the Beatles from drugs to yoga at the hands of a sort of N. V. Peale from northern India, called "the Maharishi."
29. *The Gospel of Christian Atheism*, pp. 31-57.
30. Ibid., pp. 53-61.
31. The literature is endless. For starters, Carl Braaten, *History and Hermeneutics*.
32. *The Gospel of Christian Atheism*, pp. 62-83.
33. Ibid., p. 83.
34. Ibid., p. 73.
35. Ibid., p. 86.
36. Ibid., pp. 89-131.
37. Ibid., p. 45.
38. As I asked in *A Religion Against Itself*.
39. Ibid., pp. 34f.
40. Rubenstein to the contrary, in *After Auschwitz*, pp. 258ff.
41. The title of her chief work is typical: *Christ the Representative, An Essay in Theology after the Death of God*. This work will be cited here from the English edition.
42. *Christ the Representative*, p. 10.
43. Ibid., pp. 11f.
44. Ibid., p. 11.
45. Ibid., pp. 55f.
46. Ibid., pp. 31-8.
47. Ibid., pp. 39-42.
48. Ibid., pp. 43-50.
49. Ibid., pp. 45-7.
50. Ibid., p. 55.
51. Ibid., p. 102.
52. Ibid., pp. 104f.
53. Ibid., pp. 116ff.
54. Ibid., p. 122.
55. Ibid., p. 127.
56. Ibid., p. 124.
57. Ibid., p. 10.
58. Ibid., pp. 130-3.
59. Ibid., pp. 140-2.
60. Ibid., p. 138.
61. Ibid., p. 134.
62. Ibid., p. 143.
63. Ibid., pp. 147f.

64. Ibid., pp. 144, 134f.
65. Ibid., p. 139.

NOTES—Chapter Five

1. For this, see Bouillard, vol. I, pp. 119-160, and Robert Jenson, *Cur Deus Homo?* Heidelberg dissertation, pp. 191-99.
2. *Fides quarens intellectum.*
3. "Schicksal und Idee in der Theologie."
4. For the first clear emergence of this reversal, in its one application as a principle of theological epistemology, see *Fides quarens intellectum*, pp. 65-6, 182, and passim. The most general explicit formulation of the principle is KD IV/3, pp. 45f. For further references in KD see Robert Jenson, *Alpha and Omega*, pp. 112-40.
5. E.g., KD III/2, pp. 188-98, 203.
6. KD II/2, p. 171.
7. E.g., KD IV/1, p. 57. The doctrine that reconciliation of *sinners* is the primary will behind all reality puts us in very deep water indeed. This whole complex was the main subject of my earlier Barth-book, *Alpha and Omega*. See esp. pp. 21-64.
8. E.g., KD II/2, 171-3.
9. See below, pp. 126f.
10. E.g., KD III/2, 109. See also below pp. 129-31.
11. Ibid., p. 116.
12. Ibid., p. 192-7.
13. Ibid., p. 202.
14. Ibid., p. 201.
15. KD II/1, pp. 694ff.
16. KD II/2, pp. 2-6.
17. KD II/2, p. 197. For further references, Jenson, *Alpha and Omega*, pp. 65-84.
18. See below, pp. 130 f.
19. KD II/1, pp. 6-7.
20. Ibid., p. 299.
21. KD III/1, pp. 103-258.
22. Ibid., pp. 260-5.
23. KD III/2, pp. 58, 69.
24. Ibid., p. 158f.
25. KD IV/1, pp. 610f.
26. KD IV/2, pp. 303-5.
27. KD II/2, pp. 564ff.
28. *Christengemeinde und Bürgergemeinde.*
29. Van Buren (*The Secular Meaning of the Gospel*) began as a Barthian.
30. This is the persistent worry of all Roman Catholic commentators on Barth.
31. This is the criticism raised by Gustav Wingren, *Teologiens Metodenfräge.*
32. Barth raises this himself, KD IV/1, pp. 322f.
33. Perhaps one doesn't? William Hamilton is another ex-Barthian.
34. KD IV/2, p. 185.
35. Ibid., pp. 200f.
36. KD IV/3, p. 449.
37. KD III/2, p. 261.
38. Ibid., pp. 344ff.
39. Ibid., pp. 290f.
40. Ibid., p. 269.
41. KD IV/3, pp. 419f.
42. KD II/1, p. 27.
43. KD IV/1, p. 859.
44. *Christengemeinde und Bürgergemeinde.*

45. Fragment 8. τόν σοι ἐγω διάκοσμον. For this interpretation of ἐὀικότα παντα Φατίξω, and for the whole interpretation of Parmenides' poem in terms of analogy and antithesis, I am indebted to Eberhard Jüngel, *Zum Ursprung der Analogie bie Parmenides und Heraklit.* See esp. pp. 14ff., 26ff.
46. *Timaeus,* 28A-29C, 48E-49A, 92C.
47. KD II/1, pp. 252-6.
48. Ibid., p. 256.
49. Ibid., pp. 264f.
50. Ibid., p. 266.
51. One of the very best studies of Barth is Hans Urs von Balthasar, *Karl Barth.* Nevertheless, he is directly and obviously mistaken in his main contention, that there is a turn from dialectic to analogy between the *Commentary on Romans* and Barth's later work. As we have seen, the notion of analogy plays the same role, and just as importantly, in the *Commentary on Romans* as later. And for Barth then and later, just as for Plato, it is only because of the positive relation of time to eternity, called "image" or "analogy," that there can be a dialectic at all. At this point, there has occurred no change whatever in Barth's thinking after 1920.
52. KD II/1, pp. 234f.
53. Ibid., pp. 238f.
54. Ibid., p. 241.
55. Ibid., p. 266.
56. Barth's elaborate attempts to establish such a difference fail: KD II/1, pp. 267-75 and elsewhere.
57. KD II/1, pp. 261, 267. See to this and to the whole following discussion, Eberhard Jüngel, "Die Möglichkeit theologischer Anthropologie auf dem Grund der Analogie. Eine Untersuchung zum Analogieverständnis Karl Barths," *Evangelische Theologie,* 1962, pp. 535-57.
58. KD II/1, pp. 269ff.
59. KD II/2, p. 101. Cf. Jüngel, op. cit., p. 548.
60. KD III/2, p. 269.
61. KD II/1, pp. 256, 261f.

NOTES—Chapter Six

1. E.g., KD II/1, pp. 76f.
2. Ibid., pp. 7-8.
3. Ibid., pp. 8-12.
4. Ibid., p. 9.
5. Ibid., pp. 12, 14.
6. Ibid., p. 14.
7. Ibid., p. 14.
8. Ibid., pp. 21-24.
9. Ibid., pp. 27-9.
10. Ibid., pp. 40-45.
11. Ibid., pp. 16-8.
12. Ibid., pp. 16, 58.
13. Ibid., p. 16.
14. The question is that of the *Bedingung der Möglichkeit.*
15. Above pp. 45f.
16. Ibid., p. 53.
17. Ibid., pp. 51-6.
18. See KD II/1, p. 58, in connection with the passages cited in footnotes above.
19. Ibid., p. 73.
20. Ibid., p. 76.
21. Ibid., p. 77.
22. Ibid., p. 80.
23. Ibid., pp. 80-1.

24. KD I/1, p. 358.
25. Ibid., pp. 358-60. To this discussion cf. Eberhard Jüngel, *Gottes Sein ist im Werden,* pp. 16-36.
26. Ibid., pp. 358-65.
27. Ibid., pp. 358-65.
28. Ibid., pp. 328f., 331f., 333.
29. Ibid., p. 334.
30. KD II/1, pp. 251-75.
31. See especially KD II/1, pp. 86-92, 267-75.
32. E.g., Thomas Aquinas, *Summa theologica* I, 45, 4; I, 19, 2.
33. Ibid., I, 4, 3.
34. Ibid., I, 13, 11.
35. Ibid., I, 5, 3; I, 11, 1; I, 16, 3.
36. See below pp. 155ff.
37. KD II/1, p. 258.
38. Ibid., pp. 231ff.
39. Ibid., p. 266.
40. KD I/1, pp. 332-49.
41. "Is there not in this *nunc aeternitatis,* contrary to all intention, a . . . point from which man gets God in his grasp . . . ? We think also of how . . . faith is described as 'empty space.' Is Barth not insufficiently radical here? We suspect a 'religious experience' here after all, even if a negative one." Stadtland, p. 112. Cf. pp. 11-15.
42. KD II/1, pp. 82-6.
43. Ibid., p. 83.
44. Ibid., p. 93.
45. Ibid., p. 94.
46. Ibid., p. 83.
47. Ibid., p. 100.
48. Ibid., p. 100.
49. Ibid., pp. 141ff.
50. Ibid., p. 143.
51. Ibid., pp. 144f.
52. Ibid., p. 147.
53. Ibid., p. 149.
54. Ibid., pp. 150f.
55. Ibid., p. 181ff.
56. Ibid., p. 162f.
57. Ibid., pp. 164-7.
58. Ibid., pp. 168-173.
59. Ibid., p. 266.
60. Ibid., pp. 172-8.
61. Ibid., pp. 173-8, 180-2, 285f.
62. Ibid.. p. 182-4.
63. Ibid., p. 185.
64. Ibid., p. 189.
65. Ibid., p. 185.
66. Ibid., pp. 182-90.
67. Ibid., p. 189.
68. Ibid., p. 190.
69. Ibid., p. 191.

NOTES—Chapter Seven

1. KD I/1, pp. 311, 17.
2. Ibid., p. 117.
3. Ibid., p. 316f.
4. Ibid., p. 368.

5. See P. E. Strawson, *Individuals*.
6. KD II/1, pp. 288-361.
7. Ibid., pp. 362-764.
8. KD I/1, p. 32.
9. Ibid., p. 329.
10. Ibid., pp. 319, 331, 352.
11. Ibid., pp. 311-3.
12. Ibid., pp. 321f.
13. Ibid., p. 314-5.
14. Ibid., pp. 401f.
15. Ibid., pp. 320-3.
16. Cf. Eberhard Jüngel, *Gottes Sein ist im Werden*, p. 32.
17. KD I/1, pp. 323-4.
18. Ibid., pp. 401f.
19. Ibid., p. 315.
20. Ibid., pp. 402f.
21. Ibid., pp. 332f.
22. Ibid., pp. 333f.
23. Ibid., p. 334.
24. Ibid., pp. 337f.
25. Ibid., p. 338.
26. Ibid., pp. 338f.
27. Ibid., p. 339.
28. Ibid., p. 342.
29. Ibid., p. 341.
30. Ibid., p. 342.
31. Ibid., pp. 342-4.
32. Ibid., pp. 347-50.
33. Ibid., pp. 350f.
34. Ibid., p. 350.
35. Ibid., p. 431.
36. Ibid., p. 430.
37. Ibid., p. 408.
38. The doctrine of the Trinity has, therefore, *exactly* the same function for Barth as the distinction between *dass* and *was* for Bultmann. According to Bultmann, it is the fact *that* an event in time is the revelation of God which determines the content of the revelation, not the *what* of that event in time. This is exactly what Barth's doctrine of the Trinity says. And Bultmann makes his stipulation for the same reason, to prevent the "mythology" which must result by trying to read off facts about God from the characteristics of an entity in history. The difference is that this dialectic has become innerchristological for Barth, so that he avoids that other, paralyzing kind of emptiness in our talk about God, which Bultmann, more faithful to the original dialectical theology than Barth, shares with the *Commentary on Romans*.
39. Again the parallel with Bultmann, this time already seen by Jüngel, *Gottes Sein ist im Werden*, pp. 33f.: "The critical polemical function of Barth's doctrine of the Trinity is insufficiently understood. However paradoxical it may sound, Barth has given his doctrine of the Trinity the same function as the program of demythologizing in Rudolph Bultmann's theology. . . . If one sees Bultmann's program as concern for appropriate speech about God . . . , to keep from objectivizing God as an 'it' or a 'he' and bring him to speech as 'Thou' . . . , one will not be able to miss the obvious parallel to the function which Barth gives the doctrine of the Trinity. . . ."
40. KD I/2, p. 60.
41. Jüngel, *Gottes Sein ist im Werden*.
42. KD I/1, p. 315.
43. Ibid., p. 351.
44. Ibid., p. 351. Cf. also p. 401.
45. Ibid., p. 404.

46. Ibid., p. 369.
47. Ibid., p. 369f.
48. Ibid., pp. 371-3.
49. Ibid., p. 373.
50. Ibid., p. 374.
51. τρόπος ὑπαρξέως.
52. Ibid., pp. 374-9.
53. Ibid., p. 379.
54. Ibid., p. 380.
55. Ibid., pp. 381ff.
56. Ibid., p. 382.
57. Ibid., pp. 383ff.
58. Ibid., p. 384.
59. Ibid., p. 386.
60. See further pp. 125f., 192.
61. Cf. Jüngel, *Gottes Sein ist im Werden*, pp. 36ff.
62. KD I/11, 391.
63. Ibid., p. 391.
64. Ibid., pp. 392ff.
65. Ibid., p. 395.
66. Ibid., p. 393.
67. Ibid., p. 395.
68. Ibid., pp. 394f.
69. I owe this insight to Jüngel, *Gottes Sein ist im Werden*, pp. 48-52.
70. The distinction between Jewish and hellenistic experiences of primitive Christianity is, of course, precarious. But the schema can be used, so long as we remember it is a schema.
71. This was first presented and argued by Georg Kretschmar in *Studien zur früchristlichen Trinitätstheologie*, which remains the decisive study. For possible necessary correctives, see the review by Carl Andressen in *Theologische Literaturzeitung*, vol. 84, pp. 82-67.
72. *Contra Eunomium*, Patrologia Graeco-Latina, vol. 45, col. 480.
73. Ibid., col. 484.
74. Ibid., col. 497-500.
75. Ibid., col. 680.
76. Ibid., col. 694f.
77. Ibid., col. 484.
78. Ibid., col. 680f.
79. Ibid., col. 516.
80. Ibid., col. 497/500.
81. Ibid., col. 556.
82. Ibid., col. 495/500, 516.
83. Ibid., col. 484.
84. Ibid., col. 652.
85. Ibid., col. 681.
86. Ibid., col. 488.
87. Ibid., col. 902. Cf. also col. 624.
88. Ibid., col. 902.
89. Ibid., col. 848.
90. Ibid., col. 485/8, 333.
91. Ibid., col. 477.
92. Ibid., col. 684.
93. Ibid., col. 832f.
94. Ibid., col. 821.
95. Ibid., col. 340.
96. Ibid., col. 469.
97. Ibid., col. 425/8.
98. Ibid., col. 692ff.
99. Ibid., col. 897/900.
100. Ibid., col. 900f.

101. Ibid., col. 696.
102. Ibid., col. 773/6.
103. Ibid., col. 405.
104. E.g., ibid., col. 301/9.
105. Ibid., col. 461.
106. Ibid., col. 457/60.
107. Ibid., col. 301ff.
108. Ibid., col. 852.
109. Ibid., col. 341.
110. Ibid., col. 574ff., 793.
111. Ibid., col. 341.
112. Cf. for a fine short summary of the history, Wolfhart Pannenberg, "God," RGG III, col. 1719-21.
113. E.g., ibid., col. 461, 456f., 526.
114. Ibid., col. 368.

NOTES—Chapter Eight

1. KD II/1, p. 292.
2. Ibid., p. 293.
3. The work of E. L. Mascall and Austin Farrar is a stout defense of a useless position.
4. Ibid., p. 300. Cf. p. 293.
5. KD I/1, p. 329.
6. Cf. Jüngel's admirable summaries on pp. 75f. and 107 of *Gottes Sein ist im Werden*.
7. KD II/1, p. 294.
8. Ibid., pp. 295ff.
9. Ibid., p. 296.
10. Ibid., pp. 342ff.
11. Ibid., pp. 230ff.
12. Ibid., pp. 230ff.
13. Ibid., p. 299
14. Ibid., p. 300.
15. Ibid., p. 301.
16. Ibid., p. 304.
17. Ibid., pp. 306, 334.
18. KD III/2, p. 1.
19. Above p. 19.
20. KD II/1, pp. 689ff.
21. Ibid., pp. 685-9.
22. Ibid., p. 690.
23. Ibid., p. 694.
24. Ibid., p. 695.
25. Ibid., p. 695.
26. Ibid., p. 696f.
27. Ibid., pp. 693f.
28. Ibid., p. 687.
29. Ibid., p. 690.
30. Ibid., pp. 398f.
31. Ibid., pp. 687, 689f, 698.
32. Ibid., pp. 685/687.
33. Ibid., p. 685f.
34. Ibid., pp. 687, 689, 693, 721.
35. Ibid., p. 688f.
36. Ibid., pp. 702ff, 709ff.
37. Ibid., pp. 689f.
38. Ibid., p. 308.

39. KD II/1, p. 192.
40. Ibid., pp. 192-8.
41. Ibid., p. 111.
42. Ibid., pp. 109-118, 157.
43. Ibid., p. 112.
44. Ibid., p. 109.
45. KD II/1, p. 705.
46. KD I/2, p. 65.
47. Ibid., pp. 73-6.
48. Ibid., p. 50.
49. KD II/2, p. 105.
50. Ibid., p. 157.
51. Ibid., p. 82.
52. Ibid., p. 108.
53. Ibid., p. 109.
54. Ibid., p. 110.
55. Ibid., p. 109.
56. Ibid., p. 118.
57. Ibid., pp. 123f.
58. Ibid., pp. 129f.
59. Ibid., p. 130.
60. Ibid., pp. 112f.
61. Ibid., p. 113.
62. Ibid., p. 135.
63. For my own part, I *have* said all this, in *A Religion Against Itself*, pp. 27-45.
64. KD II/1, pp. 362-764.
65. Ibid., pp. 368ff.
66. Ibid., pp. 362f.
67. Ibid., pp. 364f., 372.
68. Ibid., pp. 366f.
69. Ibid., p. 367.
70. Ibid., pp. 372ff.
71. Ibid., pp. 383-8.
72. Ibid., p. 391.
73. KD I/1, p. 404.

NOTES—Chapter Nine

1. *The Future of Belief*, p. 15.
2. Ibid., pp. 60-73.
3. Ibid., p. 131.
4. Ibid., pp. 7-51.
5. Ibid., p. 134.
6. Ibid., p. 137.
7. Ibid., p. 134.
8. Ibid., pp. 138f.
9. Ibid., p. 142.
10. Ibid., pp. 144f.
11. Ibid., pp. 153ff.
12. Ibid., p. 170.
13. Ibid., pp. 173f.
14. Ibid., pp. 174f.
15. Ibid., p. 184.
16. Ibid., pp. 175ff.
17. Ibid., p. 200.
18. Ibid., p. 184.
19. Ibid., p. 178.
20. Ibid., p. 180.

21. Ibid., p. 190.
22. Ibid., p. 193.
23. Ibid., p. 194.
24. Ibid., p. 196.
25. Ibid., p. 195.
26. Ibid., pp. 200ff.
27. Ibid., p. 206.
28. Ibid., p. 206.
29. Ibid., p. 213.
30. Ibid., p. 214.
31. Ibid., p. 177.
32. *The Reality of God*, p. 21.
33. Ibid., pp. 7ff.
34. Ibid., pp. 10ff.
35. Ibid., p. 51.
36. Ibid., pp. 48f.
37. Ibid., p. 152.
38. Ibid., pp. 51f.
39. Ibid., p. 49
40. Ibid., p. 50.
41. Ibid., p. 151.
42. Ibid., p. 59.
43. Ibid., pp. 21-42.
44. Ibid., p. 210. See, in general, pp. 206-30.
45. Ibid., p. 173.
46. Ibid., p. 173. The whole of Ogden's *Christ without Myth* is devoted to this argument.
47. Ibid., pp. 170ff.
48. Ibid., p. 172.
49. Ibid., pp. 33f.
50. Ibid., pp. 35-8.
51. Ibid., pp. 42f.
52. Cf. Jenson, "Gott als Antwort" in *Evangelische Theologie,* July, 1967.
53. Ibid., pp. 47f.
54. Ibid., pp. 57f.
55. Ibid., pp. 58f.
56. Ibid., p. 177.
57. Ibid., pp. 60, 178.
58. Ogden himself has not made as full use of Whitehead here as one might have expected from his program.
59. Ibid., pp. 151ff.
60. Ibid., pp. 57f.
61. Ibid., p. 59.
62. E.g., ibid., pp. 149ff.
63. Ibid., p. 154.
64. Ibid., p. 154.
65. Heidegger, *Sein und Zeit,* pp. 262ff.
66. This argument, of course, hits Whitehead and Hartshorne as well as Ogden. I cannot refrain from quoting the remark of a colleague, "The trouble with process theology is that it is such an attractive alternative to Christian faith."
67. It may seem trivial to mention it, but the sheer bulk of the *Church Dogmatics* undoubtedly contributes to this optical phenomenon. Anything expounded at such length will come to seem unreal to the modern eye. Huge tracts of the *Church Dogmatics* merely come across as rhetoric. But so outward a matter cannot be the whole cause.
68. KD I/2, p. 54.
69. Ibid., p. 55.
70. Ibid., p. 57.
71. Ibid., p. 58.
72. Ibid., p. 72.

73. Ibid., pp. 75f.
74. Ibid., pp. 127f.
75. Ibid., p. 73.
76. Ibid., p. 58.
77. Ibid., p. 126.
78. Ibid., p. 127.
79. Ibid., p. 113.
80. To the following, see Jüngel, "Der Möglichkeit theologischer anthropologie . . . .," esp. pp. 532-42.
81. KD III/2, pp. 256-63.
82. Ibid., p. 261.
83. Ibid., p. 262.
84. Cf. Jüngel, pp. 576-51.
85. KD III/1, pp. 378f.
86. Ibid., pp. 400f.

NOTES—Chapter Ten

1. *Luke* 24:31, 36; *John* 20:17, 26ff.
2. *John* 20:17. Cf. *Luke* 24:49.
3. *Matthew* 28:18.
4. *Matthew* 28:19f.; *Luke* 24:47f.; *John* 20:21, 21:15ff.
5. *Matthew* 28:20.
6. *Matthew* 28:16-20.
7. The God of faith is "neither an innerworldly nor an extraworldly God, but the 'God of hope' (*Romans* 15:13), a God with 'futurity as his kind of being' (E. Block) . . . , whom therefore one can have neither in nor over one, but . . . only before one. . . ." Jürgen Moltmann, *Theologie der Hoffnung*, p. 12.
8. Both preserve "the continuity of reality, the future being of which we can already now project as possibility. Hope, threat, and disappointment therefore touch only the existential mode of the realization of future reality, and no more." Gerhard Sauter, *Zukunft und Verheissung*, p. 354.
9. Cf. Heidegger, *Sein und Zeit*, pp. 235ff.
10. Here is the primitive, fundamental insight driving the movement represented by Pannenberg, Moltmann, Braaten and Sauter, which we will discuss on pp. 175-79.
11. Cf. Moltmann, *Evangelische Theologie*, 1963, p. 542. Moltmann himself thinks that future-openness will end—which surely must make his project of a "theology of hope" absurd! Cf. *Theologie der Hoffnung*, p. 177.
12. *I Corinthians* 13:13.
13. "The resurrection of Christ does not mean a possibility in this world and its history, but a new possibility altogether of world, existence and history." Moltmann, *Theologie der Hoffnung*, p. 162. Cf. also pp. 162f., 201.
14. Cf. ibid., p. 206.
15. Cf. Sauter, *Zukunft und Verheissung*, p. 52.
16. Cf. Sauter, p. 367.
17. Wolfhart Pannenberg, *Grundfragen systematischen Theologie*, p. 292.
18. KD I/2, p. 103. Cf. p. 125.
19. Ibid., p. 131.
20. It is this that one always misses in Moltmann's *Theologie der Hoffnung*. But if it is neglected, we will yet find our way back to religion, by way of the future as Altizer has done.
21. Cf. Moltmann, *Theologie der Hoffnung*, pp. 144ff.
22. Cf. Sauter, pp. 198-205.
23. Cf. Moltmann, *Theologie der Hoffnung*, pp. 122-4. But Moltmann has not discovered how to keep hold of God's *pastness*, and so says things like: "Creation is . . . not the given . . . , but its future; it is resurrection and new being." P. 149. Without the "not" this would be a true sentence. But the "not" is false.

24. *Exodus* 3:10.
25. Cf. Moltmann, *Theologie der Hoffnung*, p. 129.
26. Cf. ibid., pp. 179-84, 189-96.
27. Pp. 125f.
28. E.g., Heidegger, *Vom Wesen der Wahrheit*, pp. 14-19. Pages 14-16 of this work make especially obvious that Heidegger's "Seyn" is the secularized Holy Spirit.
29. Cf. Jenson, *Alpha and Omega*, pp. 65-111, 151ff.
30. KD I/2, pp. 222-304.
31. Ibid., I/1, pp. 490-513.
32. *Grundfragen systematischer Theologie*, pp. 265f.
33. Ibid., pp. 23ff.
34. Ibid., p. 24.
35. Ibid., pp. 387-9.
36. Ibid., pp. 146-8.
37. Ibid., pp. 148-50. See the entire essay, "Hermeneutik und Universalgeschichte," pp. 91-122 of this volume.
38. Ibid., p. 68
39. Ibid., pp. 68f., 110, 120f.
40. Ibid., pp. 42ff.
41. *Grundzüge der Christologie*, pp. 54ff.
42. Ibid., pp. 57-61.
43. Ibid., p. 62.
44. Ibid., p. 64.
45. *Grundfragen systematischer Theologie*, pp. 220f.
46. Ibid., p. 138.
47. Ibid., p. 139f.
48. Ibid., p. 139.
49. Ibid., pp. 139f., 150ff.
50. *Grundzüge der Christologie*, p. 129.
51. *Grundfragen systematischer Theologie*, pp. 286-8.
52. Ibid., p. 288.
53. Ibid., p. 393.
54. Ibid., pp. 388f. See the entire essay, *"Die Frage nach Gott,"* pp. 361-86 of this volume.
55. Ibid., pp. 392f.
56. Ibid., p. 391.
57. Ibid., pp. 393.
58. Ibid., p. 393f.
59. Ibid., p. 395f.
60. Ibid., p. 197.
61. Ibid., pp. 73f.
62. Moltmann makes a similar criticism, *Theologie der Hoffnung*, pp. 68f. Is this one of those he has now retracted? *Diskussion über die Theologie der Hoffnung*, p. 22, note 19.

NOTES—Chapter Eleven

1. Cf. P. E. Strawson, *Particulars*, pp. 30ff.
2. Just so thought Aristotle—or what else is an "entelechy"?
3. The fury of the religious against "evolution" is well taken!
4. Heidegger.
5. Hume, Sartre!
6. Ernst Fuchs, *Hermeneutik*, p. 56.
7. E.g., Gerhard Ebeling, with whom Fuchs is always paired: see *Das Wesen des christlichen Glaubens*, pp. 79-89, 178-87. Or see Hans-Gorg Gadamer, *Wahrheit und Methode*, pp. 361-465. But we could also introduce this chapter by a further discussion of the leader of the otherwise diametrically opposed school, Wolfhart Pannenberg.

8. *Hermeneutik*, pp. 268-70.
9. Ibid., p. 155f.
10. Ibid., p. 45.
11. Ibid., pp. 68-70, 130-133. Cf. here and to following *Zum hermeneutischen Problem in der Theologie*, pp. 103f., 128f.
12. *Hermeneutik*, p. 134.
13. Ibid., pp. 124ff.
14. Ibid., p. 135. Cf. also pp. 65-9.
15. Ibid., p. 136.
16. Ibid., p. 65.
17. Ibid., p. 136.
18. Ibid., p. 136.
19. Ibid., pp. 62-72, 133.
20. Ibid., p. 69.
21. Ibid., pp. 71f.
22. Ibid., p. 137.
23. Ibid., pp. 71f.
24. Ibid., pp. 139f.
25. Ibid., p. 142.
26. Ibid., p. 265.
27. Ibid., p. 142.
28. This is pure Heidegger: being is the possibility of the mutual "lightening" of "facticity" and "projection." Being is *faktisches Sein-können*.
29. Ibid., p. 143.
30. Ibid., p. 142.
31. Ibid., p. 192.
32. "Was wird in der Exegese des Neuen Testaments interpretiert?" p. 35. *Beiheft I* of *Zeitschrift für Theologie und Kirche*, pp. 31-48. *Zum hermeneutischen Problem in der Theologie*, pp. 103f.
33. *Hermeneutik*, pp. 144ff. Cf. pp. 64f., 115, 117, 119ff.
34. E.g., ibid., p. 210.
35. Ibid., pp. 146-8. Cf. pp. 116, 125, 153.
36. Ibid., p. 71.
37. Ibid., 265f.
38. Ibid., p. 139.
39. *Zum hermeneutischen Problem in der Theologie*, pp. 103f.
40. "Jesus und der Glaube," pp. 178f. *Zeitschrift für Theologie und Kirche*, 55, 2, pp. 170-84.
41. *Hermeneutik*, p. 189.
42. "Was wird in der Exegese des Neuen Testaments interpretiert?" pp. 35f.
43. Ibid., p. 229.
44. "Jesus und der Glaube," the whole.
45. *Hermeneutik*, p. 189.
46. Ibid., pp. 245f.
47. Ibid., p. 72.
48. *Hermeneutik*, p. 138.
49. Sartre!
50. Moltmann, *Theologie der Hoffnung*, p. 77.
51. Cf. Sauter, pp. 149ff.
52. KD II/1, p. 300.
53. Eberhard Jüngel, for one, has interpreted Barth in just this way. *Gottes Sein ist im Werden*, pp. 12-52, esp. p. 13 footnote. Also "Die Möglichkeit theologischer Anthropologie...," pp. 546-52.

Index

Abraham, 113, 114, 171
Adam, 189
Alcibiades, 12
Alienation, 7, 32, 33, 44, 45, 55, 69, 70, 105, 106, 189
Altizer, Thomas, 44, 58-63, 65
Anath, 56
Angels, 116
Arianism, 117-121
Aristotle, 13, 16, 21, 34, 35, 180
Astarte, 56
Atheism, 46, 60, 87, 147, 169
Augustine, 20, 21, 141

Baal, 55, 56, 118
Baptism, 119
Barth: *Church Dogmatics,* 68, 71, 72, 87, 97, 152, 155, 174, 179, 208[N67]; *Commentary on Romans,* 3-8, 10, 11, 13, 16, 23, 24, 27-31, 34, 35, 37-41, 44, 45, 48, 51-53, 55, 57, 58, 60, 61, 65-68, 71, 74, 76-78, 83, 86, 89, 95, 107, 146, 147, 152, 160, 193, 202[N51], 204[N38]; *Letter to the Romans,* 9, 11; *See Also* God: interpretations: Barth; Jesus Christ: Interpretations: Barth; Religion: Interpretations: Barth; Trinity; Interpretations: Barth
"Barthianism," 4, 6, 72
Beauty, 12, 58

Being (concept of), 77, 85, 86, 172, 180-186, 189-191
Bible, 5, 6, 20, 37, 51, 57, 79, 83, 101-105, 107-109, 164, 173, 175, 177; Ecclesiastes, 36; New Testament, 153, 161, 184, 187; Scriptures, 20, 21, 95, 99, 101, 104, 105, 108, 146
Blake, William, 59, 60
Bonhoeffer, Dietrich, 41-43, 45, 51, 57, 58
Buddha, 79
Buddhism, 51, 56
Bultmann, Rudolph, 45, 61, 126, 146, 147, 204[N38], 204[N39]

Catholic theology, 8, 139, 145
Christian religion, 3, 5, 6, 8, 9, 14, 19-23, 25, 30-35, 39-48, 51-54, 57, 59, 60, 62, 68, 70, 71, 73, 96, 109, 116, 117, 121, 122, 139, 140, 182, 199[N13]; and God, 7, 8, 10, 11, 29, 113-118, 124, 127, 140, 141; and Judaism, 55, 56
Christology, 77, 78, 89, 154
"Christomonist," 68
Church; *see* Religion; Theology
Communication; *see* Language
Communism, 123; *see also* Marx, Karl
Cox, Harvey, 44, 45
Creation, 72, 165, 168, 193, 209[N23]

213

Crucifixion; *see* Jesus Christ: death (crucifixion)
Cyrus, 104

Dagon, 118
Daniel, 168
Death, 14, 17, 18, 30, 37, 38, 41, 42, 73, 106, 174, 176, 179; and damnation, 170; and eternity, 9, 38; and future, 54, 164, 171, 191; and resurrection, 165; and salvation, 11-13; division between man and God, 8, 14, 25; *see also* God: death of; Jesus Christ: death (crucifixion)
Dewart, Leslie, 139-146, 151
"Dipolar" theism, 149, 151, 166

Ecumenical movement, 32
Eros, 12, 13, 15, 16, 19, 20, 25, 114, 115, 118, 119; *see also* Love
Eternity, 30, 32, 38, 44, 52, 67, 86, 118; Abstract eternity, 53, 71; and time, 8-17, 19, 20, 22, 24-29, 33, 40, 47, 53, 56, 69-78, 96, 127, 128, 130, 147, 152-154, 171; as reality, 11-13, 130-132; knowledge of, 55; *see also* God: and eternity; Future: and eternity
Eunomius, 118-120
Eve, 24
Evolution, 181
Existentialism, 11, 57, 58, 81, 87, 147, 149, 173, 184

Faith, 4, 5, 7, 14, 30-32, 35, 37, 39, 44, 47, 52, 56-59, 61, 68, 72, 75, 89, 108, 119-121, 147, 162, 182, 186, 187; and God, 11, 46, 47, 60, 145, 147, 166, 169, 173, 209[N7]; and hope and love, 161; and religion, 7, 8, 19, 40-43, 46, 56, 68, 71, 79, 91, 168
Feuerbach, Ludwig, 32, 33, 35

Freedom, 34, 35, 62, 115, 172, 177, 182; and God, 135, 153, 155, 159, 174, 191; and reality, 34, 35; from the past, 17, 167, 182, 187; of history, 143; of the future, 183
Freud, Sigmund, 58
Fuchs, Ernst, 183, 184, 186-189
Future, 61, 62, 77, 189; and eternity, 31, 87, 91; and history, 176, 177; and language, 185, 188-190; and past, 16-18, 29, 36, 46, 47, 62, 63, 128, 129, 132, 133, 143, 148-150, 159, 162, 166-171, 174, 179, 182-193, 209[N8]; and present, 18, 19, 55, 128, 129, 148, 160-162, 165-167, 169, 177, 180, 181, 188, 193; *see also* God: and the future; Jesus Christ and the future

God: the Father, 20, 70, 72-74, 80, 82, 86, 89, 103, 104, 106-113, 117-119, 124, 128-132, 135, 145, 149, 155, 158, 159, 169, 173, 174, 191-193; The Son, 10, 70, 73, 74, 82, 84, 86, 89, 103, 104, 108-113, 116-119, 121, 122, 124, 128-132, 135, 145, 149, 155, 173, 174, 184, 191, 192; the Holy Spirit, 82, 108-113, 116-119, 121, 122, 125, 126, 128-131, 135, 145, 149, 173, 174, 191, 192
God: and communication, 190-192; and the devil, 182; and eternity, 9, 20, 24, 26-30, 46, 69, 99, 119-122, 128, 130, 132, 143, 145, 149-155, 157, 171; and the future, 13, 16-18, 30, 62, 65, 96, 119, 126, 128-130, 144, 149, 157, 159, 162, 163, 165-169, 171-175, 177-179, 190-193, 209[N7]; and history, 8, 28, 29, 37, 51, 55, 60, 61, 72, 103, 113, 114, 126, 127, 168, 171, 172, 175-178; and lan-

214

God: and communication,—*cont.* guage, 190-193; and Jesus Christ, 4, 7, 9, 14, 17, 26, 28, 38, 52, 58, 59, 64, 65, 69-74, 76-78, 80, 82-84, 86, 88-90, 95, 97-99, 103-107, 114-116, 119, 121, 124-126, 128-131, 144, 145, 147, 150-155, 157, 162, 169, 170, 176, 177, 190-193; and man, 3, 4, 6-10, 14-17, 20, 21, 24-27, 29, 30, 38, 40, 52, 53, 64, 69-75, 77, 78, 80-85, 87-92, 100, 101, 103-106, 108, 114-116, 118-121, 126, 130-133, 141-144, 146-153, 155, 172, 177, 179, 182, 199^{N2}; and the past, 13, 128-130, 149, 157, 166-169, 171, 173, 174, 191, 192, 209^{N23}; and the present, 13, 128-130, 141, 143, 149, 153, 171, 191; and time, 13, 28, 48, 127-129, 141, 143-145, 147, 151-153, 155, 162, 168, 169, 187

God: attributes of; *see* God: identification

God: death of, 36, 60-63, 65, 66, 96, 171; *see also* Death; Jesus Christ: death (crucifixion)

God: definition of; *see* God: identification

God: deity of, 27, 119, 155, 177

God: identification, 15, 46-48, 62, 65, 97-100, 108, 118-132, 144; attributes of God, 133-135, 145, 146, 171; definition of God, 29, 30, 115, 120, 125, 140-146, 148, 173, 177; as Lord, 96, 101-103, 105-109, 169, as Creator, 24, 69, 72, 85, 168, 192, 193, 209^{N23}; as a person, 126, 127; as negation of the creature, 3, 37; as Presence, 16, 35; as antireligious, 95, 97; as ungodly, 16

God: interpretations: Barth, 3-11, 13-16, 19, 28-31, 37, 38, 45-48, 67-74, 77-92,

God: interpretations:—*cont.* Barth—*cont.* 95-99, 101-113, 121, 123-135, 151-157, 170, 173, 174, 191, 193, 203^{N41}, 204^{N38}, 204^{N39};

Altizer, 58-62; Aristotle, 13, 21, 35; Augustine, 20, 21, 141; Bonhoeffer, 41, 42, 51; Bultmann, 45, 126; Dewart, 139-145; Eunomius, 118-120; Fuchs, 187, 189; Gregory, 117-121; Hamilton, 57, 58; Hegel, 35; Ogden, 145-151; Origen, 20, 117; Pannenberg, 175-179; Plato, 15, Rubenstein, 36-38, 51, 62, 63; Sölle, 63-65

God: Kingdom of God, 6, 10, 17, 70, 73, 143, 158, 176, 177

God: knowledge of, 14, 20, 26, 30, 81-83, 87-91, 99-101, 107, 117, 118, 134, 139, 144, 177

God: Meaning of; *see* God: identification

God: nature of, 98, 118-120, 127, 141, 171

God: objectivity of, 80-82

God: of past history, 22, 23, 31, 33, 35-37, 54, 61, 95, 145, 178; death of God of past history, 135, 174, 193

God: of religion, 9, 37, 46, 80, 101, 113, 114, 135, 169, 170, 190

God: reality of, 8, 17, 27, 83, 115, 148, 149, 169, 175, 192, 193

God: revelation of, 4, 9, 99-108, 111, 112, 119, 125, 147, 152, 153, 158, 159, 176, 177, 191; *see also* Revelation

God: unity of, 102, 108-110

God; *see also* Freedom: and God; Faith and God; Hope: God of; Love: God's Love; Trinity (of God)

Gospel, 8, 10, 22, 23, 30, 31, 45-47, 55, 61-63, 71, 118, 120-122, 132, 143, 145, 151, 157, 158, 160-163, 165, 167, 174, 182, 190, 191, 193; and the future, 53, 165, 169, 184; and religion, 51, 52, 57, 62; history of, 96, 177; story of Jesus, 183, 189
Grace, 9, 10, 21, 78, 88, 119, 191
Greek religion, 47, 51, 120, 140, 141, 143
Gregory of Nyssa, 117-121
Guilt, 22, 36, 42, 55, 174

Hamilton, William, 57, 58
Harnack, Adolf von, 5
Hartshorne, Charles, 147, 208^{N66}
Heaven; *see* God: Kingdom of God
Hegal, Georg Wilhelm, 34, 35, 59-61, 104, 122
Heidegger, Martin, 150
Hell, 45
Hellenic religion, 19, 115, 139, 141-145, 205^{N70}
Hermann, 5
Hinduism, 51
Holy Spirit; *see* God: the Holy Spirit
Hope, 17, 61, 160, 164, 174, 179; and the future, 165, 166, 168, 170, 177, 188; and the present, 166, 168; faith, hope and love, 161, 162; God of, 168, 170, 209^{N7}; language of, 189, 193
Human nature, 181, 182

Idolatry, 118
India: religions of, 55, 110
Isaac, 113, 114
Isaiah, 172
Islam, 110
Israel, 16, 17, 22, 36, 37, 56, 132, 158, 168, 170, 171, 175; *see also* Judaism

Jacob, 113
Jahweh (Jahveh) (Jahve), 16, 56, 98, 114

Jeremiah, 27
Jesus Christ, 4, 5, 7, 9, 10, 14, 19, 20, 26, 30-32, 38, 42, 43, 46, 58-64, 68-70, 81, 105, 152, 167, 176, 183, 184, 187; and the future, 62, 161-163, 166, 176, 183; appearances after resurrection, 158, 159, 162, 164, 166, 170; Barth's interpretation, 4, 5, 7, 9, 14, 38, 68-78, 104, 131, 132; death (crucifixion), 10, 17, 18, 38, 70, 75, 106, 119, 130, 132, 157, 160-164, 166, 170-172, 174, 179, 183, 189, 192, 193; language of, 187, 189, 193; man's identification with, 63, 64, 69, 132; resurrection, 8, 17, 18, 31, 75, 106, 130, 150, 153, 157-167, 170, 176, 192, 209^{N13}; *see also* God: the Son; Love: Jesus's love
John, 114
Judaism, 16, 51, 53-56, 114, 116, 117, 176, 205^{N70}; *see also* Israel
Justice, 11, 12, 58

Kierkegaard, Søren, 8

Language (communications), 182-193
Leary, Timothy, 43
Liberalism, 5, 6, 164
Logos, 20, 21, 131
Love, 17, 62, 169; and faith and hope, 161, 162; and the future, 164, 165; and religion, 57, 58, as language (communication), 187, 188; defined as (God is), 30, 148, 161, 163, 164, 174; God's love, 127, 134, 135, 142, 147, 171, 174, 191, 192; Jesus' love, 163-165, 168, 187, 189, 193; *see also* Eros
Luke, 158

Marx, Karl, 32-35, 58, 164
Matthew, 158

Metaphysics, 10, 41, 42, 47, 70, 139, 146, 148, 154, 172, 181
Methodism, 41, 42
Michaelangelo, 24
Modalism, 109
Moltmann, Jurgen, 175 209[N11], 209[N23]
Monotheism, 140
Morality, 22, 145, 147, 184
Mortality, 41
Moses, 171
Mythology, 115, 116, 147, 160, 164, 177, 204[N38]

Nature: and religion, 55, 56
Nietzsche, Friedrich, 59
Nihilism, 182

Ogden, Schubert, 139, 145-151, 199[N22], 208[N66]
Origen, 19, 20, 71, 116, 117

Pannenberg, Wolfhart, 171, 175-179
Parmenides, 11-14, 16, 27, 29, 75, 76, 86, 141, 202[N45]
Past: and the future; *see* Future: and past
Paul, 114, 161
Piety, 5, 41
Pilate, Pontius, 70, 104
Plato, 11-15, 18, 19, 21, 22, 75, 76, 118, 152, 180, 202[N51]
Platonism, 14, 20, 27, 29, 116, 141
Polytheism, 109, 118
Prayer, 190, 191
Predestination, 28, 29, 31, 71, 130, 182
Prophets, 17, 18, 36
Protestant theology, 8, 139, 144

Reality, 39, 115, 116, 141, 142, 148, 167, 172, 176, 177, 179, 192, 193; as freedom, 34, 35; as history, 19, 21, 28, 34, 35,

Reality—*cont.*
67, 175, 177, 178, 184; of future and past, 168, 188, 189, 209[NS]; *see also* Eternity: as reality; God: reality of
Reformation, 139
Religion: and church, 40, 41, 113-115; and civil community, 73, 75; and eternity, 56; and the gospel, 46, 53; and history, 4, 21-24, 51-53, 67, 68, 71, 72; and love, 57, 58; and Marxism, 32, 33; and Metropolis, 45; and nature, 55, 56; and technology, 160; and time, 54; as confidence in life, 147; as polemic concept, 39-43; birth of, 25; function of, 32; meaning of, 26, 199[N2]; negative, 10; platonic, 27; primitive, 113-115, 118, 120, 121
Religion: interpretations:
Altizer, 44, 59-62; Bonhoeffer, 41-43, 51; Cox, 45; Dewart, 139, 140, 142; Feuerbach, 32, 33; Gregory, 120; Hamilton, 57, 58; Hegel, 34; Marx, 32, 33; Origen, 19, 20; Plato, 12; Rubenstein, 54-56
Barth, 6-11, 14, 15, 25, 30-32, 39-48, 52, 53, 67, 68, 79, 91, 95, 199[N2];
Religion; *see also* Buddhism; Christian religion; Faith: and religion; God: of religion; Greek religion; Hellenic religion; Hinduism; India: religions of; Islam; Judaism; Theology
Repentance, 167
Resurrection; *see* Jesus Christ: resurrection
Revelation, 45, 91, 97, 99-106, 147, 152, 153, 158, 159, 175-177, 191; *see also* God: revelation of
Rubenstein, Richard, 36-38, 51, 54-56, 62, 63

Safenwil: Barth as pastor in, 5, 6
Salvation, 11, 12, 30, 31, 42, 60, 118, 119
Schleiermacher, Friedrich, 104
Scriptures; *see* Bible
Secular life, 145, 148
Self-understanding, 181, 184-187, 191-193
Sin, 9, 18, 21, 25
Socialism, 6
Socrates, 8, 10-14, 16, 18-20, 22, 118, 180, 181
Sölle, Dorothee, 63-65
Soul, 42, 121
Spirit, 34, 35, 60, 86, 114-117; *see also* God: the Holy Spirit
Spiritual pluralism, 43
Spiritual reality, 21

Technology: and religion, 160
Theology: anti-religious, 44, 97, 170; contemporary, 4, 7, 39, 40, 52-66, 184, 199[N13]; natural, 48, 79-81, 86-92, 95, 100, 102, 109, 129, 145, 147, 148, 151, 160; *see also* Catholic theology; Protestant theology; Religion
Thought, 11, 34
Time, 61, 63, 64, 189, 193; and being, 184-186; as illusion, 11, 12, 44; as past, present and future, 169; cosmic, 169, 170,

Time—*cont.*
188; discontinuity, 126; historical, 169, 170, 172, 188, 189; *see also* Eternity: and time; God: and time
Transcendence, 20, 34, 154; of God, 60, 159, 162, 177, 190; self-transcendence, 7, 8, 19, 43, 52, 71, 121, 127, 128, 135, 144, 189, 192
Trinitarianism, 140
Trinity (of God), 97, 98, 105, 106, 122, 127, 128, 135, 150, 171-173; origin of doctrine, 47, 97, 116, 117
Trinity (of God); interpretations: Barth, 83, 84, 86, 89, 91, 95-98, 101, 102, 104, 106-113, 121, 123-125, 129-132, 135, 153, 156, 173, 174, 191, 192, 204[N38], 204[N39]
Bultmann, 204[N38], 204[N39]; Dewart, 140, 142, 145; Gregory, 118, 119, 121; Ogden, 149-151; Origen, 117
Truth, 3, 11, 19, 75, 172, 175; and power of Mind, 13; and self-understanding, 186, 187; in Jesus, 176; of God, 82
Work: righteousness, 41
Worship, 15, 26, 41, 57, 117, 118, 143, 144, 159

www.ingramcontent.com/pod-product-compliance
Lightning Source LLC
Chambersburg PA
CBHW071907290426
44110CB00013B/1310